Margaret Fulton Christmas

PHOTOGRAPHY MARK ROPER

Margaret Fulton Christmas

WITH SUZANNE GIBBS

Hardie Grant Books

This paperback edition published in 2009
First published in 2008 by
Hardie Grant Books
85 High Street
Prahran, Victoria 3181, Australia
www.hardiegrant.com.au

Cataloguing-in-Publication data is available from the National Library of Australia.
ISBN 9781740667739

The publisher would like to thank the following for their generosity in supplying props for the book: Collect Home, Country Road, Dedece, Domain Flowers, Empire Vintage, Gregory Hatton for his timber christmas tree, Izzi and Popo, Kris Coad Ceramics, Manon, Market Import, Moss Melbourne, North Carlton Ceramics, Safari Living, Seneca Textiles, Sharon Witherow for the use of her vintage decorations, The Essential Ingredient and Trash on Bay.

The authors wish to acknowledge as their chief source of material for Christmas festivals *European Festival Food* by Elizabeth Luard, Transworld Publishers.

Designed by Trisha Garner and Michelle Mackintosh
Food styling by Deborah Kaloper
Prop styling by Leesa O'Reilly
Edited by Paul McNally
Indexed by Lucy Malouf
Typeset by Megan Ellis
Set in Caslon and Corporate A BQ
Printed and bound in China by C & C Offset Printing
Cover photograph Mark Roper

10 9 8 7 6 5 4 3 2 1

FOREWORD

All families have their own traditions. Although I am Scottish, my family largely follows the English Christmas. Because my daughter, Suzanne, and I are food writers, we have been interested in the festive cooking, traditions and foods of other nations. Having written Christmas features for magazines for thirty and sixty years respectively, we have both cooked more Christmas dinners than we have had Christmas Days. We test and recook the recipes for the cameras and just when we think it's all over, our own family Christmas begins. However, it is such a joyful time that we get into the project with unexpected enthusiasm.

We know it's time to get going when friends start dropping hints about how much they enjoyed those mince pies we gave them last year. 'You couldn't make two Christmas puddings while you're at it? One for you and one for us?' 'I do love your shortbreads/toffee walnuts/gingerbread men/speculaas' – the list goes on. We're asked for recipes for all those special treats, for the stuffings, for the times for the turkey. What about the new cuts of turkey – do we recommend them? And what do we suggest for a lighter pudding? Or for a seafood Christmas dinner, or barbecue, or picnic?

Can you imagine our reaction to the idea of a Christmas book? A book dedicated to the notion that almost any festive food you could possibly want could be found in the one special place? We would include drinks, gifts, first-course dishes, morsels to nibble and of course the treats of Christmas – those traditional cakes and biscuits made to perfection, keeping alive family customs.

Let us say it has been enormous fun. Never have we enjoyed writing a book as much as we have this one.

A very merry Christmas to you all,

Margaret Fulton   *Suzanne Gibbs*

INTRODUCTION

CHRISTMAS IS COMING

What shall we have for Christmas dinner this year? Every November the family discussion turns to this. The merits of turkey? We had it last year, but it *was* good. Goose? Too fatty. Duckling? Sounds good, with turkey breast for those who prefer white meat. Perhaps tiny whole chickens – one for each person? Or roast pork with crispy crackling? Seafood?

Once the main dish is settled, the next question is how to cook it, then what we shall have with it – crispy potatoes? Don't forget the stuffing, and make plenty of gravy – everyone has their say.

Our whole family sits around the table planning the Christmas dinner – it's the most joyous meal of the year so we want to get it right. To help with this great quest, we've gathered the best recipes we know for the dishes that take pride of place on the Christmas table, as well as all the trimmings, vegetables, salads, puddings, sweetmeats and drinks.

THE TRADITIONS OF CHRISTMAS

Every country, village and family is a law unto itself as to how Christmas is celebrated – what we eat, when the tree goes up (and comes down), which decorations are favoured, when we open the presents and when we put on our paper hats, pull the Christmas crackers and read out the message inside. I find it fascinating to know the traditions behind Christmas and why they are kept alive.

Christmas took a long time to settle into 25 December as the day to celebrate. The festival of renewal has survived for at least 4000 years. When we welcome the birth of the Christ Child with evergreens, the exchanging of gifts and goodwill presents of fruits, cakes, candles, and gold and silver ornaments, we are carrying on ancient traditions. Even our Christmas crackers and thin paper hats and crowns are reminders of the King of Revels – appointed as the master of these ceremonies 2000 years ago.

ADVENT

Advent, the four weeks that lead up to Christmas, starts the Christmas festivities. In Sweden, families go to church to sing carols and people decorate their homes and streets. In Germany, the advent wreath is hung in the window,

with its four red candles lit. In Provence, a handful of seed corn is scattered on a piece of wet flannel, which is set by the fire to germinate in time to decorate the table for Christmas Eve. In Rome and Naples, bagpipe players come from the mountains to play haunting tunes before the many street shrines where lamps are kept burning on the first Sunday in Advent.

Christmas fairs are still held in northern Europe. In Britain, the St Ives pig fair fell on the Saturday before Advent – to celebrate, gingerbread men and pig-shaped pastries with currant eyes were made. Gingerbread was popular at the fairs, but was later overtaken by sugared almonds and macaroons, which young men bought for their sweethearts. Spices featured in much of the Christmas food in the 1500s as the sailors and traders ventured to the Spice Islands and brought back a rich harvest.

ST NICHOLAS

The eve of 6 December, the Festival of St Nicholas, is the traditional present-giving day over much of northern Europe. St Nicholas was originally the patron saint of sailors and later took care of children as well and, like Santa Claus, slipped gifts to young favourites under cover of darkness. Dutch families hide presents all over the house in the lead-up to St Nicholas's Eve. Marzipan is the great treat and, in preparation, Dutch pastry shops blaze with beautiful marzipan fruits and delicious spiced biscuits and cakes.

SINTE KLAUS AND SANTA CLAUS

In the 17th century the Dutch Sinte Klaus migrated to the USA. He was re-exported back to Europe as the incarnation of the polar-based Santa/Father Christmas we know today – red jacket with snowy ermine trim, with Rudolf and sleigh in tow. Father Christmas's empire is expanding rapidly; he is the much-loved, rotund, cheerful old gentleman eagerly anticipated by children.

THE FESTIVE FOODS OF EUROPE

It's never too soon to start making delicious things and storing them up for Christmas. We take inspiration from the European festive foods – Christmas cake, mince pies, and whole nuts to crack at the table.

THE YULE LOG AND SPICED BISCUITS

In France they celebrate with a yule log (*bûche de Noël*). The origin of the yule log is believed to be derived from the old custom of sending

a log to your host's house on Christmas Eve so you could be sure to enjoy the Christmas dinner before a roaring fire.

In Holland the festive season would be most disappointing without the spicy speculaas biscuits, and no self-respecting Scot would bring in the new year without shortbread.

Throughout Scandinavia, Germany and Austria, children rush to bake and decorate the gingerbread men or the angels or stars made from a spiced biscuit to hang on the Christmas tree. The Sicilians make the most beautiful hand-tinted marzipan fruits to serve at family festivals.

Throughout Europe the assortment of festive dishes to celebrate the happy season is incredible. Christmas treats like ricciarelli, panforte and marzipan fruits make wonderful gifts for Christmas. These traditions wear well and everyone appreciates the thought and care put into them.

CHRISTMAS IN GERMANY

When Queen Victoria married Prince Albert, he brought some of the German traditions to England, which we have, in turn, absorbed. The Christmas tree, with its decoration of small, lit candles, was one of these customs, as was the habit of stacking presents around the base of the tree. Christmas presents date from the 1500s, when the infant Jesus would send a sackful of

presents to be given out. Each child gets five presents: something delicious to eat, something to learn with, something to spend, something to play with and something new to wear.

In Germany, Christmas Eve is the night for magic, present giving, and eating the traditional fasting meal of baked carp or eel. It is on this night, so the story goes, that the forests blossom and the pure of heart can understand the language of animals. This witching hour extends into the twelve days between Christmas and Epiphany.

On Christmas Day, roast goose with apples, red cabbage and potato dumplings takes pride of place at the table. A *spätzlesuppe* (noodle soup) is made with a boiling fowl or a piece of shin beef. Stollen is the traditional Christmas fare – a rich fruit bread, it is either dusted with icing sugar or painted with a thin white icing while still warm, and then decorated. Spiced biscuits and cakes are a specialty of Germany's bakers, but home-baked are often the best.

SCANDINAVIAN CHRISTMAS SMÖRGASBORD

In Scandinavia, Christmas is the longest and most important holiday of the year. The Scandinavian cold table is taking a big hold in countries like Australia, especially when temperatures can be scorching. The traditional dishes include ham, jellied brawn and trotters, a large cod, pickled herring with sour cream and

potatoes, almond creamed rice and lovely spiced cake like the *kransekake* – a Christmas wreath cake made of ever-decreasing rings of almond macaroon. Treacle biscuits are baked and often decorated by children to hang on the tree.

The Christmas tree looms large – a live fir tree decked with handmade or special gold and silver ornaments that are kept for generations. The tree is watered and on 13 January, Knuts Day in Sweden, it is taken out again and planted.

TWELFTH NIGHT
Twelfth Night, the night that precedes Epiphany, is the eve of the day the Three Kings, or Three Wise Men, arrived in Bethlehem to lay their gifts before the Holy Infant. Lucky Mediterranean children enjoy two festivals

of gift-giving – the uniform celebration on 25 December and Twelfth Night. In Italy, Befana, the kind witch who walks on the rooftops, brings toys to good children and rods to naughty ones on Twelfth Night. In France, Epiphany is celebrated with a pastry not unlike pithivier, but round, in which a bean or tiny ceramic figure is hidden – whoever gets it is king for the day and wears the golden crown the pastry cook mounts on the cake.

All good things must come to an end. On the Twelfth Night, which falls on 5 January, we take down the Christmas tree and decorations. The rich cakes and spicy biscuits served bring the festivities to a rousing conclusion.

For Hugh Fulton of Glasgow, his wife Dorothy and their most joyful family who embody the very spirit of Christmas. Respectors of tradition, rejoicing and sharing with pleasure — a deep, ancestral emotion.

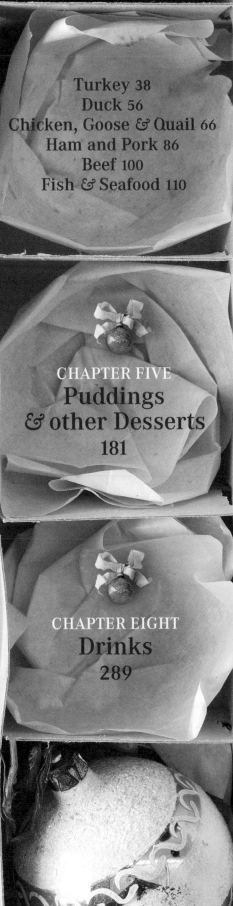

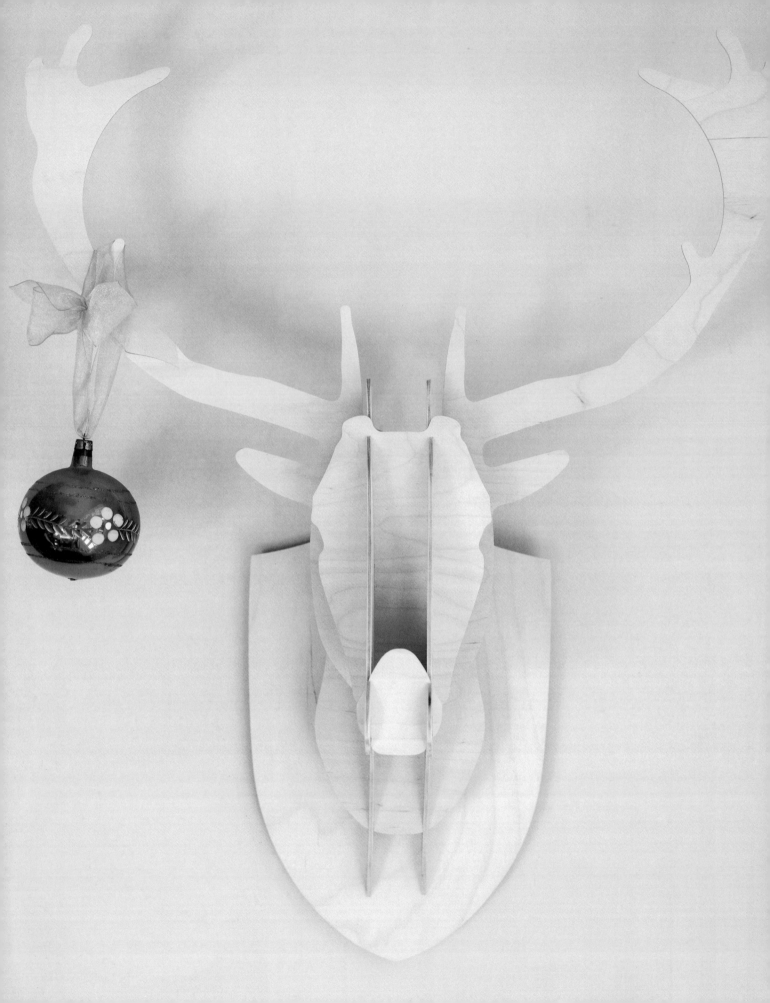

CHAPTER ONE
Starters & Appetisers

Starters & Appetisers

Christmas time means turkey with all the trimmings, ham glazed to glittering perfection, puddings full of plump fruits, little treats like spiced cookies, biscuits, nougat and nuts. With so much to take care of, the last thing the cook often thinks of is little nibbles, snacks and a first course or starter.

A few nuts, good olives and some piping hot pastries stored in the freezer are very useful come Christmas morning. In recent years, smoked salmon and gravlax have been readily available, and along with baby mixed greens, good rye or black breads or last-minute blinis (Russian pancakes), have been a mainstay for such times. For some, oysters are the ultimate treat. Most of us enjoy the surprise element of a little bite-sized nibble to enjoy with a drink to break the ice.

It is always a great pleasure to sit down to an inviting plate, perhaps very thin slices of smoked salmon, some quarters of lemon and brown bread and butter, or some simple and light dish that will stimulate, but not destroy, the appetite and set the mood for the delicious meal to follow.

Although a selection of recipes follows, there is an infinite variety of ways that they can be presented. It is a simple matter to select what will be just right to start your Christmas celebrations on the right note.

1–2 bunches asparagus, tough ends removed	6 large eggs
2 tablespoons olive oil, plus a little extra	½ cup freshly grated Parmesan cheese
1 clove garlic, crushed with salt	freshly ground black pepper, to season
¼ cup water	finely chopped oregano or marjoram, to taste

Asparagus Frittata

The savoury omelette cakes of France, Italy and Spain make the perfect Christmas breakfast – family members won't mind a break from present wrapping, opening and giving, to build strength for a busy day ahead. Asparagus makes a superb frittata, but other vegetables can be used, such as zucchini, green beans, spinach or mushrooms.

Heat a large frying pan and gently pan-fry the asparagus with the garlic in the oil for about 5 minutes, uncovered, until softened and lightly coloured. Add the water and cook, half-covered, until the asparagus is just tender, but still a little crisp. Drain and set aside.

Meanwhile, lightly beat the eggs in a bowl and add the Parmesan, pepper and herbs. Add a little more oil to the pan in which the asparagus was cooked and reheat. Pour in the egg mixture and cook over a moderate heat for 2 minutes. Arrange the asparagus decoratively on the eggs. Continue cooking until partially set, then place underneath a hot griller until an even, light golden brown. Slice into wedges to serve, hot or cold.

Serves 6–8

---

375 g zucchini, coarsely grated	1 cup grated Cheddar cheese, or a mixture of Cheddar and Parmesan cheeses
3 rashers bacon, finely chopped	
1 large onion, finely chopped	¼ cup rice bran oil or light olive oil
1 cup self-raising flour	salt and freshly ground black pepper, to season
5 eggs, lightly beaten	1 tomato, sliced
	sliced smoked salmon or ham, to serve

Tomato and Zucchini Bake

My granddaughters make this dish for Christmas breakfast. The family can help themselves and cut a wedge of it and enjoy it with the first tea or coffee of the day. As often happens, family is a bit haphazard about coming to the table together – it's a busy time on Christmas Day.

Preheat the oven to 200°C. Lightly grease a 14 x 21 cm loaf pan. Line the base and two long sides with baking paper.

Combine all the ingredients together in a bowl, except the tomato, and season to taste. Spoon into the prepared pan and decorate with the tomato slices. Bake for 40 minutes, until a skewer inserted comes out clean. Stand in the pan for 5 minutes before turning onto a wire rack to cool slightly. Serve warm or cooled with smoked salmon or ham.

Serves 10

1½ cups sour cream

100 g red salmon roe

1 tablespoon grated red onion

salt and freshly ground black pepper, to taste

chopped Continental parsley or snipped chives, to serve

Caviar Bowl

Perfect to welcome guests for a Christmas gathering at any time of day, caviar is a great accompaniment to a glass of chilled Champagne. Luxurious and pretty, salmon roe is a great way to bring on the celebrations.

Serve with water biscuits, melba toast or, for more of a flourish, with chilled vegetables such as carrot, zucchini or celery stalks, radishes, cauliflower florets or mushrooms.

Fold all the ingredients lightly together and serve chilled.

Keep a few spoonfuls of salmon roe to top. Sprinkling over chopped parsley or snipped chives also gives it a great finish.

Serves 6–8 as a spread or dip

several crisp lettuce leaves

48 oysters on the half shell, well chilled

¾ cup light sour cream

1 small jar red or black caviar, lumpfish or salmon roe

buttered brown bread, crusts trimmed and cut into
    triangles, to serve

Oysters Czarina

This is a marvellously festive dish with a chiffonnade of shredded lettuce underneath
(posing as seaweed) and caviar on top. Allow 6 oysters per serve.

Choose caviar to suit your budget – lumpfish roe is the cheapest option, followed by flying
fish roe, and then by fresh salmon roe. Of course, if you want something extra special,
imported Beluga caviar is top of the range.

Roll the lettuce leaves together into a fat cigar and cut across finely into thin
shreds. Remove the oysters from their shells and arrange a little shredded
lettuce in each shell. Top each lettuce mound with an oyster and put a small
dab of sour cream on top. Dollop a little caviar over the sour cream and
arrange the oysters on dinner plates. Serve with 2 dainty buttered brown
bread triangles to each plate.

Serves 6–8

36 oysters on the half shell, well-chilled

2 tablespoons finely chopped coriander

1 tablespoon finely snipped chives

1 tablespoon light soy sauce

juice of 1 large lime

½ teaspoon sugar

¼ cup oil

freshly ground black pepper, to season

buttered brown bread, crusts trimmed and cut into
    triangles, to serve

Oysters with Coriander Dressing

For a casual nibble with drinks, arrange these oysters on a platter then hand it around
with tiny wooden cocktail forks and paper napkins, so people can serve themselves.

To serve these oysters as a first course, allow 6 oysters per serve, and arrange on dinner
plates. Butter some brown bread, trim the crusts, and cut into fingers or triangles to serve
with the oysters.

Combine the coriander with the remaining ingredients (apart from
the oysters), seasoning well with freshly ground black pepper.

Arrange the oysters on 6 dinner plates and drizzle each one with some
of the coriander dressing. Serve with buttered bread triangles on the side.

Serves 6

4 thick asparagus spears

400 g smoked salmon

¾ cup cream cheese or crème fraîche

⅓ cup thickened cream

pinch of cayenne pepper

freshly snipped chives, to garnish

baby salad greens, lemon wedges and toast, to serve

Salmon and Asparagus Terrine

This dish is one of the lightest, prettiest ways to get the Christmas meal off to a good start. An added bonus come busy Christmas Day is that it can be made ahead of time and chilled until ready to serve.

Remove the tough ends of the asparagus. Cook the asparagus in a large saucepan of boiling, salted water for 3 minutes. Drain, cool in iced water and drain again.

Finely chop half of the smoked salmon. Combine the cream cheese or crème fraîche, cream and cayenne pepper in a bowl until smooth. Fold through the chopped salmon.

Line an 8 x 26 cm bar cake tin with plastic wrap. Line the base and sides with the remaining salmon, extending the salmon over the sides (enough for it to cover the top). Spread half of the cream mixture into the prepared tin. Top with the asparagus, followed by the remaining cream mixture. Fold the extending salmon back over the cream to fully enclose. Cover with plastic wrap and refrigerate for at least 30 minutes.

Once fully chilled, cut into 8 thick slices to serve. An attractive way of serving this is to place each slice on a bed of baby salad greens or straight on a plate, top with snipped chives and serve with lemon wedges and toast.

Serves 8

2 red apples, unpeeled and thinly sliced into wedges

juice of ½ lemon

4 tender stalks celery, thinly sliced on the diagonal

1 cup baby frisée, endive or other salad green

2 teaspoons extra-virgin olive oil

1 teaspoon balsamic vinegar

2 Lebanese cucumbers, thinly sliced in ribbons (see Tip)

16 slices smoked salmon or gravlax (page 18)

crusty bread, to serve

DRESSING

⅓ cup good mayonnaise

2 tablespoons sour cream

2 teaspoons white wine vinegar

salt and freshly ground black pepper, to season

Salmon, Cucumber and Celery Salad

A light smoked salmon salad makes a welcome first course and can look so pretty when freshly arranged on entrée-sized plates. Have everything ready in bowls in the refrigerator to be put together at the last moment.

To make the dressing, combine all the ingredients together in a bowl, seasoning to taste. Toss the apple wedges in the lemon juice. Add the apples and celery to the dressing and toss to coat.

Toss the frisée, endive or salad greens in a bowl with the olive oil and balsamic vinegar. To serve, pile ribbons of iced cucumber and the apple and celery mixture on eight entrée plates. Top with gently curled salmon slices and finish with the dressed mixed leaves. Serve with slices of crusty bread.

Serves 8

TIP Use a vegetable peeler to peel strips off the cucumber, drop into iced water to crisp, then drain. The cucumber and tender celery give a texture contrast to the delicate smoked salmon and creamy dressing.

500 g Atlantic salmon or ocean trout fillet, skin removed

1 small red onion or spring onion, finely diced

¼ cup vodka or gin

salt and freshly ground black pepper, to season

ginger mayonnaise (add 2 teaspoons grated fresh ginger to
homemade Mayonnaise, page 274)

pumpernickel or rye bread, to serve

baby salad greens, to serve

Salmon Tartare with Ginger Mayonnaise

Atlantic salmon and ocean trout are such a treat, and this dish is a simple way to enjoy them as a first course. The fish is not cooked, but rather marinated for a short while.

Finely dice the salmon or trout flesh. Put into a bowl with the onion and vodka or gin. Season with salt and a good grinding of pepper. Mix lightly, cover and refrigerate for 30 minutes or longer.

To serve, place a couple of spoonfuls of salmon or trout tartare on each of the eight entrée plates with a spoonful of the ginger mayonnaise just before serving. Serve with slices of pumpernickel or rye bread and baby salad greens.

Serves 8

ALTERNATIVE Tuna Tartare: Cut sashimi-quality tuna into tiny cubes and toss with finely diced red onion, capers and chilli. Serve on rounds of fried bread or pumpernickel as a refreshing and simply made cocktail canapé.

⅔ cup crème fraîche or sour cream

250 g sliced smoked salmon

1 bunch chives, finely chopped

watercress sprigs, to garnish

PANCAKES

½ cup plain flour

pinch of salt

1 large egg, lightly beaten

1 cup milk

Smoked Salmon Pancake Rolls

These rolls make a delightful easy-to-handle little package to accompany a welcoming drink as people gather for Christmas dinner.

To make pancakes, sift the flour with the salt into a bowl. Whisk in the egg. Stir in half of the milk, until smooth. Stir in the remaining milk and leave to stand for 30 minutes.

Heat a 20 cm non-stick frying pan over a moderate heat. Brush with a little melted butter. Add ¼ cup of the batter and tilt the pan to cover the base. Cook for 1 minute, until bubbles appear. Turn the pancake and cook for a further minute. Repeat with more melted butter and the remaining batter to make 6 pancakes.

Lay a double thickness of plastic wrap on a work surface and top with two pancakes, side by side, overlapping slightly. Spread with a third of the crème fraîche and top with a third of the smoked salmon slices, then a third of the whole chives.

Use plastic wrap to help roll the pancakes up tightly like a Swiss roll. Wrap tightly in plastic wrap and chill for 30 minutes. Repeat with the remaining pancakes, crème fraîche, smoked salmon and chives.

When ready to serve, cut into 3 cm slices and arrange on a serving platter. Garnish with sprigs of watercress and serve.

Makes 16 pieces

TIP Pancakes can be made a day ahead. Store in a freezer bag in the freezer or refrigerator with squares of greaseproof paper between pancakes, until required.

2 equal-sized fillets of salmon (skin and scales on)
     totalling about 2 kg

grated rind of 1 lemon

1 large bunch dill, chopped

½ cup salt

½ cup sugar

1 tablespoon freshly ground black pepper

½ cup vodka

Salmon Gravlax Robert

This dish is a superb starter and a speciality of my son-in-law Robert (where the dish gets its name). Prepare this dish a few days before Christmas, when it will be perfect to serve up.

Ocean trout is a very suitable alternative for salmon. A cleaned 3 kg ocean trout will provide 2 equal-sized fillets totalling about 2 kg. A clear, flat, tight-fitting plastic container about the size of the fish fillets is ideal for this dish, because marinating is achieved by simply rotating the sealed container in all directions.

Using tweezers, remove any protruding pin bones from the fish (the bones that stick out of the middle of the fillet).

Make a soggy mixture of the lemon rind, dill, salt, sugar, pepper and vodka. Spread a quarter of the mixture in the container and lay one fillet, skin side down, on top of it. Spread half of the mixture on the flesh of the fillet. Lay the second fillet, skin side up, on the fillet in the container and spread the last quarter of the mixture on the skin. Seal the lid and place in the refrigerator. Marinate the fillets by turning the container every 12 hours for 2 days (so, half the time the sealed container is stored lid-side down).

Leave a sprinkling of the dill on the fillets before carving. Start carving from the tail end, holding the knife tilted to produce thin slices as you would smoked salmon, cutting the flesh away from the skin as you do. Accompany with rye or black bread, and a mustardy mayonnaise, dill or horseradish mousse sauce.

Makes around 20 servings

TIPS Cover the fillets in plastic wrap if you are not using a sealed container.
Near-freezing cold Champagne does nicely with gravlax.

2 cups baby rocket

8 thin slices rye bread, lightly buttered

16 slices smoked salmon or gravlax (page 18)

1 tablespoon baby capers, drained, rinsed

DILL SAUCE

2 tablespoons Dijon mustard

pinch of salt

2 teaspoons caster sugar

1 teaspoon white wine vinegar

¼ cup light olive oil

2 tablespoons chopped dill

1 teaspoon lemon juice

Smoked Salmon with Dill Sauce and Rye

This is an easy dish to prepare as finger food or a starter. Keep the salmon, greens and dill sauce refrigerated until just before needed.

To make the dill sauce, combine the mustard, salt and sugar in a small bowl. Add the vinegar and slowly whisk in the oil until slightly thickened. Add the dill and lemon juice.

To assemble, pile each plate with rocket and top with two slices of salmon, repeating with each

serve. Just before serving, spoon over a little dill sauce. Scatter with a few capers and serve with the remaining sauce and buttered rye bread.

Serves 8

- -

4 small rounds pita or tortillas

olive oil, for brushing

watercress or baby rocket, to serve

200–250 g (12 slices) smoked salmon, halved first if large

2 Lebanese cucumbers, shredded or cut into julienne

1 tablespoon sliced pickled pink ginger

DRESSING

1 tablespoon rice wine vinegar

2 teaspoons soy sauce

1 teaspoon grated ginger

2 tablespoons peanut oil

1 tablespoon sesame oil

Smoked Salmon with Asian Dressing

Preheat a griller to moderate. Brush the pita bread or tortilla rounds with olive oil and cut into 1.5 cm strips, and grill until pale golden. Turn and brush other side with oil, grilling until just golden. Cool and store in an airtight container until ready to serve.

To make the dressing, combine the vinegar, soy sauce and ginger in a bowl. Gradually whisk in

the peanut and sesame oils. Set aside the dressing until ready to serve.

Arrange 4 or 5 toasted pita strips on each of 6 plates in a square lattice to form a base for the salad. Arrange watercress or rocket on top, then 2 salmon slices, curled attractively, cucumber and a few slices of pickled ginger. Lastly, drizzle with the dressing and serve.

Serves 6

90 g unsalted butter

⅓ cup buckwheat flour

⅔ cup plain flour

½ teaspoon salt

½ teaspoon baking powder

1 large egg

¾ cup milk, or use a mixture of half buttermilk, half milk

250 g smoked salmon slices or gravlax (page 14)

⅓ cup crème fraîche or light sour cream

2 tablespoons baby capers

sprigs of watercress or dill

freshly ground black pepper, to taste

lemon wedges, for squeezing over

Blinis with Smoked Salmon or Gravlax

This is a perfect treat before Christmas dinner – or any other dinner or lunch for that matter. Our family requests Robert, my son-in-law, to make his very excellent gravlax (page 14) as a special treat, which he makes 2 or 3 days ahead. A batch of proper little Russian pancakes – blinis – made with buckwheat flour is made just before we eat, and he also makes a creamy horseradish sauce by adding 1 tablespoon horseradish to 4 tablespoons crème fraîche or light sour cream. Smoked salmon or gravlax can be served on dark rye or black bread as a little pre-dinner savoury or at a drinks party as an alternative to blinis.

Melt the butter and skim off most of the white foam that rises to the surface. Sift the buckwheat and plain flours with the salt and baking powder into a large bowl. Make a well in the centre and add the egg, milk and 2 tablespoons of the melted butter. Whisk the wet ingredients together, gradually drawing in the dry ingredients, until a smooth batter is formed.

To cook the blinis, heat some of the remaining melted butter in a large frying pan. Drop the batter into the pan, 1 tablespoon at a time, to form small pancakes. Cook each for 1–2 minutes or until covered with bubbles. Turn and cook the other side until golden. Repeat with remaining batter. To serve, top warm blinis with the smoked salmon, ½ teaspoon crème fraîche or sour cream, a few baby capers and a few leaves of watercress or dill. Finish with a few twists of the pepper mill and a squeeze of lemon.

Makes about 24

32 large cooked king prawns (about 2.2 kg in total)

salt and freshly ground black pepper, to season

1 tablespoon extra-virgin olive oil

1 tablespoon lemon juice, plus wedges, to serve

rocket or baby salad greens, to serve

AVOCADO SALSA

2 Lebanese cucumbers, cut into small cubes

½ teaspoon salt

2 stalks celery, diced

½ red onion, finely chopped

1 avocado, diced

1 green chilli, seeds removed, finely sliced

¼ cup lemon juice

salt and freshly ground black pepper, to season

Prawns with Avocado Salsa

This dish shows its Mexican influence with a fairly hot salsa – but this seems to sharpen the appetite and refresh the palate, which is altogether a good introduction to a Christmas meal.

Remove the heads and shell the prawns, but leave the tails intact. Slit down the centre back on each prawn and remove the dark intestinal tract. Add the prawns to a bowl, season lightly to taste and drizzle with the oil and lemon juice. Cover and chill for 30 minutes.

To make the salsa, put the cucumber in a colander. Sprinkle with the salt and cover with a plate. Set aside to drain for 30 minutes, then rinse and pat dry with paper towel. Combine the cucumber with celery, onion, avocado, chilli and lemon juice. Season to taste and chill until required.

To serve, make a light bed of rocket or other baby greens on each plate, top with salsa then 4 prawns and a lemon wedge on the side for squeezing over.

Serves 8

1.5 kg cooked king prawns

lime wedges, to serve

CHILLI DIPPING SAUCE

2 tablespoons finely chopped coriander

1 small red onion, finely chopped

1 green chilli, seeded, finely chopped

½ cup tomato sauce

¼–½ cup sweet or Mexican chilli sauce

Tabasco, to taste

freshly squeezed lime juice, to taste

Prawns with Chilli Dipping Sauce

When offering a little something with pre-dinner drinks, delicious prawns seem to be just the thing. For the best flavour, select only the best quality king prawns.

Remove the heads and shell the prawns, but leave the tails intact. Slit down the centre back on each prawn and remove the dark intestinal tract. Arrange the prawns on a serving platter on ice, if you like.

To make the dipping sauce, combine all the ingredients in a bowl. Spoon the dipping sauce into one or two smaller bowls, and offer lime wedges in another bowl. Offer paper napkins and disposable cocktail forks.

Serves 8

TIP Keep the dipping sauce covered in the fridge for up to 1 week.

	COCKTAIL SAUCE
1.5 kg cooked king prawns	¾ cup good mayonnaise
1 Lebanese cucumber	1 tablespoon tomato sauce
1 mango	1 teaspoon Worcestershire sauce
1 ripe avocado, diced	few drops of Tabasco
juice of ½ lemon	
witlof or tender lettuce leaves, to serve	
lime or lemon wedges, for squeezing over	

Tropical Prawn Cocktails

This dish is a new twist on an old favourite and makes a welcome start to a rich meat or poultry meal. As few people today have those seafood cocktail glasses of the '60s, I suggest using small glasses or ceramic bowls.

To prepare the cocktail sauce, combine the ingredients together, mixing lightly.

Remove the heads and shell the prawns, but leave the tails intact on a few (for decoration). Slit down the centre back on each prawn and remove the dark intestinal tract. Lightly peel the cucumber and cut into dice. Cut the 2 sides from the mango, keeping the knife close to the stone. Cut each half in two and slip a small knife between the flesh and skin, remove the flesh and dice. Toss the diced avocado in the lemon juice to prevent discolouring. Store these ingredients separately in small covered containers until ready to put the prawn cocktails together.

When ready to serve, gently mix together the diced ingredients. Place a witlof or lettuce leaf in each of 8 serving glasses. Spoon the diced mixture in the glasses and top with the prawns. Spoon some of the cocktail sauce over each and serve with lime or lemon wedges if wished.

Serves 6–8

Crudités

If having pre-dinner drinks in the garden, guests will be sure to enjoy a platter of fresh vegetables. A favourite hors d'oeuvre of provincial France, this simple arrangement of crisp, young, fresh, raw vegetables is popular with everyone. The prepared vegetables should be crisped in iced water. Serve vegetables arranged on a platter with Aïoli (garlic-flavoured mayonnaise) (page 275) for dipping.

PREPARING VEGETABLES

Carrots: Wash, peel and trim Dutch baby carrots; cut larger carrots into quarters or strips. Drop into iced water to crisp.

Radishes: Use only firm, round, bright red radishes. Trim top leaves, leaving small leaf intact. (This makes it easier for guests to eat radishes with their fingers.) Wash radishes well. Place in iced water, halve if large.

Spring onions: Wash, remove outside leaf and trim off root and green tops, about 5 cm from the fork of the leaves. Keep in iced water until ends curl.

Tomatoes: Use very firm, small cherry and grape tomatoes of different colours. Wash and chill.

Celery: Wash and cut fresh stalks into 12 cm lengths. For a retro look, fray ends by making 2 cm cuts 5 mm apart, lengthwise at each end of each stalk. Drop into a large bowl of iced water and leave for 45 minutes to 1 hour to allow the stalks to curl and become crisp.

Cauliflower: Trim florets from cauliflower and wash. Place in iced water.

Baby turnips: Trim off green tops, leaving a few young leaves. Wash and chill in iced water.

Sugar peas or snow peas: String, plunge into a saucepan of boiling salted water for 1 minute, drain and chill in iced water.

---

180 g Cheddar cheese, finely grated	1 teaspoon salt
185 g butter	2 tablespoons grated Parmesan cheese
1½ cups plain flour	milk, for glazing
1 teaspoon paprika	poppy seeds or sesame seeds, to decorate

Cheese Biscuits

Preheat the oven to 180°C. Using an electric mixer, cream the cheese together with the butter until soft. Sift the flour, paprika and salt, then fold into the creamed mixture together with the Parmesan cheese. Mix well to form a dough, then turn out onto a floured board.

Divide the dough in two and wrap each half in plastic wrap to chill for an hour or so. Roll out one half on a lightly floured surface. Use biscuit cutters to cut out animal shapes and place on baking trays. Brush each with a little milk and sprinkle with poppy or sesame seeds. Bake for 10–12 minutes, until pale golden. Cool on wire racks and store until ready to serve. Repeat with the remaining dough.

Makes about 80

40 stuffed green olives, drained	½ teaspoon paprika
75 g soft butter	pinch of cayenne pepper
125 g tasty Cheddar cheese, grated	pinch of salt
⅔ cup plain flour	

Hot Olive and Cheese Puffs

A bite-sized, just-baked pastry is a great welcome with Christmas pre-dinner drinks. These can be made ahead of time, arranged on a baking tray and popped in the oven when you need them.

Preheat the oven to 200°C. Thoroughly dry the olives with paper towel. Combine the butter and cheese in a bowl. Sift in the flour, paprika, cayenne and a pinch of salt. Work together with a spatula to form a dough.

Wrap each olive in a teaspoon of dough. Arrange in a single layer on baking trays and bake for 15 minutes, until golden. Serve hot with drinks.

Makes 24

---

1 cup plain flour	½ teaspoon salt
1 cup water or milk, or a mixture of both	4 eggs
100 g unsalted butter	100 g Gruyère or other Swiss-style cheese, grated
1 teaspoon sugar	beaten egg, to brush

Gougères

These festive pastries can also be made ahead of time, by shaping them on a baking tray and freezing them when risen. When they are firm and frozen they can be transferred into freezer bags ready for baking any time.

Preheat the oven to 200°C and grease 2 baking trays. Sift flour onto a piece of greaseproof paper. Put the water and/or milk, butter, sugar and salt into a saucepan. Bring to a rapid boil and, using the greaseproof paper as a funnel, pour the flour all at once into the boiling mixture. Over a gentle heat, incorporate the flour quickly and thoroughly with a wooden spoon and beat until the mixture balls around the spoon and leaves the sides of the pan (a bit of muscle is needed here). This process dries the paste and cooks the flour.

Remove from the heat, transfer the mixture to a bowl and cool to lukewarm. Beat in the eggs, one at a time, using an electric mixer with a paddle beater or, if using a wooden spoon, beat each egg lightly first. If the paste is very stiff, beat an extra egg and add gradually, until a pliable consistency is obtained. Beat the paste until well combined, shiny and smooth.

Add the cheese to the paste and mix lightly. Use 2 spoons to drop small balls of the mixture onto baking trays. Brush with a little beaten egg and bake for 20 minutes, until puffed and golden. Serve piping hot.

Makes 30–40

200 g pitted black olives, plus extra to serve

6 anchovy fillets, drained and rinsed

¼ cup capers, drained

95–100 g canned tuna in oil, drained

juice of 1 lemon

⅓ cup olive oil

rye bread, black bread or crisp bread, to serve

Tapenade

This has to be one of the most useful savoury spreads to have in store for the busy festive season. Along with a little bowl of nuts, it is enough to set guests up with a friendly drink before dinner.

Crush the olives in a mortar with a pestle or chop in a food processor. Add the anchovy fillets, capers, tuna and half the lemon juice. Pound or process until the mixture has formed a fairly smooth paste.

While still pounding, or with the processor still running, add the oil in a slow, steady stream. Taste and add more lemon juice if needed. Transfer to a small serving bowl, decorate with a few extra black olives and serve with buttered rye, black bread, or crisp breads. Put a small spreader on the plate and serve.

Makes about 3 cups

- -

2 sheets frozen ready-rolled puff pastry

2 x 56 g cans rolled, stuffed anchovies

1 egg yolk, beaten

Anchovy Turnovers

How to produce marvellous hot savouries with a minimum of time and effort? Canned stuffed anchovies and ready-rolled puff pastry make it possible.

Roll the pastry to make it a little thinner and cut out 24 x 5 cm circles. Wet the edge of each circle with a little water, place a drained anchovy on one side and fold the other side over, pressing with the wetted tines of a fork to mark and seal.

Chill the turnovers for 30 minutes, then brush the tops with beaten egg yolk and bake in a 230°C oven for 15 minutes or until puffed and golden.

Makes about 24 turnovers

Devilled Almonds

Steep 2 cups almonds in just-boiled water for 5 minutes. Remove and drain well. Slip off the skins, if liked. Heat 2–3 tablespoons vegetable oil in a frying pan over a moderate heat and cook the almonds, stirring constantly, until golden. Drain on paper towel and sprinkle with a little salt and chilli powder – about ⅛ teaspoon chilli powder to 1 teaspoon salt. Dust off excess salt and chilli powder and serve in small bowls. Nuts can be stored in airtight containers until ready to serve with drinks.

Curried Walnuts, Pecans or Cashews

Heat 2 tablespoons vegetable oil in a frying pan over a moderate heat and add 2 teaspoons each curry powder and Worcestershire sauce. Stir the mixture and when hot, add 2 cups walnuts, pecans or cashews. Remove from the heat and stir until the nuts are coated, then spread on a baking tray lined with foil. Bake in a 160°C oven for 10 minutes until the nuts are crisp. Store in an airtight container until ready to serve with drinks.

Mixed Italian Olives

Cut slashes in the flesh of 500 g mixed green and black olives with a sharp knife, remove stones if liked, and place in a sterilised jar. Finely chop ½ small green chilli, ½ small red chilli, 3 stalks of celery and 2 cloves of garlic. Add to the jar with the olives. Add ¼ cup each of olive oil and wine vinegar and 1 sprig oregano (or a good pinch of dried oregano). Cover and leave at room temperature for at least 2 days, then store in the refrigerator until required. Drain and dry on paper towel, if desired, and serve as part of an antipasto plate.

1 large ripe pineapple

2 tablespoons caster sugar

juice of 1 lemon

mint sprigs or tarragon sprigs

DRESSING

1 large egg

¼ cup tarragon vinegar

2 tablespoons caster sugar

pinch of salt

¼ cup cream, lightly whipped

Pineapple Japonaise

It is often difficult to find the right course to precede a rich meal. The fresh taste of pineapple is an excellent choice on such an occasion – it has a refreshing taste and is not too heavy on the palate. In this recipe, each chunk of pineapple is coated with the merest suggestion of a light cream dressing.

Cut the pineapple into four lengthwise, remove the core carefully with a sharp knife and cut out the flesh. Cut into chunks and arrange on 6–8 plates. Sprinkle with caster sugar and lemon juice. The pineapple can be stored in a container in the fridge until needed.

To make the dressing, beat the egg and add the vinegar, sugar and salt. Cook in the top of a double boiler over gently simmering water and stir continuously until thick. Remove from the heat and allow to cool. When cold, fold in the whipped cream and adjust the seasoning. Just before serving, spoon the dressing over the pineapple and scatter with a few mint or tarragon sprigs.

Serves 6–8

TIP This creamy dressing is also delicious with chilled pears that have been peeled and quartered.

1 small watermelon

1 cup gin

mint leaves, to decorate

Watermelon with Gin

It's almost too easy! The gin does something magical to the flavour of the watermelon, and may be saved for later use in a fruit punch. And the pretty colour just says Christmas.

Cut the watermelon in half, remove the seeds, and scoop out balls of the firm flesh with a melon-baller. If you don't have a melon-baller, cut the flesh into bite-sized cubes.

Pour the gin over the watermelon balls in a bowl, mix lightly, cover with plastic wrap and leave to marinate for several hours in the refrigerator.

At serving time, drain the watermelon well, arrange the balls in chilled glasses, and decorate with fresh mint leaves.

Serves 6–8 as a refreshing first course or a light dessert

TIPS Look for seedless melons to make this dish easier to prepare. To take this treat on a picnic, keep the melon balls in a plastic container stored on ice in an esky. This is a welcome dish on a hot summery day. Make a separate container of watermelon with mint for children.

| 6 raw beetroot |
| 6 cups fat-free chicken stock |
| 1 continental cucumber, peeled and diced |
| 2 tablespoons snipped chives or chopped dill |
| salt and freshly ground black pepper, to season |
| 1 cup light sour cream, natural yoghurt or buttermilk |
| 1 lemon, thinly sliced, to garnish |

Summer Beetroot Soup

This bright red soup looks dramatic garnished with dill, lemon and cucumber – and, even better, is delicious and wonderfully refreshing served cool on a hot Christmas Day. But, if the weather cools down, or you're visiting relatives in the northern hemisphere, you can also serve this soup piping hot.

Add the beetroot to a saucepan and fill with enough water to cover. Simmer the beetroot for 40 minutes or until tender. Remove from the heat and drain. When cool enough to handle, use hands to slip off the skins. This should be easy if the beetroot are cooked sufficiently.

Purée two quartered beetroot with half the chicken stock in a food processor and dice the others. Add the remaining chicken stock until desired consistency. In a bowl, combine the puréed beetroot and stock with the diced beetroot, cucumber and chives or dill, reserving a little for garnishing. Stir well and chill.

Season to taste with salt and freshly ground black pepper and stir in three-quarters of the sour cream or yoghurt, or all of the buttermilk. Have some soup bowls ready and chilled, then place 1–2 ice cubes in each. Ladle in the soup and garnish with any or all of the following: the remaining sour cream or yoghurt, lemon slices and the reserved garnishes.

If serving the soup hot, heat the beetroot soup with the diced beetroot and garnish with the lemon, cucumber, sour cream and chives or dill.

Serves 6–8

TIP This is perfect for an outdoor Christmas picnic – take it in one or two thermos flasks or a suitable container with a lid and keep it chilled in an esky.

| ½ cup almonds, blanched and skinned (see Notes) |
| 1 clove garlic, peeled |
| 6 cups chicken stock |
| 1 small onion, stuck with 2 cloves |
| 1 bay leaf |
| pinch of ground nutmeg |
| salt and freshly ground black pepper, to taste |
| 45 g butter |
| 2 tablespoons plain flour |
| 1 cup light cream |

Almond Soup

This Spanish soup is enjoyed chilled in the summer, hot in the winter, and is perfect for hot climates and Christmas celebrations. You can use store-bought ground almonds, but they tend to give a grainy finish so that the soup needs to be put through a fine sieve. I prefer to prepare the whole almonds myself.

Using a mortar and pestle, pound the almonds and garlic to a smooth paste, or purée in a food processor. Combine the ground almonds, stock, onion and bay leaf in a saucepan. Simmer, covered, for 20 minutes. Remove the onion and bay leaf, pour the mixture into a jug and add the nutmeg, and salt and pepper to taste.

Melt the butter in a clean saucepan, add the flour and stir over a medium–low heat; slowly blend in the stock mixture. Stir until boiling, then reduce the heat and simmer for 5 minutes. Add the cream and reheat, but do not boil. Serve cold or hot.

Serves 6–8

NOTES To blanch and skin the almonds in this recipe, pour boiling water over the almonds in a bowl, stand for 5 minutes, then slip off the brown skins. Toasted slivered almonds and a few grapes make a delightful garnish for this soup. Chill grapes for cold soup.

750 g ripe tomatoes	2 cloves garlic, crushed
1 cup white wine	½ teaspoon ground cumin
2 cups chicken or vegetable stock	salt and freshly ground black pepper, to season
¾ cup dry white breadcrumbs	1 red onion, finely diced
2 tablespoons olive oil	1 small green capsicum, finely diced
¼ cup white wine vinegar	1 Lebanese cucumber, finely diced

Gazpacho

The refreshing, spicy, chilled soup from Spain could well have been created to combat summer heat waves. This garlicky and often highly seasoned soup-cum-salad makes a wonderfully refreshing way to begin a Christmas feast in the Australian heat. It can be accompanied by separate bowls of garnishes such as diced cucumber, capsicum or chopped hard-boiled egg to be sprinkled over each serving. Sometimes water or stock is used in place of the wine.

Peel the tomatoes by first dropping them in boiling water, waiting 8 seconds then lifting and plunging into a bowl of iced water. Lift from the water, make a small slit in the base and the skin should peel off easily.

Cook half the tomatoes in a saucepan over a moderate heat with the wine and stock until soft, breaking up the tomatoes with a spoon. Push the mixture through a sieve or purée in a food processor until smooth. Add the breadcrumbs, olive oil, vinegar, garlic, cumin, salt and pepper to the processor and process lightly until combined. Transfer to a heatproof bowl, cool and refrigerate until well chilled.

Remove the seeds from the remaining tomatoes and cut into small dice. Add the diced tomato to a bowl with the onion, capsicum and cucumber, and mix well. To serve, ladle the soup into serving bowls. Serve topped with the diced tomato mixture. If liked, add 2 or 3 ice cubes to each bowl of gazpacho.

Serves 6

NOTE The wine may be substituted with the same amount of stock if desired.

CHAPTER TWO
Mains

Turkey

Many people would feel cheated if Christmas dinner wasn't celebrated around a large golden festive turkey with its promise of plenty of white meat, dark meat, a choice of two stuffings, loads of gravy, all the trimmings and familiar vegetables served with a new twist.

Turkey breeding has changed over the years so the present day bird has more tender breast meat in proportion to dark meat, than the same-sized bird of years ago.

Turkeys are now available from a tiny 2.5 kg up to a giant 12.5 kg bird. It is also possible to buy half turkeys, turkey breasts (known as 'buffes'), half breasts and turkey hind quarters – so there's a turkey option to fit almost every family's size and budget. Order the one that's right for you.

Thawing the turkey

A large frozen turkey will take up to three days to thaw completely in the refrigerator. It is important that the turkey is properly thawed before it is stuffed and cooked and that the stuffing is added on the day of roasting.

Stuffing the turkey

Stuffing should be mixed lightly, so as to not be too compact. This ensures that room is left for expansion during cooking. Make the stuffing ahead of time and store it in the refrigerator until you're ready to stuff and cook the turkey.

Roasting the turkey

The turkey is best placed on a rack in a roasting pan, leaving extra room for cooking vegetables underneath, or in a separate pan. The use of a trivet or roasting rack also helps the turkey to get that lovely brown roasted look all over.

Keeping the turkey moist

Cover the turkey and pan completely with foil for most of the cooking to prevent the bird drying out during cooking. The foil is removed temporarily each time the turkey is basted, and completely for last 30 minutes of cooking to help promote browning. Oven bags are another good option.

Cooking the turkey in an oven bag

Turkey-sized oven bags are available and come with packet instructions. Turkeys will cook faster using this method. The oven bag will retain all the moisture in the meat and leave your oven clean. A 2–3 kg turkey takes 1½ hours; a 3–4 kg turkey takes 2 hours; and a 4–6 kg turkey takes 3 hours.

How long to cook?

A turkey positioned on a rack on the lowest shelf of a preheated 180°C oven will take 35–40 minutes per 1 kg to cook. Weigh the stuffing separately and include in the total weight to calculate the cooking time of the stuffed bird.

What size to buy

WEIGHT	SERVES	COOKING TIME
2.5 kg	6–8	1 hr 40 mins–2 hrs
3–4 kg	8–10	2 hrs–2 hrs 40 mins
4–6 kg	10–14	2 hrs 40 mins–4 hrs
6–8 kg	14–16	4–5 hrs

Is it cooked?

Invest in a meat thermometer for checking doneness. They are relatively inexpensive and available from most kitchen stores. A meat thermometer helps to ensure the turkey is cooked through. Insert the meat thermometer into the inner thigh area, close to the breast, without touching bone. It should register 80°C when cooked.

Resting the turkey

'Resting' is a term you will find in many cook books. Roasted meats are often 'rested' in a warm place for 15–20 minutes before carving. This allows the juices to be reabsorbed by the tissues, giving the meat a succulent tenderness. When carved, less juice escapes and the slices shrink less.

How to carve turkey

Slice down each side of the breast with straight strokes. Remove the stuffing with a large spoon. Place the knife between the thigh and the body and cut through the joint. Press each leg outward with the knife and bend back to cut through the hip joint. Separate each thigh and drumstick, and slice off the dark meat; remove the wings.

Serving the turkey

Slices of white meat are usually arranged at one end of a platter, with dark meat at the other. Stuffing can be served on separate heated plates or arranged on the platter with the sliced meat. If serving your guests, carve off a little white and a little dark meat to each person with some stuffing, and spoon the gravy over. Serve the vegetables in separate dishes, and have a jug of extra gravy on hand for those who like plenty.

| 1 x 3–4 kg whole turkey, at room temperature |
| 1 quantity Pork, Apple and Sage Stuffing (opposite) |
| 1 quantity Lemon and Parsley Stuffing (opposite) |
| 15 g butter, softened |
| freshly ground black pepper, to season |
| Turkey Gravy (page 42) |

Roast Turkey with Two Stuffings

Roast turkey is a Christmas favourite with its stuffing, crispy skin, moist tender white meat and richly flavoured dark meat. Make sure there's plenty of gravy, crispy roast potatoes and serve with traditional cranberries. Should you fancy a different stuffing, consult the Stuffing section (pages 78–85).

Pat dry the turkey with paper towel. Spoon the pork, sage and apple stuffing into the turkey breast. Bring the neck flap over to the back and secure with a poultry pin. Spoon the parsley, thyme and lemon stuffing into the body cavity. Press the bird into a good shape with both hands.

Place the turkey on its back, with the legs facing you. Position the centre of a piece of string below the breast at the neck end, bringing down over the wings to cross underneath the bird. Bring the string forward and upwards to tie the ends of the drumsticks and parson's nose together.

Preheat the oven to 180°C. Spread the butter over the turkey and season with pepper. Place the turkey on a rack in a large roasting pan, propping up the legs with crumpled foil if necessary. Cover the pan with a tent of greased foil.

Roast until done (see page 39). Baste every 25 minutes with the pan juices and remove the foil for the last 30 minutes to brown. Remove to a heated platter, cover loosely with foil and leave in a warm place for 20–30 minutes while finishing off vegetables and gravy. Alternatively, roast the turkey in an oven bag, following the packet directions.

Remove the string and poultry pin. Carve from the top of the breast with straight, even strokes, downwards. Cut between the thigh and body of the bird through the joint. Remove the leg by pressing it outwards with a knife and bending it back with a fork. Separate the thighs and drumsticks and slice off the dark meat; remove the wings. Carve the crop stuffing into thin slices and remove cavity stuffing with a spoon.

Serves 8–10

½ cup apple juice or cider

4 thick slices white bread, cubed

500 g pork mince (pork sausages may be used)

2 apples, peeled, cored and diced

1 small onion, finely chopped

1 tablespoon chopped Continental parsley

2 teaspoons chopped sage

1 egg, lightly beaten

salt and freshly ground black pepper, to season

Pork, Apple and Sage Stuffing

Pour the apple juice over the bread in a large bowl and set aside
to soak for 15 minutes. Add the pork mince, apples, onion and
herbs, and mix well. Add the beaten egg, season well and mix
together thoroughly. Use to stuff the crop (breast) of the turkey.

Makes 5 cups

---

3 cups day-old roughly torn white bread

1 small onion, finely chopped

¾ cup chopped Continental parsley

1 tablespoon thyme leaves

grated rind and juice of 1 lemon

30 g butter, melted

1 egg, lightly beaten

salt and freshly ground black pepper, to season

Lemon and Parsley Stuffing

Process the bread in a food processor to make crumbs. Spread the
breadcrumbs on baking tray and dry in a 160°C oven for about
20 minutes. Combine the breadcrumbs, onion, herbs, lemon rind,
juice and butter in a bowl. Add the egg, season to taste and toss lightly
with a fork to mix. Use to stuff the cavity (main body) of the turkey.

Makes 4 cups

| 30 g butter |
| 2 tablespoons plain flour |
| 3 cups Turkey Stock (see below) |
| 1–2 tablespoons dry sherry or port |
| salt and freshly ground black pepper, to season |

Turkey Gravy

After baking a turkey, pour off the excess turkey drippings, leaving about ¼ cup. Add the butter and melt over a moderate heat. Stir in the flour and cook for 3 minutes, until browned lightly. Stir in the stock, scraping up the crusty pan residue. Bring to the boil then simmer for 3 minutes, until thickened. Stir in the sherry or port and strain.

Adjust the seasonings, adding salt and pepper if necessary, and skim excess fat from the top. Serve piping hot in a gravy boat or jug.

Makes 3 cups

Turkey Stock

It's worth buying 1 kg chicken pieces, such as wings or drumsticks, to make a good stock for gravy. Add the turkey neck and gently simmer with ½ onion, 1 bay leaf, 1 stalk celery and 5 cups chicken stock or water until reduced to 3 cups. Strain and use to make turkey gravy.

For reduced-fat gravy, pour off all but the crusty residue from the turkey roasting pan and add the stock. Bring slowly to boil, stirring, then thicken with 1–2 tablespoons cornflour mixed with a little water or stock.

Makes 3 cups

TIP To avoid lumpy gravy, the 'roux' (fat and flour mixture) should be hot and the liquid added cold.

1 x 4 kg turkey, at room temperature
60 g butter
freshly ground black pepper, to season
2 cups chicken stock
½ cup water

Turkey with Orange, Herb and Nut Stuffing

Some claim the stuffing is the best part of the Christmas turkey – and it might be hard to argue with that when making this deliciously fresh tasting, nutty stuffing. If using walnuts, make sure they are fresh or use canned ones.

To make the stuffing, dry the breadcrumbs, without browning, on a baking tray in a 160°C oven. Melt the butter in a frying pan over a moderate heat and cook the onion for 5 minutes, stirring, until soft. Transfer to a large bowl and add the remaining stuffing ingredients. Season to taste and mix thoroughly. Add a small amount of cream if the stuffing doesn't hold together.

Preheat the oven to 180°C. Remove the neck from the turkey cavity and keep it aside for gravy. Wash the turkey inside and out and dry well with paper towel. Spoon the stuffing into the crop, being careful not to pack it too tightly, and press outside of the breast to mould the stuffing to the original shape of the turkey (any remaining stuffing can be placed in the cavity). Bring the neck flap over the stuffing to back and secure with a small skewer.

Turn the turkey over and fold its wings back behind it. To truss, put the turkey on its back. Run string around the wings and underneath to cross over the back. Turn the turkey over and bring the string up to tie the legs together, keeping them close to the body.

Dot the bird with the butter and sprinkle with pepper. Position in a baking dish, pour the stock and water into the dish, and cover the turkey with foil (if you have a rack it should go first in the baking dish and the bird placed on top). To cover the entire bird, join two sheets of foil by folding the edges together. Cover the turkey and seal the foil to the edges of the baking dish. Roast the turkey for 45 minutes, basting frequently. Reduce the heat to 160°C and roast for a further 1 hour 40 minutes, basting frequently, until tender and golden brown.

ORANGE, HERB AND NUT STUFFING

6 cups fresh white breadcrumbs
40 g unsalted butter
1 large onion, finely chopped
grated rind of 1 orange
¾ cup orange juice
½ cup mixed fresh herbs, such as Continental parsley, thyme and chervil
½ cup chopped nuts, such as macadamias, pecans or walnuts
1 egg, beaten
salt and freshly ground black pepper, to season

Continue roasting until a meat thermometer inserted into the thickest part of the thigh registers 80°C. If you don't own a thermometer, pierce the thickest part of the thigh with a fork or fine skewer. The fork should go in easily and the juice run out clear. If the juice has a pink tinge, further cooking is required.

About 1 hour before the end of cooking, remove the foil and continue to cook, uncovered, basting regularly with the pan juices. Add parboiled, peeled potatoes if you like.

Once cooked, turn off the heat and rest the turkey for 15 minutes in the oven with the door ajar, or out of oven, well covered with foil, while making the gravy (page 42). This resting period allows the meat to firm up and makes carving easier.

Serves 8–10

TIP Wait to stuff the turkey until you're ready to begin roasting – bacteria can start to grow inside a waiting, stuffed turkey.

Trussing a turkey means tying the legs and wings together to give the bird a tight look and nicer presentation. Trussing isn't necessary for cooking, and can actually make the legs and thighs take longer to cook, since the bird is pressed against itself.

1 x 8 kg whole turkey breast ('buffe')

60 g butter, melted

2 cups chicken stock

½ cup water

Cumberland Sauce (page 278)

STUFFING

45 g unsalted butter

1 large onion, finely chopped

500 g pork or veal mince

4 cups fresh white breadcrumbs

½ cup chopped Continental parsley

1 tablespoon chopped thyme, sage or tarragon

grated rind of 1 lemon

¾ cup apple juice

salt and freshly ground black pepper, to season

1 egg, beaten (if required)

Roast Turkey Buffe

A large turkey breast, often sold as turkey buffe, is a splendid sight on a Christmas table, and is often the choice of those who prefer white meat. It also stars on a Christmas buffet table when it can be served cold with salads. It is relatively simple to carve it into attractive slices, with the aid of a good, sharp knife.

Preheat the oven to 220°C. To make the stuffing, melt the butter in a frying pan over a moderate heat. Cook the onion for 5 minutes, stirring, until soft. Add the mince and cook for 3 minutes, until changing colour. Transfer to a large bowl with the remaining stuffing ingredients. Season to taste and mix gently. Add a lightly beaten egg if the mixture isn't holding together. Refrigerate until ready to cook the turkey.

To stuff the turkey breast, mould the stuffing under the breast and hold it into position with foil and string. Place the turkey on a rack in a large roasting pan. Brush with the melted butter and pour the stock and water into the pan. Roast for 45 minutes, basting several times. Reduce the oven temperature to 180°C, cover the turkey with foil and continue roasting for 2¼ hours, basting occasionally, or until a meat thermometer inserted into the middle registers 90°C. If you don't own a thermometer, pierce using a fork or fine skewer. If the fork goes in easily and juice runs out clear, the turkey is cooked. If the juice has a pink tinge, further cooking is required.

Once cooked, turn off the heat and rest the turkey for 15 minutes in the oven with the door ajar, while making the gravy (page 42). Set the turkey on a large platter. If serving the turkey hot, decorate with some choice vegetables, or if serving cold for a buffet, give the turkey a fresh look with salad greens. Serve a bowl of Cumberland Sauce if liked.

Serves 8–10

½ tablespoon paprika

½ teaspoon salt

½ turkey breast, cut into steaks

1 red chilli, seeded, finely chopped

1 tablespoon olive oil

¼ cup lime or lemon juice

1 red onion, cut into thin rings

1 red capsicum, cut into thin rings

sprigs of coriander, to garnish

Escabeche of Turkey

This tasty turkey dish is a colourful addition to any Christmas table.

Combine the paprika and salt and rub into the turkey breast; place in a shallow dish. Combine the chilli with the olive oil and half of the lime or lemon juice. Pour the chilli mixture over the turkey, toss through, cover and refrigerate for four hours or overnight, turning once or twice.

Preheat a grill to high. Cook the turkey for about 20 minutes, until tender, brushing frequently with the marinade and turning once or twice.

Meanwhile, toss the onion rings in the remaining lime or lemon juice. Arrange the cooked turkey steaks on a platter, scatter with the onion and capsicum rings, and coriander sprigs. Sprinkle with any remaining lime juice from the onion rings.

Serves 6–8

NOTE Young limes are readily available, as is coriander. They form an integral part of this Mexican turkey dish.

Use rubber gloves or extreme care, when seeding and chopping the chilli. If you don't use gloves, ensure you wash your hands meticulously after handling the chilli.

2.2 kg turkey breast roll

1 tablespoon olive oil

1 cup dry white wine

APPLE, PRUNE AND PISTACHIO STUFFING

60 g butter

2 spring onions, finely chopped

1 granny smith apple, coarsely grated

2 cups cubed day-old bread, toasted

⅓ cup pistachios

½ cup chopped pitted prunes

½ cup chopped Continental parsley

2 teaspoons chopped thyme leaves

salt and freshly ground black pepper, to season

Roasted Stuffed Turkey Breast

A variation of Jannie's turkey recipe (page 50), the apple, prune and pistachio stuffing adds a sweet American-style flavour to this Christmas bird. For vegetables to include, consult the vegetables chapter, but crispy roast vegetables are a must.

Preheat the oven to 200°C. To make the stuffing melt the butter in a frying pan over a moderate heat and cook the onion for 5 minutes, until soft and golden. Add the apple and cook for a further 4 minutes, until soft. Combine the onion and apple mixture in a bowl with the bread cubes, pistachios and prunes. Fold through the parsley and thyme and season well with salt and freshly ground black pepper.

Place the turkey breast roll, skin side down, on a board. Starting from one long edge, fill the stuffing along the centre of the turkey, then roll the turkey up along long edges to secure the stuffing. Secure with poultry skewers and tie at 3 cm intervals with string into a neat roll.

Heat the olive oil in a baking dish in the oven for 5 minutes. When hot, add the turkey roll and turn to coat with the oil. Roast for 45 minutes. Add the wine to the dish and roast for a further 45 minutes, basting the turkey frequently with the wine and cooking juices. Stand in a warm place for 15 minutes before removing the string and cutting into slices. Make gravy while the turkey is resting, and arrange vegetables on the platter or in serving dishes.

Serves 6–8

TIP Turkey breast rolls are available at most butchers. Make sure you place your order at least one week ahead to allow for delivery.

½ turkey breast, boned (about 1.4 kg boned weight)

10 large rashers bacon or prosciutto slices (optional)

stuffing of choice, see Pork, Apple and Pistachio Stuffing (page 80), or consult the Stuffings section (pages 78–85)

Jannie's Stuffed Turkey Breast

This dish is perfect for a smaller Christmas party – like a mini roast turkey! Our dear family friend Jannie, a wonderful cook, makes this as part of a Christmas Day banquet – hence the name. A traditional stuffing makes this dish.

Preheat the oven to 180°C. Prepare the selected stuffing. Pat the turkey dry with paper towel. Place the turkey breast, skin side down, on a board. Starting at a long edge, slice horizontally through the centre, not quite through to the other side, to make a large pocket. Fill the turkey pocket with the prepared stuffing.

Lay 2 sheets of overlapping foil on a bench (large enough to be used as a parcel for the stuffed breast). Cover the foil with baking paper then position the turkey breast in the middle. If using, cover the top of the turkey with overlapping slices of bacon or proscuitto, then place another sheet of baking paper over the breast. Wrap the foil up to form a compact log, twisting the ends to form a sealed bonbon parcel.

Bake on an oven tray for 1½ hours. Remove from the oven and leave to rest in the foil for at least 45 minutes (this will keep it hot while it rests). Slice thinly and serve with cranberry sauce, roast potatoes and vegetables.

Serves 6–8

TIP This is a lovely dish, with or without the bacon or prosciutto wrapping, which sometimes goes a bit grey. If you are not using the bacon, put a bit of melted butter on the breast before rolling it up.

2.2 kg turkey breast roll

salt and freshly ground black pepper, to season

1½ tablespoons Dijon mustard

6–8 large English spinach leaves

100 g sliced double-smoked ham

1 tablespoon chopped sage

1 stalk celery, cut into chunks

1 onion, quartered

1 bouquet garni

watercress sprigs or chopped Continental parsley, to garnish

grated rind of lemon or lime, to serve

LIME MAYONNAISE

1 whole egg, plus 2 egg yolks

juice and grated rind of 1 lime

1 tablespoon Dijon mustard

½ cup light olive oil

salt and freshly ground black pepper, to season

Poached Turkey Breast Roll with Lime Mayonnaise

The best thing about turkey cooked this way is that it is easy to cook and carve, and the preparation can be done the day before. It also avoids the possibility of overcooking the bird, since it cooks more evenly. Only 1 hour is required for a half-breast weighing about 2 kg. It is served cold, sliced and served with a big bowl of lime mayonnaise and salad greens. This dish is perfect for a buffet table or to take on a picnic.

Place the turkey roll, skin side down, on a board. Season inside with salt and freshly ground pepper and spread with the mustard. Top with the spinach, ham and chopped sage. Roll the turkey breast to enclose the stuffing and tie securely at 3 cm intervals with kitchen string.

Put the turkey breast in a large saucepan with the celery, onion and bouquet garni with just enough water to cover. Bring slowly to the boil, cover and simmer gently for 50–60 minutes. Remove from the heat and leave the meat to cool in the liquid. Remove to a plate to cool completely. Cover with plastic wrap and refrigerate.

Meanwhile, to make the lime mayonnaise, process the eggs, lime juice and Dijon mustard in a food processor until just combined. With the motor running, add the oil, a tablespoon at a time, processing well after each addition, until the mixture starts to thicken. Continue processing, adding the olive oil in a thin, steady stream until all incorporated and the mayonnaise is thick and glossy. Season well with salt and freshly ground black pepper and stir through the lime rind.

Remove the string and cut the turkey into thin slices, arrange on a platter and garnish with watercress sprigs or parsley and a little grated lemon or lime rind to serve.

Serves 8–10

2.2 kg turkey breast

1 carrot, cut into chunks

1 stalk celery, cut into chunks

1 onion, quartered

handful of Continental parsley sprigs

1 small bay leaf

rind of 1 lemon

watercress sprigs or chopped Continental parsley, to garnish

TUNA MAYONNAISE

185 g can tuna in oil, drained

4 anchovy fillets

¼ cup baby capers, drained

¾ cup Mayonnaise

lemon juice, to taste

salt and freshly ground black pepper, to season

Turkey Tonnato
(Poached Turkey with Tuna Mayonnaise)

A visitor to Italy will often be offered *vitello tonnato*, a cold dish of poached veal with a mayonnaise-type sauce made with canned tuna, anchovies and mayonnaise – it's delicious! We have found that for a light lunch it is perfect made with turkey breast instead of veal and served with a lightly dressed green salad. This is a perfect choice for a Christmas buffet table or cold Christmas dinner.

Roll the turkey to make a neat oval parcel and tie into a good shape with kitchen string at 3 cm intervals. Place the turkey breast in a large saucepan with the carrot, celery, onion, parsley and bay leaf then add just enough water to cover. Bring slowly to the boil, cover and simmer gently for 40 minutes. Remove from the heat and leave the meat to cool in the liquid.

Meanwhile, make tuna mayonnaise by processing the tuna, anchovies, 2 tablespoons of the capers and 2 tablespoons of the cold turkey cooking liquid to a paste in a food processor. Add to a bowl with the mayonnaise and mix thoroughly. Add enough lemon juice, salt and pepper to taste. If necessary, add a little more of the cooking liquid to make a coating consistency.

Cut the turkey into thin slices, arrange on a platter and spoon over the tuna mayonnaise. Sprinkle with the remaining capers, watercress sprigs or parsley and grated lemon rind to serve.

Serves 8

TIP The beauty of this dish is that it can be made well ahead of time.

| 1 whole uncooked stuffed turkey (page 39) |
| oil, for brushing |
| cut potatoes, pumpkin and sweet potatoes, to serve (optional) |

Turkey in the Barbecue

Enjoy a carefree cool kitchen on Christmas Day. Fans of the hood-covered barbecue wouldn't cook a turkey in any other way. It gives you moist and tender breast meat, flavoursome dark meat and a crispy skin every time. For best results, ensure you are familiar with your barbecue and fully understand its uses.

The real secret of barbecuing a whole turkey lies in keeping the meat moist during cooking. This can be achieved by brushing it during cooking with stock, juices or butter, or loosely covering the turkey with foil, lifting the foil only to spoon over the juices.

First prepare the barbecue and position the barbecue grill racks. If you're using a charcoal barbecue, light the fire lighters (if using) and leave the coals to heat up, with the lid off, for about 45 minutes. If you have a gas barbecue, follow the manufacturer's instructions and preheat the temperature to 180°C.

Brush the turkey with oil, loosely wrap it in foil and place on a rack in an aluminium baking dish in the centre of the barbecue, cover the barbecue lid and cook for about 25 minutes per 1 kg and an extra 30 minutes. If you're including vegetables, add them to the barbecue 45 minutes before the turkey is cooked, turning them during cooking.

Unlike other meats, turkey must be cooked through. Care must be taken, especially when barbecuing, that the outside is not burned and the inside raw. To overcome this, cook the bird slowly, in a lower heat, by the indirect method of cooking with the roasting hood down.

Serves 8–10

TIP Turkey cooks beautifully in the barbecue, but don't use one bigger than 5 kg. I find a 3–4 kg turkey works well and takes about 1¾–2½ hours to cook.

GRAVY

Use a good homemade chicken stock to make a delicious gravy. The gravy can be made in the kitchen. Pour off all but ¼ cup of drippings from the pan in which the turkey was cooked. Add 2 tablespoons plain flour and stir over a low heat for about 5 minutes, until the flour browns. Remove from the heat and gradually add 3 cups chicken stock, stirring until smooth. Bring to the boil, stirring continuously. Season with salt and freshly ground black pepper to taste and simmer until slightly thickened.

VEGETABLES

Roasted potatoes and other vegetables can be cooked with the turkey. To include potatoes, first peel and halve, then cook in boiling salted water for about 10 minutes. Drain and score lightly with a fork then add to the roasting pan for the last 30 minutes of roasting the turkey, turning several times during cooking. Continue to roast while the turkey is resting.

If there isn't enough room in the roasting pan, boil the potatoes as above for about 20 minutes; drain. Remove the turkey from the barbecue (it has to rest for 20 minutes). Put the potatoes in a fresh roasting pan with ¼ cup of the fat from the turkey and roast for 20 minutes, turning several times – you will have lovely crisp roast potatoes.

Duck

A glazed and glistening roast duck, with its crispy skin and luxurious flavour, is perfect for a Christmas spread.

A bird prized by gourmets for its rich flavour and succulence, duck can be prepared in a great variety of ways. If this is your choice for the Christmas table it is probably best – and certainly convenient for the carver – to serve half or a quarter of a whole young duckling for each person. A good young duck has creamy skin and a plump breast with a pliable breastbone. Roasting or cooking over a dry heat allows the fat to cook off the bird, also making the skin crisp. Cooking in an oven bag keeps the flesh moist, and the bag is opened at the end to crisp the skin.

It is important to realise that although a duck can almost look as big as a large chicken, it has a larger frame, more fat and less meat than a chicken the same weight. So, allow about 375–500 g raw duck per person.

Duck breasts are available at good poultry shops and butchers, the marylands (leg quarters) being used for duck confit. The breasts are excellent for easy cooking and entertaining.

Weight and temperature chart for roast duckling

WEIGHT	SERVES	COOKING TIME
Size 14: 1.4 kg	2–3	1 hour 5–15 minutes
Size 16: 1.6 kg	3-4	1 hour 5–25 minutes
Size 20: 2 kg	4	1 hour 25–30 minutes
Size 25: 2.5 kg	5–6	1 hour 35–45 minutes

Oven temperature

Set the oven at 230°C for the first 20 minutes of cooking time then reduce the heat to 190°C. Allow less time for a rare duck, which the French and many gourmets prefer.

To cook in oven bags, follow the instructions in the recipe for Duck with Cherries (page 58).

To grill duck breast

Grilled duck breast is simply delicious. As the duck breast is often fatty, the skin is scored or pricked in several places; the fat runs off during grilling. Rub the skin with a little freshly ground black pepper and sea salt. Place the breasts, skin side up, under a preheated grill and grill for 8–10 minutes; pour off excess fat as it gathers to prevent it catching alight. Turn the breasts and cook for a further 2–3 minutes. Transfer to a hot platter, cover loosely with foil and stand in a warm place for 5 minutes. Serve with a green salad and Mango–Chilli Salsa (page 61).

To carve a duck

Remove trussing strings and set the bird on a board. Cut straight down through the breastbone and back. (Use scissors or poultry shears to cut through bone.) Lay each half on a board and make a slanting cut between ribs to separate the wing and leg, making two good portions of each half. With scissors or shears, trim away any carcass bone. The portion should be two wings and two legs with a good portion of breast attached to each wing portion.

Cutting a duck

A whole young duckling may be cut into four — two breasts and two hind quarters with legs — trimmed and treated the same way; allow an extra 15 minutes cooking for legs.

Duck stock

Heat a little oil in a saucepan and brown the duck neck and giblets (if available). It is worth buying 4 or 5 chicken wings to enrich the stock. Pour off all the fat and add 3 cups water, a bouquet garni and simmer for 1 hour. Strain before using.

1 x 2 kg duck

olive oil

4–5 chicken wings

celery leaves

½ onion, chopped

1 strip of lemon peel

salt and freshly ground black pepper, to season

2 teaspoons plain flour

1 large clove garlic

250 g perfect red cherries, stoned

⅓ cup dry sherry or Raspberry Vinegar (page 294)

Roast Duck with Cherries

Roast duck is often served with fruit, which helps to counteract the rich flavour and extreme fattiness of the bird. Peaches, oranges and pineapple can all be used – cut the fruit into even-sized pieces and glaze as with the cherries in this recipe, or heat the fruit in butter or port then add to the sauce. As duckling is so rich and the flavour so good, it needs only simple accompaniments – crusty roasted potatoes or simply steamed new potatoes, green peas and a mixed green salad fit the bill.

To prepare the duck stock, remove the neck from the duckling and cut off the wing tips. Heat the oil in a small pan and brown the neck and wing tips of the duck with the chicken wings. Cover with water and add the celery leaves and chopped onion. Half cover with a lid and simmer gently for about 1 hour. Set aside until needed.

Meanwhile, wipe the duck inside and out with paper towel. Put some celery leaves and the lemon peel in the cavity and season all over with salt. Prick the skin of the duck and tie the body with kitchen string into a neat shape.

Combine the flour, salt and pepper in a large oven bag and shake the bag to coat the inside. Put the prepared duck and the garlic in the oven bag, tie up the opening and prick the bag once near the opening. (Instead of using an oven bag, you can wrap the duck in foil.) Place on a roasting rack in a baking dish and cook in a preheated oven at 230°C for 10 minutes, then reduce the heat to 220°C and cook for a further 1 hour.

Remove the duck from the oven bag and pour the juices into a jug. Sit the duck on the roasting rack and return it to the oven for a further 10 minutes, to crisp and brown the skin. Set the duck aside to keep warm. Put the baking dish over a gentle heat and lightly sauté the cherries until heated through in a little duck fat taken from the juices in the jug. Remove the cherries with a slotted spoon and set aside. Pour in the sherry or vinegar, reduce the liquid by half over a high heat, then add the strained duck stock and the reserved jug juices which have been skimmed of fat. Reduce over a moderate heat until a syrupy sauce has been formed, then return the cherries to the dish.

Present the duck whole on a warmed serving dish or carve the breast into thin slices and cut off the leg and wing joints with a little of the breast meat. Spoon a little of the sauce over the duck and scatter with the cherries. Serve the remaining sauce separately.

Serves 4

TIP This duck is cooked in an oven bag. If you prefer to roast it in the oven, see method for Duck à l'Orange (page 62).

Canned cherries may be used; drain and prepare as above. If desired, add ½ cup of the syrup to the duck stock for the gravy.

1 x 2–2.5 kg duck
salt and freshly ground black pepper, to season
1 cup wild rice
45 g butter
sprigs of watercress or mint, to serve
½ quantity Mango–Chilli Salsa (below)

Roast Duck with Wild Rice and Mango-Chilli Salsa

For a special Christmas dinner serve the whole leg or wing section and cut several slices of the breast meat for each person. Any leftover is delicious cold.

Preheat the oven to 250°C. Split the duck in halves using poultry shears and a strong knife, removing all the noticeable fat. Season the duck and place, skin side up, on a rack in a pan. Roast for 10 minutes to render some of the fat from under the skin. Reduce the oven to 180°C and continue cooking for about 30 minutes, until tender, or done to taste. Set aside in a warm place.

Meanwhile, bring a large saucepan of salted water to the boil and sprinkle in the wild rice. Boil, stirring a few times, until tender, about 30 minutes. Drain the rice, toss thoroughly with the butter and lay out in an ovenproof casserole dish. Cover and bake for 15 minutes in the oven with the duck, stirring and fluffing the rice twice. Uncover the rice, stir again, and bake for a further 15 minutes, stirring twice more to ensure that the rice grains are separate and firm.

To serve, remove the whole legs and wings with some of the breast meat attached and slice the remaining breasts slightly diagonally across. Place a leg or wing piece on each plate on a bed of the wild rice with some of the the breast slices and spoon some salsa on each plate. Garnish with watercress or mint sprigs.

Serves 4

MANGO–CHILLI SALSA

Cook 1 small red onion, 1 seeded and finely chopped serrano chilli, 3 tablespoons oil and 1 tablespoon water in a saucepan over a gentle heat for about 10 minutes, until the onion is transparent without colouring. Cool then add to a bowl with 2 cups cubed mango. Drop ½ cup mint leaves in boiling water for 30 seconds. Drain, refresh in iced water, drain again and squeeze dry, then finely chop. Add to the onion and mango mixture and stir in a little lime juice, and salt and pepper to taste. Leave to stand for an hour before serving.

Makes about 3 cups.

	ORANGE SAUCE
2 x 2.5 kg ducks	⅓ cup sugar
rind of 1 orange, pared	¼ cup sweet red wine vinegar
salt and freshly ground black pepper, to season	1½ cups chicken stock
	1½ tablespoons arrowroot mixed with 2 tablespoons port
	rind of 1 orange, cut into shreds
	½ cup port
	2 tablespoons orange liqueur such as Cointreau or Grand Marnier
	15 g butter

Duck à l'Orange

This is the best loved of all duck dishes. The duck is roasted and then served with an orange sauce, which varies from cook to cook. This recipe includes port as well as Cointreau, which makes a particularly delicious sauce. When red-fleshed, or blood, oranges are in season use them, as they add a different note to this great dish.

Preheat the oven to 220°C. Remove all the excess fat from the inside of the ducks and insert the pared orange rind into the cavities. Season with salt and pepper and truss the ducks. Pat dry with paper towel and place the ducks, breast side up, in a roasting pan. Bake for 20 minutes, until the ducks have browned lightly and released some of their fat. Remove the ducks and pour off the excess fat. Lower the temperature to 190°C and return the ducks back to roast for an hour.

Meanwhile, for the sauce, boil the sugar and vinegar over a high heat until it forms a thick syrup. Remove from the heat and gradually stir in the chicken stock. When smooth, put back over the heat and bring to the boil. Gradually add the arrowroot mixture and the orange rind. Simmer the sauce for about 4 minutes or until the sauce is clear and thickened.

When the ducks are cooked, remove the trussing string and place them on a serving dish and keep warm. As duck is awkward to carve, it might be best to carve them in the kitchen (see page 53).

Remove all the fat from the baking dish, leaving the juices in the bottom. Place over the heat and stir in the port, scraping up the pan juices, allowing it to reduce by half. Strain into the prepared sauce base and bring to a gentle simmer, then stir in the orange liqueur. Adjust the seasoning and when ready to serve, remove the sauce from the heat and swirl in the butter. Spoon a little of the sauce over the ducks to give them an attractive glaze and serve the remainder in a sauceboat.

Serves 8

NOTE *The flesh of the oranges may be cut into segments and added to the sauce at the last moment.*

2 ducklings, quartered

salt and freshly ground black pepper, to season

10 fresh figs, halved

2 tablespoons sugar

1 tablespoon balsamic vinegar

½ cup duck stock or chicken stock

Duck with Grilled Figs

This is a stunning combination – and somewhat auspiciously, good figs are available at Christmas time.

Preheat the griller to very hot or the oven to 250°C. Season the duck pieces and place, skin side up, on a rack in a pan. Grill or roast for 10 minutes to render some of the fat from under the skin then let the duck cool.

Cook the duck pieces, skin side down, in a large frying pan over a high heat for 3 minutes, reduce the heat and cook until the duck is done to taste, about 4–5 minutes. Let the duck rest in a warm place for 5 minutes to allow the juices to be reabsorbed into the meat.

Sprinkle the figs with the sugar and place under a very hot griller for 1–2 minutes until caramelised, then set aside. Alternatively, use a gas torch to caramelise the figs.

Heat 1 tablespoon of the duck fat in a frying pan with the balsamic vinegar and stock, and cook over a high heat for about 3 minutes, until the sauce has slightly thickened.

To serve, arrange the duck breasts and legs on 4 warmed serving plates, surround with the grilled figs and spoon over the sauce. A dish of Creamy Mashed or Mousseline Potatoes (page 154) could accompany this dish.

Serves 4

4 duck breasts

1–2 tablespoons light olive oil

1 tablespoon red wine vinegar

good pinch of sugar

¼ teaspoon ground cinnamon

salt and freshly ground black pepper, to season

⅔ cup blueberries or raspberries

1 tablespoon balsamic vinegar

Duck Breasts with Blueberry and Balsamic Sauce

This is a terrific dish for special occasions, so it's a perfect Christmas dinner for a small and busy family – and it only takes 15–20 minutes to cook. Serve this duck dish with a bowl of creamy mashed potatoes, asparagus or baby green beans, Beetroot and Orange Salad (page 164) or a simple green salad.

Trim the back bone and breast bones from the duck breasts. Heat the oil in a large frying pan over a gentle heat and fry the duck breasts, skin side down, until the skin is golden. Turn over and add the red wine vinegar, sugar and cinnamon and season with salt and pepper. Cover and cook gently for 10 minutes, until the duck breasts are tender and still juicy inside. Add half the berries and continue cooking for 5 minutes, until the berries have melted into a delicious sauce. Finally, swirl in the balsamic vinegar, let it bubble for a few seconds and check the sauce for seasoning. Just before serving, add the remaining berries and heat through.

Serve the duck breasts cut into thick slices over freshly steamed asparagus spears with the sauce to the side. Serve with creamy Garlic Potato Purée (page 154).

Serves 4

Chicken, Goose & Quail

How times change. When I was a girl, a chicken dinner was a treat – always roasted, we splurged on one maybe once a month, and always one for Christmas dinner. Now chicken is on the menu often twice a week and we Australians enjoy it grilled, stir-fried, roasted, and in so many other ways. So, this bird has been sidelined as a Christmas bird for many families, replaced by the enormous turkey or the more fatty goose. Quail, as well, is now a popular Christmas option, each person getting their own bird. An organic, free-range chicken is still an excellent choice for Christmas though – and like goose and quail it will fit in the oven of most households! Many families insist on a fatty goose for Christmas, which will often be forgotten the rest of the year and only be enjoyed when the stockings are hung and the tree is sparkling.

Whichever bird you choose for your Christmas meal, there are many wonderful ways to prepare them. Roasting seems most appropriate for Christmas, and all these birds go beautifully with your more traditional Christmas vegetable options – crispy potatoes, green peas and Brussels sprouts.

Chicken

We've learned how versatile chicken can be, but I still sometimes crave chicken the way it was – firmer to the bite, the chicken tasting so good on its own you hardly needed to do anything else but roast it with a little sea salt, pepper and butter or olive oil. Such chicken can still be enjoyed today, but you have to pay more for it. Personally, I prefer to have it less often and pay the price for a good-quality organic chicken – one that has scratched around and pecked the ground, and had some sort of life.

A free-range organic chicken is the way to go, especially for Christmas dinner.

What size to buy

Chickens are sold by weight – the size also relates to the weight.

WEIGHT	COOKING METHOD	SERVES
450–500 g	Perfect for splitting and grilling	1
Size 10: 750 g–1 kg	May be grilled and roasted. May also be split for a barbecue or grill	2
Size 12: 1–1.25 kg	Perfect size for sautéed dishes	3–4
Size 15–20: 1.5–2 kg	For roasting	4–6
Size 18: 1.8 kg	For roasting	6

Goose

Goose is a traditional English and German bird. It is a gamey and rich meat which also contains a lot of fat – and many people love it.

The skin on goose craves to be cooked to a crisp, while the goose itself needs gentle treatment. A red currant glaze helps to give the goose a nice sweetness and a festive pink colour with the juices inside the meat.

Carving the goose

Remove the trussing string and poultry pins and place the bird on a board. Cut off the legs. Remember that the leg joint is set differently to a chicken, right under the back of the bird. Raise the wing and breast by slipping the knife under them and along the carcass down to the wing bones, which are severed at the joint. Slice off a piece of breast with each wing bone attached. Cut the rest of the breast into slanting slices.

To serve, arrange the legs at one end of a hot serving dish, the wings at the other end and the breast pieces in the centre. Spoon gravy over the meat and serve the rest separately in a sauceboat.

Quail

Quail is a small pale-fleshed game bird, which has a delicious gamey taste. It is usually tender and should be cooked quickly in a hot oven or on a grill or barbecue. Allow one or two per person (depending on appetites) for a main course.

Quail can be eaten with a knife and fork, but it is easier to eat wings and drumsticks with fingers. For this reason, finger bowls should be offered when quails are served.

	GLAZE
1 x 3 kg goose	⅔ cup red currant jelly
3 large cooking apples	1 tablespoon grated ginger
salt and freshly ground black pepper, to season	1 teaspoon grated lemon rind
12 large prunes, stoned	1 clove
rind of 1 lemon	½ cup water
2 tablespoons plus 2 teaspoons plain flour	
¼ cup brandy	
1 cup chicken stock	

Red Currant Glazed Roast Goose

For centuries, roast goose has been served traditionally throughout Europe and England at Christmas. Each country has its own favourite stuffing – apple and prune for the Danes, sage and onion for the English and a truffle or two for the French.

Goose was also traditionally served on Michaelmas Day (29 September). Legend has it that Good Queen Bess (Elizabeth I) was indulging her fondness for goose when she was brought the news of the Spanish Armada's defeat. To celebrate, she decreed that roast goose should be served on this day each year in commemoration of this great event.

To make the glaze, simmer the red currant jelly, ginger, lemon rind, clove and water in a saucepan over a gentle heat for 5 minutes, then set aside in a small bowl.

Remove any excess fat from the inside of the goose and wipe the inside of the cavity and outside skin with damp paper towel. Using kitchen scissors or poultry shears, remove the oil sac from the parson's nose (or bishop's nose). This has a strong taste and if not removed can flavour the flesh of the bird.

Peel, core and roughly chop 2 of the cooking apples, season with salt and pepper and mix with the prunes and lemon rind. Spoon this stuffing into the cavity. Place a whole apple in

the body cavity to give the goose a good shape, then truss it. This stuffing is often discarded.

Lightly dust the goose with 2 tablespoons of the flour and place in a lightly greased roasting pan over a high heat. Sear the goose, then pour the brandy over and set it alight to flame the bird. This adds flavour and at the same time sears off the tiny pin feathers.

Place in a 200°C oven for 15–20 minutes, then cover the pan with a lid or foil, reduce the oven temperature to 170°C and continue to cook for about 2 hours, brushing with the glaze every 30 minutes. Remove the lid or foil and cook for a further 30 minutes.

4 granny smith apples

8 large prunes, stones removed

Glaze (page 68)

Poached apples stuffed with prunes

Cut the apples in two, remove the core and any pips. Place a prune in the centre of each apple half and spoon over 1 teaspoon of the glaze on each. Place the apples on a lightly greased ovenproof dish and cover the bottom of the dish with a little water. Cover the dish with a lid or foil and poach gently in a 170°C oven for 10 minutes. Serve with goose.

NOTE If the oven space is limited, this dish may be cooked over a gentle heat in a flameproof dish.

When the goose is cooked, remove it from the oven and place it on a serving platter or a carving board and remove the trussing string. Keep it warm while it rests.

To make the gravy, skim 2 tablespoons of the fat from the pan juices into a cup and discard any extra fat. Blend the fat to a smooth paste with the remaining 2 teaspoons of flour. Place the roasting pan over a gentle heat and add the remaining apple, which has been peeled, cored and chopped very finely. Cook gently for 2–3 minutes, until the apple is soft. Add the hot stock, then blend in the paste of flour and goose fat and bring to the boil, stirring and scraping all the pan juices. Simmer for a further 2–3 minutes. Mash the stuffing and add a little to the gravy. Serve the gravy separately in a sauceboat. Discard the stuffing, as it could be too rich.

Surround the roast goose with the poached apple halves stuffed with prunes. This dish goes well with sides of Braised Red Cabbage (page 144), Mousseline Potatoes (page 154) and Green Peas with Mushrooms (page 148).

Serves 8

1.8 kg (size 18) free-range organic chicken

60 g butter or ¼ cup olive oil

salt and freshly ground black pepper, to season

6 tarragon or Continental parsley stalks

3 strips orange rind

1 cup chicken stock

½ cup white wine

500 g baby new potatoes or 4 large desiree potatoes, peeled and quartered

Lemon and Parsley Stuffing (page 73)

French Roast Chicken Dinner

Ensure you buy a large, free-range organic roasting chicken and this meal will be special enough to serve for Christmas. The French way of roasting chicken is to add stock to the baking dish and to baste the chicken with the stock throughout the cooking process. The chicken may appear pale, but miraculously the skin turns a lovely golden brown at the end of the cooking and the flesh is kept beautifully moist. The potatoes taste good too, having taken in some of the flavour of the chicken. Should you also decide to stuff the chicken, I've included one of the best stuffings I know.

Preheat the oven to 200°C. Put a little butter or oil, salt, pepper, tarragon or parsley stalks and orange rind inside the cavity of the chicken. If you fancy stuffing the chicken, refer to the recipe for Lemon and Parsley Stuffing (page 73).

Truss the chicken (see instructions over the page) and rub all over with remaining butter or oil. Turn the chicken on its side on a roasting rack in baking dish with ½ cup of the chicken stock. Add the potatoes to the dish and roast the chicken for 20 minutes. Turn on the other side, baste with stock and turn the potatoes.

Reduce the heat to 190°C and cook for a further 50 minutes, turning and basting every 15 minutes and adding more stock when necessary (about

another ½ cup). Towards the end of cooking, add the wine and turn the chicken on its back for the last 15 minutes to brown the breast. Turn the potatoes from time to time. There should be just enough stock to keep the juices in the pan from scorching.

To test, run a fine skewer into the thigh joint of the chicken. The juices should be clear, with no pink. Remove the chicken from the pan and discard the string. Keep in a warm place to rest.

Remove the potatoes and keep warm while making gravy, or you can simply deglaze the pan. If so, place the baking dish over a moderate heat, add 1 cup chicken stock or white wine and scrape up the sediments to mix with the liquid.

Let it bubble for a few minutes to become syrupy. Pour into a jug and keep warm to serve with the chicken.

You may like to carve some of the breast meat and cut the remaining chicken into joints. Arrange the chicken on a heated serving dish, surrounded with the potatoes. Serve with the stuffing, Glazed Carrots (page 150) and French Peas (page 135), or other young cooked green vegetables, and the pan sauce or gravy.

Serves 6

IF YOU WANT TO MAKE GRAVY
Pour off all but 2 tablespoons of the pan juices and put the pan over a gentle heat. Add 1 scant tablespoon flour and stir well, until lightly browned. Add 1½ cups chicken stock or stock and water, and stir until thickened. Season with salt and pepper. Pour into a small saucepan to keep warm or pour into a jug or gravy boat.

Cream Gravy: Make as above but just before serving stir in ¼ cup cream and cook a little, just until thickened.

Mushroom Gravy: Pour off all but 2 tablespoons of the pan juices and put the pan over a gentle heat. Add 8–10 sliced button mushrooms to the pan and cook for 3–4 minutes, stirring and turning together to cook evenly. Proceed as for gravy, stirring in ¼ cup cream at the end.

TO TRUSS A CHICKEN
Put the chicken on its back, pull the skin over the neck and secure by folding the wing tips back over the skin. Run kitchen string across the outside end of the breast, around the wings, cross under the back, then bring the string back up to tie the legs together, keeping them close to the body.

If you want to stuff the chicken, put some of the stuffing into the neck end – don't fill it too tightly – and some into the body cavity. Allow plenty of space for the stuffing to swell and stay light.

3 cups fresh white breadcrumbs

1 small onion, finely chopped

15 g butter

¾ cup chopped Continental parsley

2 teaspoons grated lemon rind

1 egg, lightly beaten

salt and freshly ground black pepper, to season

lemon juice or chicken stock, to moisten

Lemon and Parsley Stuffing

I love this lemon and parsley combination for a stuffing.

Spread the breadcrumbs on a baking tray and dry in a 160°C oven, but do not colour. Cook the onion with the butter over a low heat for about 5 minutes, until softened. Mix with the breadcrumbs, parsley and lemon rind. Add the egg, salt and pepper and a little lemon juice or stock to bind. Toss together lightly with a fork – don't over-mix.

4 x 600 g spatchcock, excess fat removed

salt, to season

2 rashers bacon, rind removed, halved

8 sage leaves

4 sprigs of rosemary

40 g butter

2 tablespoons oil, plus extra, for greasing

8 thin slices prosciutto

Roast Spatchcock

Serving a whole spatchcock per person makes a great festive meal for Christmas. Each person gets their very own chicken, but for smaller appetites, one spatchcock can serve two. The spatchcock are cooked in a large brown paper bag, which you can make from brown wrapping paper or baking paper. You can also use oven bags or foil.

Season the cavities of the spatchcock with salt, then stuff half the bacon with the sage leaves and rosemary inside each cavity. Truss the spatchcock into a neat shape with kitchen string. Heat a quarter of the butter and oil in a frying pan over a moderately high heat and quickly brown one spatchcock all over. Repeat with remaining spatchcock. Remove from the pan, cool slightly and then cover each with 2 slices of the prosciutto.

Brush the insides of 4 paper bags large enough to enclose a spatchcock with oil, enclose the spatchcock in the parcel and tie securely with string. If using baking paper, fold loosely around the spatchcock, folding the edges to make a seal. Place the bags in a baking pan and bake in a preheated 180°C oven for 15 minutes. Pierce each bag in a couple of places with a sharply pointed knife and continue cooking for a further 1 hour. Cut open the bags for the last 10 minutes to allow the skin to brown and crisp.

Remove from the oven and discard the bags, allowing any juices in the bags to drain into a hot jug. Line a warm platter with the slices of prosciutto and arrange the spatchcock on top, whole or jointed. Offer a bowl of steamed new potatoes to serve with the spatchcock and some choice vegetables such as peas or asparagus, followed with a green salad. Offer some of the hot chicken juices or make a gravy (page 71).

Serves 4

	GREEN PEA MOUSSELINE
6–8 quail	500 g shelled green peas, fresh or frozen
salt and freshly ground black pepper, to season	1 iceberg lettuce, shredded
2 strips orange rind, pared thinly	60 g butter
6–8 sprigs of thyme and Continental parsley	salt and freshly ground black pepper, to season
60 g butter	½ cup cream
2 tablespoons olive oil	4 slices ham or prosciutto (optional)

Quail Borghese

This is a delicious dish for a special occasion, like a Christmas dinner – it looks spectacular at the table. The mousseline of green peas may be made ahead of time and the quail prepared and ready for the oven. Think of offering finger bowls, as fingers will be needed to eat the quail.

Pat dry the quail with paper towel and season with salt and pepper. Put a small piece of orange rind and a sprig of thyme and parsley inside each bird. Tie the birds into a neat shape with kitchen string. Heat the butter and oil in a heavy flameproof casserole dish and brown the quail on all sides. Cover the casserole and bake the birds in a 230°C oven for 15–20 minutes, basting several times during cooking with the juices.

To prepare the pea mousseline, cook the peas with the shredded lettuce and butter in a heavy-based saucepan over a gentle heat until tender, shaking the pan from time to time. Season with salt and pepper to taste and purée in a mouli or food processor or push through a sieve. Return to the pan, taste and adjust the seasoning. Fold in the cream and heat gently. This may be done ahead and reheated when ready to serve.

Spoon the pea mousseline into a heatproof serving dish. Cut the ham or prosciutto, if using, into julienne strips and sprinkle over the purée. Remove the string from the quails and arrange them on the purée. Return to a 180°C oven for 10 minutes.

Serves 6–8

6–8 quail

salt and freshly ground black pepper, to season

1–2 teaspoons chopped mint

30 g unsalted butter

1 cup white grape juice

1 cup seedless grapes

Quail with Grapes

Quail are delectable treated this way and because you may need to use your fingers, be sure to provide finger bowls.

Pat dry the quail with paper towel and season with salt, pepper and mint. Melt the butter in a large heavy-based frying pan over a moderately high heat until foaming. Add the quail and cook for 3–4 minutes on each side, until the juices run clear when the thighs are pierced with a skewer. Transfer the birds to a warm serving plate and keep warm while making the gravy. If your frying pan is not large enough, you may have to add more butter and cook the quail in batches or use 2 frying pans.

Pour off any excess butter from the pan, add the grape juice and stir over the heat, scraping up any brown bits on the base of the pan. When reduced and syrupy, heat the grapes in the sauce then spoon the sauce over the quail. If liked, serve with a small mound of steamed wild rice or long-grain rice, or a combination of both.

Serves 6–8

TO ROAST QUAIL IN THE OVEN
Preheat the oven to 200°C. Pat dry the quail with paper towel. Rub soft butter over the birds and season with salt and pepper. Place in a baking dish with 40 g butter and bake for 7–10 minutes on each side, basting every now and then, until they are tender. Proceed with the recipe.

Stuffings

75 g butter	½ cup chopped pitted dessert prunes
1 small onion, finely chopped	½ cup chopped Continental parsley
1 granny smith apple, coarsely grated	2 teaspoons chopped sage leaves
2 cups cubed toasted day-old bread	salt and freshly ground black pepper, to season
¼ cup pistachios	

Apple, Prune and Pistachio Stuffing*

Melt the butter in a frying pan over a moderate heat and cook the onion, stirring, for 5 minutes, until soft and golden. Add the apple and cook for a further 4 minutes, until soft. In a bowl, combine the onion and apple mixture with the bread cubes, pistachios and prunes. Fold through the parsley and sage and season well with salt and freshly ground black pepper.

Makes enough to stuff a turkey

* SEE ALSO *ROAST STUFFED TURKEY BREAST* ON PAGE 49

- -

3 cups cubed day-old bread	grated rind and juice of 1 lemon
1 small onion, finely chopped	30 g butter, melted
¾ cup chopped Continental parsley	1 egg, lightly beaten
1 tablespoon thyme leaves	salt and freshly ground black pepper, to season

Lemon and Parsley Stuffing*

Process the bread in a food processor until it forms crumbs. Spread the breadcrumbs on a baking tray and dry in a 160°C oven for about 20 minutes.

Combine the breadcrumbs, onion, herbs, lemon rind, juice and butter. Add the egg, season to taste with salt and freshly ground black pepper and toss lightly with a fork to mix. Use to stuff the cavity (main body) of turkey.

Makes enough to stuff a turkey

* SEE ALSO *ROAST TURKEY WITH TWO STUFFINGS* ON PAGE 40

6 cups fresh white breadcrumbs

40 g unsalted butter

1 large onion, finely chopped

grated rind of 1 orange

¾ cup orange juice

½ cup mixed fresh herbs, such as Continental parsley,
thyme and chervil

½ cup chopped nuts, such as macadamias, pecans
or walnuts

1 egg, beaten

salt and freshly ground black pepper, to season

Orange, Herb and Nut Stuffing*

Dry the breadcrumbs, without browning, on a baking tray in a 160°C oven.
Melt the butter in a frying pan over a moderate heat and cook the onion for
5 minutes, stirring, until soft. Transfer to a large bowl and add the remaining
stuffing ingredients. Season to taste and mix thoroughly. Add a small
amount of cream if the stuffing doesn't hold together.

Makes enough to stuff a turkey

* SEE ALSO *TURKEY WITH ORANGE, HERB AND NUT STUFFING* ON PAGE 44

- -

½ cup apple juice or cider

4 slices white bread, cubed

500 g pork mince

3 stalks celery, finely chopped

2 apples, peeled, cored and diced

1 small onion, chopped

1 tablespoon chopped Continental parsley

2 teaspoons chopped thyme

½ cup shelled unsalted pistachios

1 egg, beaten

salt and freshly ground black pepper, to taste

Pork, Apple and Pistachio Stuffing

Pour the apple juice or cider over the bread cubes and allow to stand for
30 minutes. Mix together the pork mince, celery, apples, onion, herbs and
pistachios with the soaked bread. Blend together well with the egg and
season well with salt and freshly ground black pepper. Use to stuff the crop
(breast) of turkey.

Makes enough to stuff a turkey

| 2 cups soft white breadcrumbs |
| 60 g butter |
| 3–4 tablespoons chopped Continental parsley |
| 1 teaspoon chopped thyme or lemon thyme |
| 1 teaspoon chopped marjoram |
| 2 eggs, beaten |
| salt and freshly ground black pepper, to season |
| grated rind and juice of 1 lemon |

Fresh Herb Stuffing
(For a Small Turkey or Large Chicken)

This recipe may sound simple, but the result is deliciously fresh-tasting and interesting. If you don't have fresh herbs, don't substitute with dried herbs in this recipe – choose a different stuffing.

Spread the breadcrumbs on a baking tray and dry in a 160°C oven for about 20 minutes. Melt the butter and combine in a large bowl with the toasted crumbs and the remaining ingredients. If the lemon is large and very juicy, use the juice of only half the lemon. Allow the mixture to cool, and stuff the bird just before roasting.

Makes enough to stuff a small turkey or large chicken

4 cups day-old bread, cut into small cubes	¾ cup pine nuts
185 g butter	⅓ cup chopped Continental parsley
1 onion, chopped	½ teaspoon chopped thyme leaves
2 granny smith apples	salt and freshly ground black pepper, to taste
1 cup chopped, pitted dessert prunes	

Apple and Prune Stuffing
(For Goose or Large Duckling)

Spread the bread cubes on a baking tray and dry in a 160°C oven for about 10 minutes. Melt the butter in a heavy frying pan and sauté the onion until soft. Peel, core and cube the apples and add to the pan, cook for a further 2 minutes. Combine the onion mixture with the toasted bread cubes and the prunes in a bowl. Use the onion pan to lightly toast the pine nuts. Add to the bread mixture with the parsley and thyme. Blend together well and season well with salt and freshly ground black pepper.

Makes enough to stuff a goose or large duckling

- -

2 tablespoons olive oil	1 cup sliced mushrooms
500 g pork and veal mince	1 tablespoon salt
1 large onion, chopped	freshly ground black pepper, to season
1½ cups chopped celery	grated nutmeg, to taste
4 cups fresh white breadcrumbs	pinch of dried thyme
4 cups cooked, mashed sweet potato	pinch of ground cloves

Sweet Potato Stuffing
(For Turkey)

Heat the oil in a large frying pan and cook the pork and veal mince until lightly browned, stirring to brown evenly. Remove from the pan with a slotted spoon and add the onion and celery to the fat remaining. Cook for a few minutes, stirring, then add the breadcrumbs, sweet potato, mushrooms, salt, pepper, nutmeg, thyme and cloves. Stir over a gentle heat until well combined, then stir in the browned pork and veal mince. Take off the heat and allow to cool before filling the turkey. The mixture may be refrigerated in a covered bowl, and used to stuff the turkey just before baking.

Makes enough to stuff a turkey

4 granny smith apples

1 cup soft white breadcrumbs

½ small onion, chopped

30 g butter, melted

½ cup seeded raisins or sultanas

salt and freshly ground black pepper, to season

1 teaspoon sugar

Apple and Raisin Stuffing (For Goose)

Wash the apples and hollow out as much as possible from the top with a sharp spoon, leaving a shell of apple. Make sure all the core and seeds are removed, but take care not to pierce the base of the apple. Chop the apple flesh finely, and mix with the remaining ingredients. Spoon into the apple shells. Place around the goose for the last 45 minutes of cooking.

Makes 4 stuffed apples

½ cup raisins

¾ cup Cognac or brandy

¼ cup chopped spring onions

125 g butter

½ teaspoon salt

1½ cups cooked rice

¼ cup chopped, shelled pistachios or pine nuts

Cognac Raisin and Rice Stuffing (For Duck)

Soak the raisins in the Cognac or brandy for 10 minutes. Sauté the spring onion in the butter until tender. Combine the raisins, spring onions and butter, salt, rice and nuts in a large bowl and toss lightly to combine.

Makes enough to stuff a duck

2 onions, sliced

60 g butter

2 cups fresh white breadcrumbs

1 teaspoon dried sage

2 teaspoons finely chopped Continental parsley

salt and freshly ground black pepper, to season

1 beaten egg or a little milk, to bind

Sage and Onion Stuffing (For Duck – a Traditional Stuffing)

Simmer the onions for 5 minutes in salted water. Drain and stir in the softened butter. Add the breadcrumbs, sage and parsley, season with salt and freshly ground black pepper, and bind together with beaten egg or milk.

Makes enough to stuff a duck

- -

3 rashers streaky bacon, rind removed, diced

1 cup diced celery

1 cup finely chopped onion

750 g pork sausage mince

2 tablespoons chopped Continental parsley

3 cups lightly-packed soft white breadcrumbs

1 egg, lightly beaten

grated rind of ½ lemon

salt and freshly ground black pepper, to season

Sausage and Bacon Stuffing (For Turkey)

Sauté the bacon, celery and onions in a large frying pan over a moderate heat for about 10 minutes, add the mince and stir until combined.

Mix the sausage mixture lightly in a large bowl with the parsley, breadcrumbs, egg and lemon rind. Season with salt and freshly ground pepper.

Makes enough to stuff a turkey

NOTE This amount of stuffing is sufficient for a turkey weighing 5-6 kg. Use it to stuff the neck cavity or body cavity, but don't pack too tightly. Any leftover stuffing may be baked in a separate ovenproof dish or made into balls and placed around the turkey for the last 30 minutes of baking.

12 large dessert prunes	1 tablespoon finely chopped herbs (Continental parsley, thyme, sage)
½ cup red wine mixed with ½ cup water	
30 g butter	grated rind of ½ lemon
1½ cups finely chopped celery	salt and freshly ground black pepper, to season
1 large onion, finely chopped	½ beaten egg
250 g dried chestnuts or 290 g canned whole chestnuts	

Prune, Chestnut and Celery Stuffing (For Turkey)

Soak the prunes in the wine for 2 hours. Gently simmer the prunes and wine in a saucepan until tender. Drain and reserve the liquid. Cut into quarters.

Melt the butter in a frying pan and sauté the onion and celery until tender. Quarter the chestnuts and add to a bowl with the prunes, onion and celery, and remaining ingredients, adding a little prune juice if necessary.

This stuffing is suitable for the crop or neck of the turkey. To use it as a stuffing for a whole turkey, add 4–6 cups fresh breadcrumbs, enough stock or orange juice to moisten and a whole egg to bind.

Makes enough to stuff a turkey

- -

1⅓ cups long-grain rice	½ cup chopped mixed fresh herbs (chervil, tarragon, dill, mint, Continental parsley, chives)
45 g butter	
1 onion, chopped	salt and freshly ground black pepper, to season
4 rashers streaky bacon, rind removed, diced	

Rice Stuffing with Herbs (For Vegetables)

Use as a stuffing for vegetables, such as red or green capsicum, tomatoes, cucumbers, squash, marrow or wrapped in cabbage or vine leaves. It is also excellent as a stuffing for a roast chicken.

Cook the rice in boiling salted water until almost tender then drain. Melt the butter in a frying pan and cook the onion until translucent. Add the bacon and fry, stirring, until lightly coloured. Remove from the heat and stir in the cooked rice, herbs, salt and freshly ground black pepper.

Makes about 3 cups

Ham & Pork

Since I was a child, the youngest of six in a very social and busy family, I have relished the air of excitement in preparing for a celebration. I have never outgrown this, and no matter how small the occasion, I still get a lot of pleasure in anticipating and planning the food for guests. For Christmas celebrations, you will often find ham or pork at our table.

It was a great celebration the day I learned to cook roast pork with crispy crackling and tender succulent meat the way my mother used to make. I thought it was all due to her management of the temperamental, but wonderful fuel stove. With today's superb temperature-controlled ovens it is something we can all manage – it's all a matter of timing and temperatures. If you choose to cook pork without the crackling, the oven temperature is moderate throughout the cooking but the times remain the same (see page 92 for instructions).

Carving ham

Use a very sharp knife, preferably with a long, thin blade. The easiest way to carve a ham is to cut a wedge out first, about two-thirds along the leg, and carve slices each side. This allows a good distribution of lean and fat, and makes manageable slices. Cold ham is cut in thin slices, but a hot ham may be cut into thicker slices. Before carving, wrap a sheet of foil around the knuckle. The carver can cover this with a clean napkin, and hold the ham without getting greasy.

Storing ham

Cover with a clean tea towel or store in a light cheesecloth bag that has been dipped in a solution of 2 cups water with 1 tablespoon vinegar, then squeezed out. If covering with a tea towel, replace it about every three days to keep the ham moist and fresh. It is also a good idea to cut the ham in several large pieces, wrap the pieces in foil and store until needed. When the bone is stripped, freeze the bone for making soup later on.

Glazed or baked ham?

For a spectacular looking ham with a glaze that sparkles and glows, there are many glaze recipes to choose from. The process of glazing usually takes 30–60 minutes and involves removing the skin from the ham, scoring the fat underneath and spreading the glaze over the surface. Ingredients for glazes vary but can include mustard, marmalade, honey, spices (often cloves), pineapple rings and green and red glace cherries.

I prefer a baked ham where the meat is baked under foil to steam in the fumes of stout, basting every so often, the ham surface is scored and a spiced mixture is spread over the top. It emerges from the oven the most glorious spectacle and the slightly caramelised sugary bits and the flavour of the meat are truly memorable.

Glazes for ham

Marmalade glaze

Combine ½ cup Dijon mustard, ½ cup marmalade, ½ cup brown sugar, 2 tablespoons ground ginger and ¼ cup orange juice. Brush on the ham to glaze after scoring the fat (for method, see recipe for Baked Guinness Ham, page 88). Insert cloves in the centre of the diamonds if you like.

Red currant and balsamic glaze

Combine ½ cup red currant jelly, 1 tablespoon Dijon mustard, ½ cup brown sugar and 2 tablespoons balsamic vinegar. Brush on the ham to glaze after scoring the fat (for method, see recipe for Baked Guinness Ham, page 88). Insert cloves in the centre of the diamonds if you like.

Brandied red currant glaze

Combine ¾ cup red currant jelly and 2 tablespoons each brandy and lemon juice. Heat the jelly if lumpy. Brush on the ham to glaze after scoring the fat (for method, see recipe for Baked Guinness Ham, page 88). Insert cloves in the centre of the diamonds if you like.

Baked Guinness Ham

Come Christmas or New Year, there is usually a baked glazed ham on our buffet table. Most often the ham is baked with the flavours of stout, sugar and spice, with the edges caramelised, so that each slice, with a lot of lean and a little fat, is a perfect mix of flavour.

I got this recipe from the Irish Tourist Board years ago and thought they were way ahead of the times using such unlikely ingredients. Although the ham is already cooked before being baked, further cooking with the stout helps to flavour the meat before the glaze is added. Baking continues at a higher temperature, with the sweet and spicy caramelised glaze really making this a special occasion dish. Look at doing a more economical picnic ham (the shoulder with the bone still attached) or a half leg for smaller family gatherings. Accompany the ham with a big bowl of still warm boiled new potatoes, tossed in butter, with a grinding of pepper and chopped parsley. Crusty bread, a large green salad and a choice of mustards are the other essentials. [CONTINUED OVERLEAF]

	GLAZE
1 x 5–6 kg leg of ham	1 cup sugar
2 cans or 1 large bottle Guinness extra stout, reserving 2–3 tablespoons for the glaze	2 teaspoons dry mustard
whole cloves (optional)	2 teaspoons each ground cardamom and ground ginger
	extra 2–3 tablespoons Guinness stout

Baked Guinness Ham [CONTINUED]

Preheat the oven to 160°C. Cut the skin around the thick end of the knuckle (this can be made into a scallop pattern) without cutting into the fat and flesh. Ease the skin from the fat by slipping the thumb of one hand under the skin, and firmly sliding it back and forth. Turn the ham over and ease away the rest of the skin, which should come off in one piece. Place the ham, fat side up, in a roasting pan with the stout, reserving 2–3 tablespoons for the glaze. Cover with foil, crimping the edges onto the roasting pan, making it as airtight as possible, and bake for 1½ hours. Lift the foil and baste the ham with the drippings several times during cooking.

Remove from the oven, lift the foil and pour off the liquid into a saucepan. Using a sharp knife, score the fat with 4 cm interval diagonal cuts, first one way, then the opposite way, to form a diamond pattern.

Spread half the glaze mixture over the ham and stud a clove in the corner of each diamond if you like. Increase the oven temperature to 200°C and bake for a further 30–40 minutes, basting every 10 minutes with the remaining glaze. If serving hot, leave the ham in the turned-off oven for 30 minutes. If serving cold, cool and store in refrigerator overnight and serve thinly sliced. Place the ham on a stand or large serving platter and garnish with watercress or parsley.

Serves 20

2.5 kg boned loin of pork, rind on

12 pitted dessert prunes

12 almonds

12 anchovy fillets

coarse salt and freshly ground black pepper, to season

Apple Sauce (page 276), to serve

GRAVY

1 tablespoon plain flour

1 cup chicken or vegetable stock

Roast Pork with Prunes, Almonds and Anchovies

The Danes often roast a loin of pork with a prune stuffing. This one is unusual – each prune is stuffed with an almond and rolled in an anchovy fillet. Anchovies are known to do wonders for the flavour of meat.

Score the pork rind with a sharp knife. Unroll the pork loin, skin side down. Place an almond in the cavity of each prune and wrap an anchovy fillet around each one. Arrange the stuffed prunes along the centre of the pork loin. Season well with freshly ground black pepper. Roll up and tie with kitchen string.

Rub a little salt into the rind of the pork and place on a rack in a roasting pan. Roast in a preheated 250°C oven for 30 minutes or until the rind is puffy and blistered. Reduce the oven temperature to 180°C and pour about ½ cup water into the pan. Roast for a further 1–1½ hours or until a meat thermometer registers 76°C. If you don't have a meat thermometer, it is cooked when the juices run clear when the meat is pierced with a skewer. Remove the pork and stand 10 minutes before carving.

To make the gravy, pour the excess fat from the roasting pan, leaving about 2 tablespoons and blend in the flour. Cook for a few minutes then add the stock. Bring to the boil, stirring in the crusty bits from pan for 2–3 minutes, until thickened. Season to taste and serve the gravy and Apple Sauce with the pork and a selection of your favourite vegetable dishes.

Serves 6–8

2–2.5 kg loin of pork, with the bones intact and scraped
    as for a rack of lamb (ask the butcher to do this)

1 sprig rosemary

3 cloves garlic

coarse salt and freshly ground black pepper, to season

1 tablespoon fresh chopped mixed herbs

1 cup dry white wine

Apple Sauce (page 276), to serve

Roast Loin of Pork with Rosemary and Garlic

This looks magnificent, like a standing rib roast – and is special for those who love roast pork.

Ask the butcher to score the skin and some of the fat of the pork in narrow strips or a diamond pattern. Finely chop the rosemary and garlic, season with salt, freshly ground black pepper and chopped mixed herbs. Make a few slits on the underside of the pork and push this herb and garlic mixture into the slits to season the pork well. Rub the skin liberally with salt and put the pork on a rack in a roasting pan. Roast the pork in a preheated 230°C oven for 25 minutes to crisp the skin. Reduce the oven temperature to 180°C and continue to roast the meat, allowing 20 minutes per 500 g, about 1½ hours.

Transfer to a serving platter and keep warm for 10 minutes before carving. Pour off the fat from the roasting pan and add the wine to deglaze over a moderate heat. Boil for a few minutes and set aside in a bowl to keep warm and serve. Carve the pork into thick chops to serve. Serve with Braised Red Cabbage with Apples (page 144), Creamy Mashed Potatoes (page 154) or Mousseline Potatoes (page 154), Glazed Carrots (page 150), Green Beans with Almonds (page 148) or vegetables of your choice, and follow with salad greens.

Serves 8

1.5–2 kg loin of pork, boned or left on the bone with the
  chops chined (ask your butcher to do this), or 1 leg or
  shoulder of pork

6 sage leaves

1 tablespoon olive oil

sea salt

8 desiree, pontiac or Dutch cream potatoes, peeled
  and halved

Apple Sauce (page 276), to serve

GRAVY

1½ tablespoons plain flour

1½ cups chicken or vegetable stock

Traditional Roast Pork

Roast pork with its crisp crackling always seems rather special. Be generous with serving the
crackling as it really isn't all that good cold and everyone loves the crisp crunchiness of warm
crackling. Don't forget the apple sauce and gravy, or rhubarb and orange for a change –
you could even consider grilled peaches or apricots.

Preheat the oven to 230°C. Weigh the pork and ascertain the cooking time. It is
a good idea to ask your butcher to give you the exact weight. Also, ask him to
score the skin of pork in narrow strips or a diamond pattern. Pierce the flesh with
a sharp pointed knife to insert the sage leaves. Place on a rack in a roasting pan
and rub the skin all over with the oil then with the salt.

Roast for 30 minutes or until the skin is crisp and golden. Meanwhile, drop the
potatoes into a saucepan of boiling salted water for 5 minutes, drain and score
lightly with a fork.

Reduce the heat to 180°C, add the potatoes and roast until cooked through, turning
the potatoes several times, for about 45–60 minutes. If the loin is on the bone, use
a sharp knife to remove the chin bone and loosen the meat. To make carving easier,
remove the crackling in sections. Carve the meat across into thick slices.

To make the gravy, pour the excess fat from the roasting pan, leaving about
1 tablespoon and blend in the flour. Cook for a few minutes then add the stock.
Bring to the boil, stirring in the crusty bits from pan for 2–3 minutes, until
thickened. Season to taste.

Serve the pork hot with green vegetables in season, gravy and apple sauce, or one
of the following fruit suggestions.

Serves 8

OTHER FRUITS

While apple sauce is hard to beat with pork, other fruits may be used. Ripe peach or apricot halves can be dotted with butter and grilled to serve with a joint of pork, pineapple rings can be treated the same way, and many people enjoy a cranberry sauce as an accompaniment. The tart flavour of plums also goes well with the richness of pork.

One of my favourite fruit combinations to combine with a roast pork dish is rhubarb with orange. To prepare, wash and cut a bundle of rhubarb into 5 cm lengths. Add to a heavy-based saucepan with a nut of butter, the grated rind and juice from an orange and 1 tablespoon brown sugar. Cover and cook over a low heat for 8–10 minutes. Leave until cool and serve with the pork.

CRACKLING

So you want crispy crackling? Ask the butcher to remove the pork rind from the loin. Slice the rind into narrow strips. Toss the rind, 2 teaspoons sea salt and 2 tablespoons oil together in a bowl. Preheat ⅓ cup vegetable oil (rice bran oil is good) in a baking dish over a high heat. Add the rinds to the hot baking dish and roast in a preheated 220°C oven for 20–25 minutes or until crispy. Drain on crushed paper towel.

Extra crackling? Ask the butcher for an extra 500 g pork rind piece to be cut specially.

2 kg loin of pork, boned and skin removed

1 large clove garlic

salt and freshly ground black pepper, to season

½ teaspoon lemon rind

⅓ cup chopped Continental parsley

4 sprigs thyme, leaves from 2 sprigs chopped

1 bay leaf, crushed

¾ cup white or red wine

¼ cup fine dry breadcrumbs

Apple Sauce (page 276), to serve

Roast Loin of Pork Provençal

Roast pork has its steadfast devotees. This is the way it is done in the south of France. Serve this dish with Creamy Mashed Potatoes (page 154) or a scalloped potato dish, with French Peas (page 136) and Apple Sauce (page 276), and a green salad to follow.

Use a sharp knife to cut the rind from the pork and bone – it is better to ask the butcher to do this. Place the pork, fat side down, on a work surface.

Cut the garlic into 4–5 slivers. Place the slivers along the inside of the pork, season with salt, freshly ground black pepper, lemon rind, half the parsley and the chopped thyme leaves. Roll up and tie with kitchen string.

Put the meat in a non-metallic dish. Pour the wine over with the 2 whole sprigs of thyme and the bay leaf and marinate, covered in the fridge, for several hours, turning every now and then.

Meanwhile, preheat the oven to 200°C. Place the rind which has been slashed, fat side down, in a baking dish, rub with salt and roast for 30 minutes until crackling. Remove and keep warm. Reduce the heat to 180°C.

Place the pork in a baking dish, add the marinade and cover the meat with baking paper, foil or a lid. Roast in the oven for about 1–1½ hours, basting every now and then with marinade. If the liquid dries up, add a little water.

Mix the remaining parsley with the breadcrumbs. Remove the cover from the meat and spread the parsley crumbs over, pressing it down with a knife. Lower the oven to 150°C and cook for a further 30 minutes. At this point, the crackling can be returned to the oven to heat up. Baste the meat every 10 minutes with the drippings so that the breadcrumbs form a golden topping over the pork. Allow pork to stand in a warm place for 10–15 minutes before slicing and serving.

Serves 6–8

2 kg loin of pork

salt and freshly ground black pepper, to season

1 small onion, sliced

1 cup white wine or chicken or vegetable stock

1 sprig rosemary

BAKED PLUMS

750 g plums

¼ cup red or white wine

¼ cup caster sugar

Roasted Loin of Pork with Baked Plums

The tart flavour of plums goes very well with the richness of pork and rings a change from the more usual apple accompaniment. Serve with a scalloped potato dish, Green Beans with Almonds (page 148) and follow with a green salad. You can, if you like, cook the rind by placing over the pork. It will need to be scored first.

Ask the butcher to bone the loin of pork. Cut off skin and any excess fat, leaving only 6 mm to protect the meat while cooking. Season with salt and pepper, roll and tie the loin. Put the meat, fat side up, on a rack in a roasting pan and add the onion and wine or stock. Cut a few holes in the pork fat and insert a few leaves of rosemary. For crackling, refer to the recipe for Roast Pork (page 95).

Roast the pork in a preheated 180°C oven, allowing 20–25 minutes per 500 g, basting occasionally with pan juices until it is done. It may be necessary to add water to the baking dish as the liquid evaporates.

Meanwhile, make a shallow cut in each plum and arrange in an ovenproof dish. Mix the remaining ingredients with ½ cup of the roasting pan juices in a jug or bowl, stirring until the sugar is dissolved. Pour over the plums, cover the dish and bake with the pork for 10–15 minutes, until tender.

Carve the meat into fairly thick slices and serve with baked plums.

Serves 6–8

2 kg boneless centre-cut loin of pork, trimmed
   and butterflied

½ cup walnut oil

salt and freshly ground black pepper, to season

1 cup chopped Continental parsley

¾ cup walnuts, chopped

4 garlic cloves, chopped

Apple Sauce (page 276), to serve

Roulade of Pork with Walnut Stuffing

Give the butcher a day's notice to prepare for this recipe. The loin needs to be trimmed then
butterflied, cut open to take the stuffing, and the rind should be cut into fine strips – not too
deep. This is a delicious way to serve pork and is easy when entertaining.

Preheat the oven to 230°C. Lay the pork out flat, sprinkle with 1 tablespoon of the
walnut oil and season with salt and pepper. Combine the parsley, walnuts, garlic and
all but 1 tablespoon of the remaining walnut oil. Spread evenly over the meat, roll into
a neat shape and tie securely with kitchen string. Rub the pork with the remaining oil
and rub with coarse salt.

Place in a roasting tin on a rack if you have one. Roast for 30 minutes, until the crackling
is crisp and golden (for instructions, see recipe on page 95). Reduce the heat to 180°C and
cook for a further 45–60 minutes.

Transfer the meat to a serving platter and let it rest covered with foil for 10 minutes
in a warm place. Remove the string, slice and cover. Pour off the fat from the roasting
pan, deglaze with a little water or chicken stock and reduce until syrupy. Spoon over the
pork slices and serve with apple sauce. This pork dish goes well with roasted pear halves,
steamed baby new potatoes, Parsnip Purée with Peas (page 149), Green Beans with
Almonds (page 148) and a mixed green salad.

Serves 6

Beef

A wonderful roast of beef, rump or sirloin, on or off the bone is one of the best meals in the world. You can do it the way every Englishman likes it, roasted with Yorkshire puddings, roast potatoes and a nose-punching English mustard, or choose a fillet and treat it the French way with beautiful summer vegetables. This is so easy to cook and carve and provides a contrast to an otherwise rich meal.

Roasting beef

There are several prime cuts of beef that are really impressive when roasted. One is a large whole rump that may well weigh about 4.5 kg. Or you can choose a smaller cut from the rump, when you may like to ask for the point end, weighing about 2 kg. Another premium cut is a standing rib roast or rolled rib. A convenient cut is a boned rib roast which makes for easy carving.

Use a hot oven to start with to develop those nice carel flavours and then reduce the heat. With the control of temperature and timing you should get the results you want. Always remove the meat from the refrigerator in time for it to reach room temperature before cooking it.

The times for roasting prime beef may vary with the way you roast, for you have the choice of quick roasting or slow roasting.

For quick roasting the meat is browned on the top of the stove then put in a hot oven (220°C) for 20 minutes. Then the heat is lowered to (180°C) for the rest of the cooking time. If you love the crusty brown outside of the meat then this is the method you will prefer. For timing allow 15 minutes to the 500g plus 15 minutes over for medium-rare beef. Allow 20 minutes per 500g for well done meat and 20 minutes over.

For slow roasting the meat is cooked in a moderately slow oven (160°C) for the whole cooking time. This gives a moister meat with less shrinkage, but it does not give a crisp outside. For timing allow 30 minutes per 500g and 30 minutes over, this gives a medium done result.

1 standing rib of beef (3 ribs to serve 6–8,
    4 ribs to serve 8–10) or 1 rump of beef (2 kg to serve 6,
    3 kg to serve 8)

1 teaspoon freshly ground black pepper

2 tablespoons olive oil

2 teaspoons sea salt

GRAVY

½ cup white wine

1 tablespoons sherry vinegar

2 cups beef stock

salt and freshly ground black pepper, to season

10 g butter

Roast Rib of Beef

A standing rib joint from grass-fed cattle bought from a good butcher can't be beaten as a Christmas dinner feature. The joint of beef should not be overseasoned, it has enough flavour in itself along with its traditional accompaniments. Gravy and a hot horseradish relish or hot English mustard are popular adjuncts. Serve with boiled new potatoes or roasted potatoes, which can be baked in the hot oven as the beef is 'resting'. This is one of the best meals in the world.

Preheat the oven to 220°C. Bring the beef to room temperature and rub the pepper over the surface. Heat the oil in a heavy roasting pan over a moderately-high heat and brown the beef on all sides. Place the beef, curved side up, in the dish (a rump should be placed on a wire rack in the baking dish). Press the salt onto the surface fat. Roast in the oven for 20 minutes, then reduce the heat to 180°C, until done. For rare beef, allow 10–12 minutes per 500 g; for medium-rare, allow 15 minutes per 500 g, plus 15 minutes; and for well-done, allow 20 minutes per 500 g, plus 20 minutes. Remove the beef from the baking dish to a warm plate, cover loosely with a double sheet of foil and leave to rest in a warm place for 20–30 minutes.

To make the gravy, pour the excess fat from the roasting pan, leaving about 2 tablespoons. Deglaze the pan over a moderate heat with the white wine and sherry vinegar, lifting off the brown bits. Add the beef stock and any red juices from the meat and cook for a few minutes. Season to taste with salt and freshly ground black pepper. Strain into a small saucepan and, just before serving, swirl in the butter – this softens the gravy and creates a liaison. Pour into a gravy boat to serve.

Serve the beef with a selection of your favourite vegetable side dishes. One suggestion would be roast potatoes, green beans, glazed carrots and sugar-fried sweet potatoes.

YORKSHIRE PUDDINGS

Sift 1 cup plain flour and 1 teaspoon salt into a bowl. Make a well in the centre, add 1 large or 2 small beaten eggs and 1¼ cups milk, beating the centre well and gradually incorporating all the flour. Pour into a jug and refrigerate until required. When you take the roast out of the oven, increase the heat to 200°C. Heat 8–12 Yorkshire pudding or muffin pans. Put a good teaspoon of the hot meat drippings into each pan, give the batter a good beat and pour into the pans, filling them about two-thirds full. Bake in the oven for 20 minutes, reduce the heat to 180°C and cook for a further 5–10 minutes.

HOT ENGLISH MUSTARD

Mix 2 tablespoons hot dry English mustard powder with enough water to make a slack paste. Put into a small mustard pot to serve with the roast beef.

HORSERADISH SAUCE

Grate a fresh horseradish and mix with a little vinegar, or use a commercial grated horseradish. If preferred, mix it with a little cream to taste.

1.5 kg beef fillet, trimmed and tied (see Tip)

freshly ground black pepper, to season

1 tablespoon olive oil

30 g butter

½ cup brandy

GRAVY

¾ cup Madeira, wine or stock

10 g butter

salt and freshly ground black pepper, to season

Roast Fillet of Beef

For a feature of a Christmas buffet, fillet of beef is rightly considered the finest cut of this meat. Serve it sliced, at room temperature, with a good sauce. Many people choose Béarnaise (page 277), the queen of rich, buttery sauces, or a Green Sauce (see below).

Preheat the oven to 260°C. Season the fillet with pepper. Heat the oil and butter in a flameproof roasting pan. When hot, add the beef and brown well all over. Pour the brandy over the beef and set it alight. Shake the pan until the flames subside. Place the pan in the oven and reduce the heat to 220°C. Cook for 15–20 minutes. Remove the beef and allow it to rest, covered loosely in foil, for 10–15 minutes.

To make the gravy, pour the excess fat from the roasting pan, leaving about 2 tablespoons. Deglaze the pan over a moderate heat with the Madeira, white wine or stock, lifting off the brown bits. Swirl the butter around the pan. Season with salt and pepper to taste. Put the gravy into a small jug or gravy boat.

To serve, remove the string and carve the meat into 1 cm slices. Arrange on a serving dish and brush with a little of the gravy to keep the meat moist. Spoon a little of the gravy on each plate, top with a few slices of the fillet and serve with lightly cooked green beans and steamed baby potatoes or vegetables of your choice.

If you prefer, serve the fillet at room temperature with salad and a green sauce (salsa verde).

Serves 6–8

GREEN SAUCE (SALSA VERDE)

This lovely pungent green sauce of Italy often accompanies cold fish or beef fillet. Process 1 cup Continental parsley sprigs, 8 small gherkins, ¼ cup capers, 6–8 anchovy fillets, 1 tablespoon green peppercorns and the grated rind of 1 lemon in a food processor until a smooth paste, working in ⅔ cup olive oil. Alternatively, pound the mixture using a mortar and pestle.

TIP Remove surface fat and membrane covering the meat with a sharp knife. After trimming, tie the fillet neatly with kitchen string at regular intervals, so that it keeps its shape during cooking.

2 kg fillet of beef

30 g butter

½ cup brandy

salt and freshly ground black pepper, to season

1 cup finely chopped curly parsley

HORSERADISH SAUCE

1 Lebanese cucumber, peeled, finely diced

2 teaspoons chopped tarragon

1½ cups light sour cream

¼ cup grated horseradish

1 tablespoon white wine vinegar or lemon juice

2 tablespoons snipped chives

Fillet of Beef with Herbs

When so many families are buying poultry, ham or pork, you may prefer a really choice fillet of beef. It's easy to cook and carve and provides an excellent contrast to the rich foods of Christmas. For a cold Christmas dinner or a buffet spread this dish is a good choice. Serve with the Horseradish Sauce (page 104) or Béarnaise (page 277), which everyone loves, and some steamed baby new potatoes and some lovely salads – and everyone will be happy.

Preheat the oven to 200°C. Trim the beef and tie into a neat shape with kitchen string. Melt the butter in a heavy baking pan over a high heat. Cook the beef fillet for 5 minutes, turning, until browned. Add the brandy and ¼ cup water, and season to taste with salt and pepper.

Roast the beef for 25 minutes, basting frequently. Remove from the oven and cool. Place the roast on a piece of foil. Sprinkle with the parsley and roll to coat. Leave at room temperature for up to 2 hours before serving.

Meanwhile, to make horseradish sauce, combine the cucumber, tarragon, sour cream and horseradish in a bowl with the vinegar or lemon juice, adding more if necessary to taste. Stir in the snipped chives. Cut the beef into thick slices and serve with the horseradish sauce.

Serves 8

TIPS *A roasted fillet of beef is best served rare to medium-rare. Those who like it well-done should take slices from the ends. Avoid cooking the beef the day before, even if you fancy a cold fillet of beef, much of the flavour is lost once it has been refrigerated.*

1.5 kg fillet of beef, trimmed and tied (see Tips)

freshly ground black pepper, to season

1 tablespoon olive oil, plus extra, for frying

¼ cup brandy

250 g baby green beans

250 g zucchini, thickly sliced

250 g patty pan squash, cut in half

500 g cherry tomatoes

½ cup small black olives, such as niçoise olives

1 tablespoon finely chopped herbs, such as Continental
  parsley, basil, oregano or tarragon

GREEN HERB VINAIGRETTE

½ cup good-quality olive oil

1–2 tablespoons white wine vinegar

1 teaspoon French mustard

1 clove garlic, crushed

¼ cup finely chopped mixed herbs

salt and freshly ground black pepper, to season

Fillet of Beef with Summer Vegetables

This is an absolutely delicious and amazingly simple way of cooking and serving a fillet of beef.
It can be served warm or at room temperature and is a perfect solution to a Christmas dinner,
whether it be a formal indoor or outdoor casual affair. It's also a good one for the buffet table.

Preheat the oven to 260°C. Season the fillet with the pepper. Heat the oil in a
flameproof baking dish, add the beef and brown it well all over. Place the dish in
the oven and turn the heat down to 220°C. Cook for 20 minutes. Remove the
beef from the oven and allow it to cool, wrapped loosely in foil, until required.

Meanwhile cook the beans, zucchini and squash in a saucepan of boiling salted
water for 4–5 minutes, drain and set aside. Toss the tomatoes in a little extra oil
in a frying pan for 30 seconds; set aside.

To make the green herb vinaigrette, combine the olive oil, white wine vinegar,
mustard, garlic, mixed herbs, salt and pepper in a screw-top jar and shake until
well mixed.

To serve, remove the string from the beef and carve the meat into 1 cm slices.
Arrange on a serving dish. Meanwhile, toss the vegetables with the olives lightly
in enough of the vinaigrette to just coat. Spoon the salad around the beef and
sprinkle with the chopped herbs.

Serves 6–8

*TIPS To trim a fillet of beef, remove the membrane covering the meat with a sharp
knife. You can leave a little fat on if there is, to add extra flavour. After trimming, tie
the fillet neatly with string so that it will keep its shape during cooking.*

For a larger party, have two fillets, and double the amount of vegetables and dressing.

| 850 g fillet of beef |
| salt and freshly ground black pepper, to season |
| 60 g butter |
| 100 g button mushrooms, very finely chopped |
| 60 g liver pâté, jelly removed |
| 2 sheets frozen puff pastry, thawed |
| 1 egg, lightly beaten |

Beef Wellington

Named after the Iron Duke – or was it the boots that bear his name? In any case, an imaginative chef browned a fillet of beef, flamed it with brandy, topped it with pâté and wrapped it in pastry.

Season the beef with a little salt and plenty of freshly ground black pepper. Melt half of the butter in a large, heavy-based frying pan over a high heat. When foaming, add the beef and brown for 5 minutes, turning to brown all over. Transfer to a dish and refrigerate until cold.

Preheat the oven to 240°C. Line a baking tray with baking paper. Melt the remaining butter in a large frying pan over a high heat. Cook the mushrooms for 3–5 minutes, until liquid is released and completely evaporated again. Mix together the pâté and mushroom and spread evenly over the top of the beef.

Lay the beef in the centre of one sheet of pastry. Brush around the edges, close to beef, with a little beaten egg. Cover with the remaining pastry and press to seal the pastry

together all around the beef. Trim the excess of long edges, leaving about 2 cm each side. Fold the short ends under to seal. Place on the prepared tray, brush with egg and decorate if you like with pastry remnants cut into leaf shapes and brushed with egg.

Bake for 30 minutes. If the pastry is becoming too brown, cover with foil. (This will be necessary if you like your beef well done.) Reduce the heat to 200°C and bake for a further 5 minutes for rare and 10 minutes for medium. Rest for 5 minutes before cutting into 4 cm thick slices.

Serves 4

NOTE Flame the beef with ¼ cup of brandy when searing if you like.

Fish & Seafood

Having spent much of our early family life on the Hawkesbury River, north of Sydney, where we dined almost daily on rock oysters collected from the bottom of our garden, and prawns from the local fisherman, and where evenings were spent cooking the day's catch of snapper, bream, mullet, even crab sometimes, which we would eat around the kitchen table as if we were royalty, I still can't imagine Christmas without a course of seafood.

We don't often catch it ourselves these days but there's the fish market closeby where traffic jams occur in the 24 hours leading to Christmas, as families buy their favourite kind of food for feasting. There has been a boom in the fishing industry, and a wide variety of fresh seafood is close to most people's doorsteps. For those nowhere near a fish market, rapid air transport now ensures fresh fish over most of populated Australia.

Apart from availability, the other great change when it comes to fish is in the ways of preparing it. In those days on the Hawkesbury, we ate the oysters simply, with no more than a squeeze of lemon and a grinding of pepper. Salmon was not available and smoked salmon prohibitive. It was usually fish and chips or if we were being particularly creative, baked fish with a rice or breadcrumb stuffing. But as you can see from the recipes in this book, the possibilities are endless, especially in the summer months when our tastes go for food that is light and easy.

Salmon appears in many recipes – smoked salmon, salmon gravlax, even salmon roe provides the basis of many festive dishes. They are so easy to prepare and have become such a part of today's Christmas feasting. And, of course, prawns are an essential at this time. If you love an outdoors Christmas meal there's nothing better than that quintessential Australian dish of barbecued prawns.

When buying whole fish, look for bright alert eyes, glistening scales and bright red gills. Fillets should be firm to the touch and not in the least slimy. As soon as you get the fish home lay in a plastic or glass dish and cover it with foil. Store in the meat compartment of the refrigerator.

CRAYFISH

The Australian rock lobster (spiny lobster or crayfish), with its long antennae and rough, spiny carapace (shell), is one of the delights of the crustacean world. The meat, most of which is found in the tail, is sweet, firm-textured and very white when cooked. It can be used in any recipe needing lobster meat. Allow half a large or one small crayfish per serve.

Crayfish may be bought live or ready cooked. When buying cooked crayfish, make certain the tail is tightly curled into the body and snaps back when straightened, and that the crayfish is heavy for its size. The smell should be sweet and fresh. A 1–1.5 kg crayfish is ideal – larger ones tend to be rather tough so are best avoided.

The European lobster or French homard from northern seas differs from the Australian rock lobster or crayfish in that it has much larger pincer claws, containing much of the sweet juicy meat, and a smooth, shiny carapace.

To BOIL CRAYFISH

If a recipe calls for green (uncooked) crayfish, it should be killed immediately before cooking. This can be done by leaving it head first in a bucket of cold fresh water for at least 1 hour, or in the following manner.

Take a heavy, sharp, short-bladed knife. Place the crayfish on a board, underside up. Hold the crayfish with a towel and make a firm incision with the point of the knife where the tail joins the body. This will sever the spinal cord and kill the crayfish immediately. Any movement of legs or tail after the crayfish is killed is due to reflex muscular spasms.

Alternatively, put the live crayfish into the freezer and leave it for 30 minutes for each 500 g, in order to stun it.

To boil, place the crayfish in a large saucepan of fresh cold water and bring slowly to simmering point. Simmer for 10 minutes for the first 500 g weight and 7 minutes for each subsequent 500 g. Remove from the water and allow to cool.

You may use frozen green crayfish tails instead, if your prefer.

To CLEAN CRAYFISH

Use a heavy, sharp knife. Cut the crayfish in half lengthwise. Insert the point of a knife at the tail, cut towards the head and slit the underside. Remove the intestinal vein that runs the length of the crayfish, and all the soft matter in the body and at the top of the head. Retain any orange or pink roe and the thick, dark brown liquid which is the 'mustard' or 'tomalley'. The roe can be gently poached; the mustard can be used in a sauce or butter for the crayfish, or can be placed in a small bowl and cooked in a water bath, to be served separately as an accompaniment or used as a spread for canapés.

To REMOVE CRAYFISH MEAT FROM SHELL

Prise the meat from the tail and body with a sharp knife and cut into pieces. The meat may be extracted from the legs by breaking them at the joints and carefully pulling the meat out. Rinse the shell and dry well. It can then be used as a container in which to serve the meat.

500 g calamari

1 small, very firm mango, sliced into strips

2 red shallots, sliced lengthwise

1 tablespoon chopped coriander

1 tablespoon chopped mint

¼ cup cashews, roasted

1 eschalot, sliced lengthwise and deep-fried

1 clove garlic, sliced and deep-fried

DRESSING

1 small green chilli, seeded

pinch of salt

1 tablespoon palm sugar or brown sugar

2 tablespoons fish sauce

1 tablespoon lime juice

Calamari and Mango Salad

We love calamari, not just for its soft texture and delicious taste, but because it is one of the more sustainable things to come out of our seas. With the addition of fresh mango, this dish is perfect for a summery Christmas day lunch.

First prepare the calamari. Cut off the tentacles and set them aside. Wash, one at a time, under cold running water and discard the ink sacs and quills. Cut away the head and wash thoroughly. What should be left of each is the triangular body, called the tube, plus the the tentacles and the flaps. Slice across the tubes finely.

To make the dressing, crush the chilli with the salt, or using a food processor, chop the chillies, adding the remaining ingredients, processing until well blended.

Blanch the calamari in boiling salted water for 30 seconds, remove and drain. Combine the calamari with the mango, red shallots, coriander, mint and nuts. Add the dressing to the salad, tossing well to combine. Pile into bowls and sprinkle with the deep-fried shallots and garlic, and serve.

Serves 4–6

4 thick salmon steaks or ocean trout

2 cloves garlic, finely chopped

1 red bird's eye chilli, seeded and finely chopped

2 kaffir lime leaves, finely shredded

1 tablespoon fish sauce

1 tablespoon vegetable oil

MANGO SALAD

1 mango, cut into thin strips

pinch of salt

1 teaspoon lime juice

mixed salad greens

125 g snow peas, blanched

Salmon Steaks with Mango Salad

This is a lovely dish for warm weather entertaining. The tropical flavours complement the fish so beautifully.

Rinse the salmon steaks very lightly and pat dry with paper towel. Combine the garlic, chilli, lime leaves and fish sauce together in a bowl. Add the salmon and allow to marinate for 1 hour.

Meanwhile, for the mango salad, marinate the mango strips in a small bowl with the salt and lime juice for 30 minutes.

Heat a grill or frying pan over a moderately-high heat until hot, then brush the rack or pan with vegetable oil. When the oil is hot but not smoking add the fish fillets with the marinade and cook for about 6 minutes, turning once. Remove the fish and keep warm.

To serve peel away the skin of the fillets, cut in half. Arrange on serving plates piled with the mango strips, mixed salad greens and snow peas.

Serves 4

1 teaspoon sea salt
3.3 kg fresh whole Atlantic salmon or ocean trout
1 lemon, sliced
thyme sprigs

HERB MAYONNAISE

3 egg yolks
1½ tablespoons lemon juice
1½ teaspoons Dijon mustard
1 cup olive oil
1 tablespoon each finely chopped Continental parsley, chives, basil and dill
salt and freshly ground black pepper, to season

Baked Salmon with Herb Mayonnaise

This dish can be the *pièce de résistance* of a Christmas buffet table. Salmon or ocean trout has a huge advantage over the traditional roasts. It is quick and easy to cook, needs no carving, it is very good for you and, to top it off, its delicate pink flesh looks most inviting on a hot day.

Preheat oven to 180°C. Line a large baking dish with foil. Sprinkle the dish with half of the salt. Lay the fish on top and place lemon slices and thyme sprigs in the cavity. If you like, tie the fish using kitchen string. Sprinkle with more thyme and the remaining salt. Cover loosely with foil and cook for 30–40 minutes. Remove from the oven and rest for 15 minutes.

Meanwhile, to make the herb mayonnaise, blend the egg yolks, lemon juice and mustard in a food processor until combined. With the motor running, gradually add ¼ cup of the oil, 1 tablespoon at a time, processing well after each addition, until the mixture starts to thicken. Add the remaining oil in a thin, steady stream until thick and smooth. Add the herbs, process until combined and season to taste.

Make a shallow cut into the skin around the top of the tail section, along the back of the fish and across the start of the head section. Carefully pull away the skin. Transfer to a serving plate, draining off any juice. Serve at room temperature with the herb mayonnaise. Decorate with fresh herbs, lemon wedges and cucumber slices.

Serves 8–10

TIP Fish is cooked when eyes are white and a skewer inserted into the thickest part feels warm when tested on your lip or back of wrist.

To serve use a large knife and fork cut down the centre of the fish and remove serving size pieces from the head down to the bone. Ease pieces off each side of the cut avoiding bones. Turn fish to repeat with other side.

1 punnet (200–250 g) cherry tomatoes

¼ cup olive oil

2 spring onions, thinly sliced

2 cups fresh breadcrumbs (see Tip)

½ cup chopped Continental parsley

¼ cup chopped pine nuts

salt and freshly ground black pepper, to season

2 kg whole fish such as jewfish, snapper or barramundi

¼ cup oregano leaves

lemon wedges, to serve

Baked Whole Fish (Pesce al Forno)

This fish is easiest to cook in the oven but can also be done in the barbecue. It will need several layers of foil wrapped around it to make a parcel, and a fairly low heat; turn the parcel halfway through cooking.

Preheat the oven to 200°C. Roughly chop half the cherry tomatoes. Heat half the oil in a frying pan over a low heat and sauté the spring onion for 3 minutes, until soft. Add the chopped tomato and cook for a further minute. Remove from the heat and stir in the breadcrumbs, parsley and pine nuts. Season to taste with salt and pepper.

Score three diagonal cuts through thickest part of each side of fish. Fill the cavity with the breadcrumb mixture and place the fish in a baking dish. Season well and scatter any leftover breadcrumb mixture over the fish. Top with the remaining cherry tomatoes, halved, the oregano and drizzle with the remaining oil. Cover with foil and bake for 30–35 minutes, until just tender. Serve with lemon wedges.

Serves 6

TIP To make breadcrumbs, break day-old bread into chunks and whizz into crumbs using the food processor.

24 large green (raw) king prawns or scampi

¼ cup extra-virgin olive oil

few sprigs of oregano and thyme, chopped

2 tablespoons chopped Continental parsley

2 cloves garlic, finely chopped

½ red chilli, seeded and chopped

freshly ground black pepper, to season

lemon wedges, to serve

Barbecued King Prawns

Large king prawns and scampi, like all shellfish, are best eaten from their shells. If you are having a barbecue Christmas, these are a must – just ensure you don't overcook them.

Split the prawns or scampi lengthwise through the centre, devein and arrange, cut side up, on a large shallow dish. Combine the oil with the chopped herbs, garlic and chilli. Drizzle the flavoured oil over the shellfish and season with freshly ground black pepper. The shellfish can be prepared ahead up to this stage.

Preheat the barbecue to high and arrange the shellfish, cut side up, on the flat rack. Cook for 3–5 minutes, until the flesh has turned white. Remove from the heat and arrange on a large serving platter with the lemon wedges. Have a bowl on the table for the discarded shells, and finger bowls with a slice of lemon. To eat the shellfish, use a fork to pull out the tail meat. Serve with crusty bread and, if liked, a bowl of Mayonnaise (page 274) mixed with a little sweet chilli sauce.

Serves 4

¼ cup curry powder	**SATAY SAUCE**
⅓ cup light soy sauce	3 onions, chopped
2 tablespoons sugar	1 stem lemongrass, white part only, sliced
16 large green (raw) prawns, peeled, deveined, tails intact	1 tablespoon chilli powder
2 tablespoons vegetable oil	1 teaspoon paprika
½ fresh pineapple, peeled, cut into chunks	2 tablespoons vegetable oil
sliced red chilli, finely sliced red onion and mint leaves, to serve	1 cm slice of shrimp paste (belacan) (optional)
	200 ml coconut milk
	juice of 1 lemon
	¼ cup sugar
	2 cups raw peanuts, toasted, coarsely crushed
	salt, to season

Barbecued Prawn Satays

We Australians love a barbecue, so why not have one on Christmas day? These Asian-inspired prawn satays are loved by all, are easy to make and easy to eat.

Combine the curry powder, soy sauce and sugar in a bowl. Add the prawns and toss to coat. Cover and refrigerate for 1 hour.

To make the satay sauce, blend the onion, lemongrass and 1 tablespoon water in a food processor until finely chopped. Stir through the chilli powder and paprika. Heat the oil in a saucepan over a moderate heat and add the onion mixture. Cook for 5 minutes, stirring, until aromatic and the onion is soft. Add the shrimp paste, if using, and stir until melted into the mixture. Stir through the coconut milk, lemon juice and sugar, and simmer for 5 minutes. Add the peanuts, mix well and simmer for a further 5 minutes, until the sauce has thickened slightly. Season with salt to taste. Set aside until needed.

Thread the prawns onto skewers and brush lightly with oil. Preheat a chargrill pan or barbecue on high. Cook for 2 minutes each side, until pink.

Pile the pineapple onto the centre of a serving platter and top with chilli, onion and mint. Arrange skewers at each end of the platter and serve with the warmed satay sauce.

Serves 4

TIP Soak bamboo skewers in water for 1 hour before use to prevent them from burning.

100 g bean sprouts	
100 g baby spinach leaves	
2 red shallots, sliced lengthwise	
1 tablespoon chopped coriander	
1 tablespoon chopped mint	
¼ cup roughly chopped macadamia nuts, roasted	
1 small, very firm mango, sliced into strips	
200–300 g green (raw) prawns, shelled and deveined	

DRESSING

1 small chilli, seeded
pinch of salt
1 tablespoon palm sugar or brown sugar
2 tablespoons fish sauce
1 tablespoon lime juice

Asian Mango and Prawn Salad

A hot Christmas day often calls for a break from tradition, and something fresh and clean tasting for lunch. This salad is the perfect thing for such a day.

Combine the bean sprouts, spinach, shallots, coriander, mint and macadamia nuts and arrange on 4 dinner plates. To make the dressing, crush the chilli with the salt, or using a food processor, chop the chillies, adding the remaining ingredients, processing until well blended. Set the dressing aside in a shallow bowl.

Arrange the mango over the salad. When ready to serve, blanch the prawns in a little boiling salted water until they have all turned pink, remove and drain. Toss while still hot in the dressing and spoon over the salad.

Serves 4

TIP This salad can also be made with thin rings of calamari cooked exactly the same way as the prawns until just turned white and opaque.

½ cup Mayonnaise (page 274)

2 tsp chopped mixed fresh herbs (Continental parsley, thyme, chives)

½ tsp Dijon mustard

1 cooked crayfish, halved and flesh sliced

lettuce leaves

GARNISH

cucumber slices, hard-boiled egg slices, thyme or dill sprigs, or lemon wedges

Lobster (Crayfish) Mayonnaise

Because this is a time of year we often like to splash out, fabulous Australian crayfish are a superb addition to the Christmas lunch. Please refer to the crayfish preparation section on page 111. For me, the best way to serve crayfish are halved or sliced and served with a good homemade Mayonnaise (page 274).

Flavour mayonnaise with chopped herbs and mustard. Spoon over lobster meat in shells or remove and slice into 0.5 cm rounds. Serve chilled on crisp lettuce leaves, garnished with egg slices, tomato, paper-thin cucumber slices and a sprig of fresh dill and lemon wedges.

Serves 2

4 small calamari (about 250 g)

100 ml sesame oil

salt and freshly ground black pepper, to season

a few sprigs of tarragon or chervil

1 cup vegetable or chicken stock

30 g butter

1 tablespoon lemon juice

1 tablespoon white wine vinegar

1 teaspoon Dijon mustard

125 g baby spinach leaves

Grilled Calamari with Tarragon Sauce

Squid or calamari is one of the more environment-friendly commercial seafoods available. It is fast-growing, and the harvesting makes less impact on the environment than many other seafoods (trawling, for instance, can be indiscriminate and wasteful). Don't be discouraged by the cleaning of this wonderful seafood, it is relatively quick and worth the effort. The sesame oil offers a nutty addition to the flavours of the tarragon sauce and the sharp, clean spinach.

Squeeze out the ink and quills from the tubes. Wash the squid very thoroughly in cold water. Drain and pat dry with paper towel. Cut into 2–3 cm lozenge shapes. Leave the flaps and tentacles whole. Place in a bowl with 2 tablespoons of the sesame oil, season lightly with salt and pepper and keep in the fridge until ready to cook.

Keep half the tarragon leaves on the stalk, remove the remaining leaves, leaving them whole. Put the stalks in a small saucepan with the stock and reduce over a low heat until two-thirds of the liquid has evaporated. Take the pan off the heat and whisk in the butter, a small piece at a time. Strain through a sieve, season to taste, cover and keep hot.

To make the dressing, whisk together the lemon juice, vinegar, mustard, remaining sesame oil in a bowl and season with salt and pepper.

Heat a grill pan until very hot, then cook the squid pieces for 2 minutes. Turn the squid and repeat on other side. Toss the spinach in the dressing and arrange in loose piles in the centre of a serving plate. Top with the grilled squid and scatter over the tarragon leaves. Pour the sauce in a ribbon around the spinach and over the squid.

Serves 4

3 cooked crayfish (page 111)

1 onion, sliced

1 bay leaf

6 peppercorns

1 teaspoon vinegar

1 kg large king prawns, cooked

6 cooked Balmain bugs

24 fresh oysters on the shell

6 slices smoked salmon

3 lemons, cut in wedges

dipping sauces (see below)

Green Salad (page 172)

Potato Salad (page 168)

Seafood Platter

People have been enjoying food from the sea since the beginning of time. Many think seafood fresh from the markets is the best treat of all for Christmas. I know because I live very near a great fish market and it is always packed with shoppers in the lead-up to Christmas.

Split the crayfish in two. Lift out the crayfish meat with fingers, slice into chunky pieces and return to the shells. Crack any claws and keep them for plate decoration.

Shell the prawns, leaving the head and tail intact. Slit down the back and remove the black tract.

Place the bugs upside down on a chopping board, cut in half lengthwise, remove any intenstinal matter from the tails.

Arrange the seafood on a large platter or two. Cover with foil or plastic wrap and refrigerate until required.

Make the dips and store in bowls, covered with plastic wrap. Inexpensive tiny dishes are available from many kitchen shops; if liked, purchase a dozen or two and allow individual bowls for dipping.

Chill the green salad without dressing – this can be added at the last moment. Make the potato salad, but do not refrigerate.

To serve, make sure there is clear space on the table for the large platters and salads. If preferred, individual dinner plates can be made up of an assortment of seafood. The dipping sauces can be placed in bowls to

pass around or in individual dishes on each plate. Don't forget the lemon wedges. Include a few bowls to take any shells or heads and a few finger bowls with a slice of lemon to wash fishy fingers, and plenty of large paper napkins. Small entrée plates can be offered for salads if liked.

DIPPING SAUCES

Hot cocktail sauce: Combine ¾ cup Mayonnaise (page 274) with 2 tablespoons tomato sauce, 1 teaspoon Worchestershire sauce and 1 teaspoon sambal oelek in a bowl and serve.

Chilli mint sauce: Combine ⅓ cup sweet chilli sauce, the juice and rind of 1 lime, 1 teaspoon fish sauce, 1 tablespoon water and 2 teaspoons finely chopped coriander or Vietnamese mint in a bowl and serve.

Dill Sauce: see page 280

Mayonnaise (page 274) would also be a welcome addition.

500 g raw or cooked prawns, shelled and deveined

250 g scallops

500 g small mussels

400 g small calamari tubes

1 teaspoon grated lemon rind

1–2 tablespoons lemon juice

salt and freshly ground black pepper, to season

2 teaspoons snipped chives

1 teaspoon Dijon mustard

1 tablespoon finely chopped tarragon or roughly torn basil

½ cup light olive oil

500 g fresh spinach (green) tagliatelle, linguine or fettucine

1 tablespoon olive oil

250 g snow peas or asparagus tips, lightly cooked
   and cooled

1 small red chilli, thinly sliced

¼ cup chopped herbs such as Continental parsley, basil,
   chives or chervil, to garnish

8–10 red cherry tomatoes

Seafood and Pasta Salad

There are many seafood lovers who flock to the fish markets, which, where I live, stays open all Christmas Eve. Many buy fresh seafood to serve on platters or cook on the barbecue. I often make this salad for a lunch with friends – it would also be great for a Christmas meal.

This seafood and pasta salad changes from time to time, depending on what's available at the fish markets. When you're very busy, buy the seafood ready prepared. The essence of the dish lies in the freshness of the seafood and the quality of the pasta. For a special treat, add fresh lobster tail cut in chunks and decorate the finished salad with the cracked claws.

Prepare and cook the fresh seafood (see opposite). Combine the cooked seafood in a large bowl. Process the lemon rind and juice, salt and pepper, chives, mustard and tarragon or basil in a food processor until well mixed. With the motor still running, gradually add the olive oil in a slow, steady stream to make a thick, creamy dressing. Add ¼ cup of the dressing to the seafood and toss together.

Cook the pasta in a large saucepan of boiling salted water until al dente (firm to the bite), then drain thoroughly. While still warm, toss through the oil. Combine the pasta with the seafood, reserving some seafood for the garnish, snow peas or asparagus and remaining dressing. Turn onto a serving platter and garnish with slivers of red chilli and the reserved seafood. Garnish with chopped herbs and cherry tomatoes.

If you're taking this salad on a picnic, pack it in a large plastic container, keep it chilled in an esky and have bowls at the ready.

TO PREPARE AND COOK THE SEAFOOD

If using raw prawns, drop them into a large saucepan of boiling salted water over a high heat. Stir until the prawns take on a pink tinge, then reduce the heat to moderate, cover and simmer for 2 minutes. Drain, shell and devein the prawns. The tails can be left on for decorative effect.

To cook the scallops, rinse and remove any brown bits, then poach gently in salted water for about 2 minutes. Drain and cool.

Scrub the mussels thoroughly in plenty of water, tug off any seaweed and beards and rinse thoroughly. If possible, leave them to soak in enough cold water to cover for an hour or so. Then place the mussels in a large saucepan with ½ cup water over a high heat and steam, covered, shaking the pan occasionally, for 4–6 minutes or until the shells have opened. The moment they are all open, put the pan aside to cool a little. Discard any mussels that haven't opened. When cool enough, remove the mussels from their shells.

To prepare the calamari, squeeze out the ink and quills from the tubes and wash the calamari very thoroughly in cold water. Drain and pat dry with paper towel. Cut the flaps and tentacles from the tubes and slice the tubes into thin rings. Trim the base of the tentacles from the heads and wash. Pat the rings, flaps and tentacles dry with paper towel. Heat 1–2 tablespoons oil in a heavy-based frying pan and when very hot, sauté the calamari for 2–3 minutes, until the colour just changes.

Serves 6–8

CHAPTER THREE

Vegetables

Vegetables

Good vegetable dishes range from the most tender green beans, lightly cooked and tossed in butter and freshly squeezed lemon juice, to a plate of mixed young baby vegetables steamed and finished off with a drizzle of good-quality olive oil and fresh herbs.

For many of us, it is an easy matter to produce beautiful vegetable dishes as there seems to be no end to the variety and quality of vegetables in tip-top condition available at most greengrocers and farmers' markets. World-class oils, spices, aromatics and herbs, and intriguing vinegars and mustards are all there for us to use with imagination.

Vegetables can be appreciated in their own right and for the contribution they make to our feeling of well-being, and the enjoyment of meats, poultry and seafood. Vegetables are as much a part of a good meal as the wines, meat or other dishes – so take care and cook them carefully.

1 kg frozen broad beans

¼ cup extra-virgin olive oil

1 small onion, finely chopped

250 g pancetta, cut into strips (see Note)

salt and freshly ground black pepper, to season

Broad Beans with Pancetta

Broad beans are a delightful vegetable and one that freezes well. This recipe makes an easy but first-rate side dish for the festive table, and is best served with meats or poultry.

Cook the beans in a saucepan of boiling salted water for 8 minutes or until tender. Drain and remove the skins from the beans to reveal the beautiful green underneath. (If you're short of time, keep the skins on – it's up to you.)

Heat the oil in a large saucepan and sauté the onion until soft. Add the pancetta strips and cook for 2–3 minutes. Add the beans and season with a good grinding of black pepper. Cook over a gentle heat for 1 minute, season with salt and serve immediately.

Serves 8

NOTE *Pancetta, air-dried pork belly, is the Italian answer to bacon or speck – although each has its own distinctive flavour and can be used in this recipe. For a more delicate flavour, cover the strips of pancetta with water in a saucepan, bring to the boil then drain, discarding the water. Proceed with the recipe.*

60 g butter

2 rashers streaky bacon, rind removed, cut into strips

6 spring onions or eschalots, finely sliced (including some green tops of the spring onions)

½ lettuce or 6–8 outer lettuce leaves, shredded

1 kg frozen baby peas

sprigs of mint

1 teaspoon sugar

salt and freshly ground black pepper, to season

2 tablespoons water

French Peas
(Petits Pois Française)

Tiny petits pois, baby peas, are available frozen and are absolutely delicious cooked this way. Cook the whole bag of peas so there will be plenty for everyone – even seconds.

Melt the butter in a large, heavy-based saucepan with a lid and gently fry the bacon and spring onions until soft but not brown. Add the lettuce to the pan and stir over a low heat until it is bright green and juicy.

Add the frozen peas to the pan with one or two sprigs of mint and the sugar, and season with salt and pepper to taste. Add the water, cover with a lid and cook over a gentle heat for 15–20 minutes or until the peas are tender. To serve, remove the mint and serve from the pan with the pan juices and lettuce.

Serves 6–8

| ¾ cup long-grain white rice |
| ¾ cup wild rice |
| salt and freshly ground black pepper, to season |
| 10–15 g butter |

Wild and Long-grain Rice

This combination of wild and white rice is a perfect accompaniment for game meats, turkey, goose and quail.

Rinse the long-grain and the wild rice separately in a sieve under cold running water, until the water runs clear. To cook the long-grain rice, bring 1½ cups water to the boil in a heavy-based saucepan with ½ teaspoon salt. Sprinkle in the rice through your fingers so that the water does not go off the boil. Stir once, then cover with a tight-fitting lid and reduce the heat to very low. Do not lift the lid until the last few minutes of cooking. Cook very gently for 10–15 minutes or until a test grain is tender, but still firm, when bitten. Remove from the heat and fluff up lightly with a fork. For very dry, fluffy grains, set the rice aside, still covered, for 5 minutes before fluffing up.

To cook the wild rice, cover the rice with cold, salted water in a heavy-based saucepan. Bring to the boil, skim any foreign particles from the top and drain. Bring 3 cups fresh water to the boil, add 1 teaspoon salt and stir in the rice slowly. Cook without stirring for about 30 minutes, until the grains are tender, adding a little more boiling water if necessary. Fluff up with a fork.

To combine, toss the two rices together, add the butter and freshly ground black pepper.

Makes about 4½ cups

RICE

The long-grain basmati rice from Pakistan is a superb, light-textured rice with a wonderful aromatic flavour. Wild rice is the seed of a grass related to the rice family. It is an expensive but rare treat – its nutty flavour is the perfect complement to game. The combination of these two grains is terrific and to be recommended.

Asparagus

To many gourmets, the first breath of spring is really when asparagus makes its appearance on the greengrocers' shelves. Fresh asparagus is such a treat, so I ensure that I prepare this delicate vegetable with great respect. It is always a popular vegetable on the Christmas table.

COOKING ASPARAGUS

Although you can buy special asparagus cookers, I find a wide, not too shallow frying pan does a good job.

Take care to wash the vegetable thoroughly and trim the ends if tough. The test is to break off the tougher ends – they should snap. If you like, you can make a small pillow of foil so that the tips can cook at the same time as the stalks and not be overcooked. Lay the asparagus in a pan of hot salted water with the tips resting on the foil and the stalks in the water. Bring to the boil and cook for 7–10 minutes or until tender. Lift the vegetable onto a clean tea towel and serve.

Asparagus can be served as a first course, an accompaniment, in a stir-fry or salad, warm or cold. I recommend serving asparagus simply and eating it with your fingers as a first course.

3 hard-boiled eggs, chopped

1 tablespoon chopped Continental parsley

45 g butter

¾ cup fresh breadcrumbs

24–30 spears asparagus, cooked (page 138)

Asparagus Polonaise

Simple to make, this lovely dish is a wonderful way of preparing asparagus. Either have as a first course or add it to your Christmas banquet.

Mix the hard-boiled eggs with the parsley and fry the breadcrumbs in the butter until golden. Add the eggs and parsley and toss to mix through. Put the hot asparagus in a serving dish and spoon over the toasted crumbs.

Serves 6

- -

45 g butter

squeeze of lemon juice

freshly ground black pepper, to season

36 spears asparagus, cooked (page 138)

Asparagus with Lemon Butter

Serve this as an accompaniment to your roast turkey, chicken or salmon.

Melt the butter, add a squeeze of lemon juice and a grinding of pepper. Arrange hot asparagus on a serving dish and spoon the hot lemon butter over the tips.

Serves 6–8

- -

36 spears asparagus, cooked (see page 138)

½ cup freshly grated Parmesan cheese

60 g butter, melted

freshly ground black pepper, to season

Asparagus Parmigiana

Serve this lovely asparagus dish as an accompaniment to your Christmas meal.

Put the cooked asparagus in greased ovenproof dish. Sprinkle with Parmesan cheese, pour over the melted butter and season with a generous grinding of pepper. Cook under a hot griller until the cheese has melted. Serve immediately.

Serves 6–8

1 kg even-sized potatoes such as desiree, Dutch creams or pontiac, peeled and halved or quartered

¼ cup olive oil

sprigs of rosemary (optional)

sea salt and freshly ground black pepper, to season

4 parsnips, scraped lightly and halved

8 small red onions, halved

4–6 cloves garlic (optional)

Crispy Roasted Vegetables

You can hardly have a roast turkey without some crispy vegetables on the side. Potatoes and parsnips roasted this way have a wonderful crisp golden crust. The garlic and rosemary give the vegetables extra punch. Serve with any roasted meat or poultry.

Preheat the oven to 200°C. Boil the potatoes in a saucepan with enough water to cover for about 5 minutes, until just tender. Drain and cool slightly. With the lid on, shake the pan lightly so that the potatoes dry and have a slight crumbling on the surface but retain their shape.

Mix the oil, rosemary, salt and freshly ground black pepper together in a bowl. Add the potatoes, parsnips and onions and toss until well coated. Arrange the vegetables in a single layer in a baking tray. Bake for 1 hour, or until very crisp, adding the garlic cloves after 30 minutes and turning occasionally. Serve immediately.

Serves 8

½ cup olive oil

2 cloves garlic, chopped

¼ cup rice vinegar

4 leeks, washed and halved

4 small zucchini, peeled and quartered lengthwise

8 button squash, halved

8 baby eggplants, halved lengthwise

1 red onion, quartered lengthwise

1 head young garlic, halved crosswise

1 red or yellow capsicum, trimmed and cut into its natural lobes, seeds discarded

2 bunches fresh asparagus, tough stalk ends snapped off

1 large green or red chilli

SAGE AND GARLIC MAYONNAISE

1½ cups homemade Mayonnaise (page 274)

1½ tablespoons rice vinegar

1 tablespoon tamari or soy sauce

juice of ½ lemon

2 tablespoons white sesame seeds, toasted

1 small red chilli, finely chopped

2 cloves garlic, finely chopped

1½ tablespoons Dijon mustard

8 sage leaves, finely chopped

Barbecued Vegetables with Sage and Garlic Mayonnaise

Many of us select the outdoors and a barbecue for Christmas – and this dish makes a wonderful start to a relaxed meal, as each guest makes a selection of vegetables to dip in the unctuous mayonnaise.

Whisk together the oil, garlic and rice vinegar in a large bowl. Add the leek, zucchini, squash, eggplant, red onion, garlic head, capsicum, asparagus and chilli. Toss gently and marinate at room temperature for 1 hour.

Meanwhile, to make the sage and garlic mayonnaise, spoon the homemade Mayonnaise into a bowl. Stir in the vinegar, tamari or soy sauce, lemon juice, sesame seeds, chilli, garlic, mustard and sage. Cover and chill until ready to serve.

When ready to cook, remove the vegetables from the marinade and arrange on the barbecue grill over medium–hot coals, or on a pre-heated ribbed grill. You can also cook them under a domestic griller. Cook for 4 minutes on each side or until tender. Serve with the sage and garlic mayonnaise on the side.

Serves 8

TIP Tender young vegetables are an inspiration for any cook. For a large gathering I often make this platter of lightly grilled colourful vegetables and serve them with a good mayonnaise with an Asian influence. Most tender young vegetables can be cooked this way – mushrooms, potato, sweet potato or yam slices, or halved tomatoes.

1 kg sweet potatoes, yams or kumara

45 g butter

½ cup soft brown sugar

Sugar-fried Sweet Potatoes

This naughty but gorgeous way of preparing sweet potatoes makes them irresistable.

If the sweet potatoes are large, peel and cut into thick rounds. Boil the sweet potato in a saucepan until almost cooked through. Remove from the heat and drain.

Melt the butter in a frying pan, add the potatoes and sprinkle with the sugar and stir through the butter to form a kind of caramel. Turn the potatoes to coat evenly for about 5–7 minutes, until they are coated in a crunchy crust.

Serves 6–8

- -

1 kg sweet potatoes

2 red apples, such as jonathan, gala or pink lady

lemon juice, for sprinkling

60 g butter

½ teaspoon salt

½ cup light brown sugar

½ cup water

Sweet Potatoes and Apples

This is a good choice to serve with rich meats like ham, roast pork or goose. Perfect for your Christmas table.

Peel the sweet potatoes and cut into even-sized pieces. Simmer the sweet potato in a saucepan, covered, for 20 minutes or until tender. Drain and cool.

Wash and core the apples and cut into thin slices. Sprinkle with lemon juice to prevent them from discolouring.

Heat the butter, salt, sugar and water in a shallow saucepan and stir until the sugar dissolves. Boil for 3 minutes then add the cooled sweet potatoes. Simmer for 3 minutes, basting frequently with the syrup. Add the apple slices and cook for a further 2 minutes.

Serves 6–8

100 g pancetta (Italian bacon), cut into thin strips

1 large clove garlic

good pinch of chopped rosemary leaves

1 tablespoon olive oil

1 kg cabbage, preferably savoy, finely shredded

½ cup chicken stock or white wine

freshly ground black pepper, to season

Cabbage with Pancetta, Garlic and Rosemary

This is a great Italian dish to serve as part of a Christmas buffet. As the cabbage isn't boiled in water, it doesn't impart the strong unpleasant smell that some cabbage dishes tend to do.

Mix together the pancetta, garlic and rosemary. Heat the oil in a large saucepan with a lid and gently fry the pancetta mixture until aromatic and sizzling. Add the shredded cabbage and toss to coat well. Add the stock and freshly ground pepper and cover tightly with a lid.

Cook over a gentle heat for 30–45 minutes until done to taste – the cabbage is usually fairly well cooked.

Serves 4–6

- -

60 g butter

½ red cabbage, finely shredded

1 tablespoon red or white wine vinegar

2 apples, peeled and cut into thick slices

1 tablespoon sugar

salt and freshly ground black pepper, to season

Braised Red Cabbage with Apples

Red cabbage, with its beautiful colour, just seems to say 'Christmas'. Adding apples gives this dish a festive element.

Melt the butter in a heavy-based saucepan with a tight-fitting lid over a gentle heat. Add the shredded cabbage and vinegar, apples and sugar. Season with salt and freshly ground black pepper. Cover the pan and cook for 30 minutes. Serve hot.

Serves 4–6

4 eggplants, cut lengthwise into 1 cm slices

salt and freshly ground black pepper, to season

½ cup plain flour

⅓ cup olive oil

3 cloves garlic, crushed

3 x 400 g cans diced tomatoes

¼ cup shredded basil, plus extra basil leaves, to serve

½ cup grated mozzarella cheese

½ cup grated Parmesan cheese

Eggplant Parmigiana

Vegetarians will be very pleased to see this dish on the festive table or buffet.

Preheat the oven to 190°C. Lightly grease a large ovenproof dish.

Place the eggplant slices in a colander. Sprinkle generously with salt and leave for 30 minutes. Rinse under cold water and drain well on paper towel. Season the flour in a shallow dish with salt and pepper to taste. Dust the eggplant slices in the flour, shaking off any excess.

Heat the oil in a large frying pan over a high heat. Cook the eggplant, in batches, until lightly golden. Set aside. Sauté the garlic in same frying pan for 1 minute, without browning. Add the tomatoes and simmer for 10 minutes, until the mixture thickens slightly. Stir in the shredded basil and season to taste.

Spoon one-third of the tomato sauce into the prepared dish. Top with half of the eggplant slices. Repeat with remaining tomato sauce and eggplant, finishing with a layer of tomato sauce. Sprinkle with the combined cheeses. Bake for 15 minutes, until the cheese is melted and bubbling.

Rest for 15 minutes before cutting into squares. Top with the extra basil leaves before serving.

Serves 8–10

TIP If the eggplants are firm and unblemished they should not need the initial salting.

1 kg Brussels sprouts, trimmed
90 g butter
60 g hazelnuts, toasted and roughly chopped
salt and freshly ground black pepper, to serve

Brussels Sprouts with Hazelnuts

There's something about the flavour of sprouts that goes well with rich Christmas meats, goose, turkey or pork. It's not the season for them, but because they are so traditional they are often available at Christmas time.

Using the tip of a paring knife, cut a cross in base of each sprout to help cook evenly. Arrange in a steamer basket and cook covered over boiling water for about 8–10 minutes.

Melt the butter in a large frying pan over a low heat until lightly browned. Add the hazelnuts and Brussels sprouts and toss for 1–2 minutes. Season to taste and serve.

Serves 6–8

BRUSSELS SPROUTS WITH CHESTNUTS

An alternative to hazelnuts, chestnuts are a popular addition to the Christmas table. Prepare the sprouts as for Brussels Sprouts with Hazelnuts. Cook the sprouts in a saucepan of boiling salted water for about 15 minutes, then drain. Meanwhile, drain a 250 g can of chestnuts and break up half of them. Heat 40 g butter in a saucepan over a gentle heat and toss through the chestnuts for a few minutes, add the drained sprouts and toss together for 5 minutes. Season with freshly ground black pepper and serve.

Serves 6–8

500 g green beans, trimmed

50 g butter

½ cup slivered almonds

salt and freshly ground black pepper, to season

Green Beans with Almonds

Take advantage of green beans, which are at their best around Christmas in Australia, in this classic recipe that everyone will be sure to enjoy.

Cook the beans in a saucepan of boiling, salted water for 4–5 minutes, until just tender. Drain and set aside.

Meanwhile, melt the butter in a frying pan over a gentle heat until just beginning to brown. Add the almonds, toss until coated in the butter, then add the beans and toss together for 1–2 minutes. Season to taste and serve.

Serves 8

- -

1 kg shelled green peas, fresh or frozen

1 sprig of mint

1 teaspoon sugar

60 g butter

125 g button mushrooms, sliced

Green Peas with Mushrooms

This side dish is a good choice to serve with duckling, roast chicken or beef fillet.

Cook the peas in a saucepan of boiling salted water with the mint and sugar for 10 minutes. Drain, refresh and return to the saucepan with half the butter.

Meanwhile, sauté the mushrooms in a frying pan with the remaining butter until lightly browned. Add the mushrooms to the saucepan with the peas and toss lightly together.

Serves 6–8

1 kg parsnips, peeled and cut into chunky pieces

2 large potatoes, peeled and quartered

½ teaspoon salt

2 cups shelled green peas, fresh or frozen

4 spring onions, chopped

45 g unsalted butter, cut into pieces and softened

100 ml milk

salt and freshly ground black pepper, to season

Parsnip Purée with Peas

The nutty flavour of parsnips makes a fabulous vegetable purée, mellowed by the potato. Serve this as a side with grilled or roasted poultry or meats. This is a great dish worthy of pride of place at a festive table.

Add the parsnip and potato to a large, heavy-based saucepan of cold water. Bring the water to the boil, then add the salt. Boil for 8–10 minutes or until tender. Meanwhile, cook the peas in a small saucepan of boiling water until tender. Drain and transfer to a bowl of iced water.

Add the spring onions, butter, milk and drained peas to a bowl. Drain the parsnips and potato, return to the saucepan and steam over a moderate heat, stirring for about 1 minute, to evaporate any excess liquid. Purée the parsnip mixture with a food processor, season to taste with salt and freshly ground black pepper, and add to the pea mixture. Fold the mixture lightly to combine.

Serves 8

1 kg baby carrots

60 g butter

good pinch of salt

1–2 tablespoons honey or sugar

2 tablespoons chopped mint or Continental parsley

freshly ground black pepper, to season

Glazed Carrots

Glazing is a classic method of cooking carrots rather than simply boiling them. Young baby carrots need only to be scraped lightly and, if they are tiny, cooked whole. Larger carrots can be used, but are best cut into finger-length batons. Everyone loves the syrupy glaze that is left at the end of cooking.

Wash the carrots and cut off the green tops, leaving a small tuft. Put in a saucepan with 1 cup water, the butter, salt and honey or sugar. Cover the pan and cook gently for about 10 minutes, until almost tender. Remove the lid and cook briskly until the liquid in the pan has completely evaporated, taking care not to burn. Shake the pan frequently so that the carrots are thoroughly glazed with the sugar and butter. Toss with the mint or parsley and pepper, and serve piping hot.

Serves 4–6

---

500 g baby vine-ripened truss tomatoes

2 cloves garlic, thinly sliced

1 tablespoon olive oil

1 teaspoon balsamic vinegar

6–8 basil leaves

Truss Tomatoes

This is a sure way of brightening up a festive table and dinner plate – pretty truss tomatoes roasted for 10 minutes then topped with torn basil.

Preheat the oven to 180°C. Snip each truss into two, place in an oven tray, sprinkle over the olive oil, garlic and vinegar, and cook for 10 minutes.

Tear the basil leaves gently or roll into a cigar shape and cut into thin strips. Serve the tomatoes on a heated serving dish, sprinkled with the basil.

Serves 8

2 tablespoons light olive oil	1 tablespoon chopped Continental parsley
1 punnet (200–250 g) cherry tomatoes	6 basil leaves, slivered
1 punnet (200–250 g) yellow grape tomatoes	salt and freshly ground black pepper, to season
1 clove garlic, chopped	

Pan-fried Cherry Tomatoes

Serve this as a fresh-tasting vegetable side dish. The acidity of the tomatoes cuts through an otherwise rich meal at Christmas.

Heat the oil in a frying pan over a moderate heat, add the tomatoes, garlic and parsley, and cook for 2–3 minutes or until the tomatoes are heated through. Take care not to allow the skins to split. Just before serving, toss in the slivered basil and season with salt and pepper to taste.

Serves 8

---

10 asparagus spears or green beans	sprig of thyme or oregano
10 baby carrots or 2 carrots cut into sticks	sea salt and freshly ground black pepper, to season
8 florets broccoli or cauliflower	herbs such as Continental parsley, chives, basil and chervil
8 patty pan squash	1 tablespoon extra-virgin olive oil (optional)

Steamed Vegetables

Christmas dinner calls for lots of steamed, fresh vegetables, dressed with herbs and a drizzle of good olive oil. Look for a mixture of young vegetables in season. A large steamer is recommended for a big family, although collapsible steamers that spread out will take more vegetables.

First prepare the vegetables. Break the tough ends off the asparagus or top the beans if using. Trim and wash the baby carrots. Trim any thick base stalks from the broccoli or cauliflower and separate the heads into florets. Wash the squash and lightly trim the stem and end; leave whole or halve if large.

Put about 1½ cups water in the base of the steamer and bring to the boil. Lay the sprig of thyme or oregano on the steamer. Arrange the vegetables on top and sprinkle lightly with sea salt to season. Cover and steam for 5–8 minutes.

Arrange the vegetables on a serving plate or bowl and sprinkle generously with chopped herbs and freshly ground black pepper. Drizzle over the olive oil if desired.

Serves 6

8 desiree, pontiac or Dutch cream potatoes, peeled, halved

⅓ cup rice bran oil or turkey fat

salt and freshly ground black pepper, to season

Best-ever Roast Potatoes

Crispy and golden on the outside, tender and fluffy inside – just how we all seem to like them.

Preheat the oven to 200°C. Cook the potatoes in a large saucepan of boiling salted water for 8–10 minutes, until almost tender. Drain, return to the pan and shake gently to roughen the surfaces, or score with a fork.

While the turkey or other meats are resting, heat the oil or fat in a baking pan in the oven for 3 minutes. Add the potatoes, season to taste and toss to coat. Bake for 15 minutes then turn the potatoes and bake for a further 15 minutes, until golden and crisp.

Serves 8

TIP Halved parsnips and chunks of kumara can be added to the roasting pan with potatoes.

- -

1 kg desiree, pontiac or Dutch cream potatoes

1 clove garlic, halved

60–90 g butter, plus extra, for greasing

1 cup milk, or half cream, half milk

freshly grated nutmeg, to sprinkle

salt and freshly ground black pepper, to season

½ cup grated Gruyère cheese

Scalloped Potatoes

This dish is a variation of *gratin dauphinois*, a rich, filling regional dish from France. Some recipes include eggs, but the authentic recipe is made only with potatoes and thick, fresh cream. Here is a simpler version.

Peel the potatoes and slice thinly. Rub a shallow ovenproof dish with the cut clove of garlic, then grease the dish generously with butter.

Arrange the potato slices in layers in the prepared dish. Heat the milk in a saucepan until scalding, then add the nutmeg and season to taste. Pour the milk mixture over the potatoes in the dish. Sprinkle with the cheese and dot with butter. Bake in a 180°C oven for 40–50 minutes, until the potatoes are tender and golden. Serve straight from the dish.

Serves 8

6 old desiree, coliban or Dutch cream potatoes	30 g butter
¾–1 cup milk	salt and freshly ground black pepper, to season

Creamy Mashed Potatoes

A creamy mash is always a welcome addition to the Christmas table and, as oven space is limited, it is a good idea to serve them alongside traditional roast potatoes.

Overcooking potatoes, or cutting them too small, makes them water-soaked, causing them to lose all their flavour. Potatoes should break under the pressure of a fork, but not be too mushy. Another important note to remember is that adding cold milk to potato makes the mash grey and sticky – always add hot milk for the fluffiest result.

Peel the potatoes and add to a saucepan with just enough cold, lightly salted water to cover. Cook with a lid on the pan for 20–30 minutes, until the potatoes are easily pierced with a fork. Drain thoroughly and return the potatoes to the pan over a gentle heat for a few minutes, until all the surplus moisture has evaporated and the potatoes are quite dry. Mash with a potato masher or put through a potato ricer.

Once mashed, beat the potatoes with a wooden spoon until very smooth. Meanwhile, heat the milk in a saucepan until scalding. Add the butter to the potatoes, then gradually beat in the hot milk until the potatoes are light and fluffy. Season to taste and serve.

Serves 4–6

HOW TO KEEP THE MASHED POTATO HOT WITHOUT SPOILING

Cook the potatoes as described above, then mash and press down well in saucepan with a potato masher. Pack tightly, levelling the top. Add the butter, spoon about ⅓ cup hot milk over, cover with tight-fitting lid and leave in a warm place. Before serving beat well, adding more hot milk if necessary. The potatoes will keep this way for up to 30 minutes.

- -

750 g old desiree, coliban or Dutch cream potatoes	30 g butter
½ cup warm milk	salt and freshly ground black pepper, to season

Mousseline Potatoes

This potato dish, good with any roasted meat or poultry, is not unlike a creamy mash, but has a finer texture.

Boil the potatoes for 20 minutes. Drain, peel and return to the saucepan over a gentle heat to dry them out. Mash, then rub them through a sieve. Return the purée to the saucepan and beat in the warm milk, little by little, and the butter, until the mixture is light and creamy. Season to taste and serve.

Serves 6–8

8 old desiree, coliban or Dutch cream potatoes, peeled
   and halved

60 g butter

6 cloves garlic, simmered gently in a little stock until soft

¾–1 cup hot milk

salt and freshly ground black pepper, to season

Garlic Potato Purée

For those who enjoy garlic, it livens up a creamy mash of potatoes in this simple side dish.

Cook the potatoes in boiling, salted water until soft. Drain, return to the saucepan and shake the pan over a gentle heat until the potatoes are dry. Mash the potatoes with the butter and garlic flesh, which is squeezed out using a thumb and index finger. Gradually beat in enough hot milk to make the potatoes light and fluffy. Season to taste and serve.

Serves 8

- -

24 baby new potatoes

½ cup caster sugar

125 g clarified butter, melted

Sugar-browned Potatoes

Give someone the job of sugar-browning the potatoes – they will be as proud as punch when everyone starts raving.

Boil the potatoes in their jackets for 10–15 minutes or until just cooked. Let them cool a little, then peel if the skins are not a good colour.

Melt the sugar in a heavy saucepan over a gentle heat. Continue to cook the sugar slowly until it becomes a light brown caramel, stirring to prevent it from burning. Stir in the butter and add as many potatoes as possible without crowding the pan. Shake the pan from time to time until the potatoes are coated with caramel. Remove from the heat and serve as soon as possible.

Serves 6–8

CHAPTER FOUR

Salads

Salads

No meal seems complete without a salad – and Christmas time is no exception. Consider including a salad with the main meal, or for a barbecue, picnic buffet or cold table. Look for good-quality salad greens, prepare them and chill to crisp. Select everything you are going to add with care, and use good-quality vinegars and oils to make dressings.

This chapter takes you past the plain iceberg lettuce and introduces a whole new breed of salads. Rice, mangoes, beetroots, cranberries and a wide selection of vegetables, herbs and dressings add colour and flavour to the Christmas table.

½ red cabbage

½ green cabbage

2 tablespoons olive oil

1 tablespoon white wine vinegar

1 tablespoon Dijon mustard

2 tablespoons chopped celery

1 red capsicum, shredded

½ green capsicum, shredded

6 spring onions, finely shredded

½ cup light sour cream

¼ cup chopped Continental parsley

Sour Cream Coleslaw

This is a good salad to add to a barbecue spread and makes a great addition to any buffet table.

Shred the cabbage finely with a stainless steel knife or use a mandoline for very fine slices. Add the cabbage to a large salad bowl. Combine the oil, vinegar and mustard and beat with a fork until thick. Add to the cabbage and mix well.

Top with the capsicum, spring onions, and celery, and chill well. Just before serving, toss in the light sour cream, mix lightly, and top with the parsley.

Serves 8–10

1½ cups cooked basmati rice (see Tip)

1½ cups cooked wild rice (see Tip)

1 cup dried cranberries

¼ cup slivered almonds, toasted

2 spring onions, finely sliced

½ cup chopped coriander

1 tablespoon grated ginger

½ cup freshly squeezed orange juice

1 tablespoon extra-virgin olive oil

salt and freshly ground black pepper, to season

Crunchy Cranberry and Rice Salad

Cranberries are popular at Christmas time, especially in the cranberry sauce often served with turkey. Dried cranberries are great in cakes or muffins, and work well in salads, such as in this festive rice dish. Wild rice, with its intense nutty flavour, mixes well with long-grain basmati rice. This is a great salad for the Christmas buffet table or with barbecued meats.

Combine the rice, cranberries, almonds, spring onions and coriander in a serving dish.

Press the grated ginger through a fine sieve to extract as much juice as possible. Combine the ginger juice with the strained orange juice and oil. Drizzle the ginger mixture over the rice mixture and toss to coat. Season to taste and serve at room temperature.

Serves 6

TIP Cook wild rice separately as it takes longer to cook than basmati rice – follow the packet directions for cooking times. You'll need to cook ½ cup basmati rice and ⅔ cup wild rice for this recipe.

6–8 beetroot, peeled, cut into wedges

1 tablespoon honey

2 tablespoons balsamic vinegar

2 tablespoons light olive oil

salt and freshly ground black pepper, to season

½ red onion, thinly sliced

2 oranges, segmented

2 tablespoons fresh mint leaves

Beetroot and Orange Salad

So pretty on the plate, and delicious too. This colourful salad is a lovely fresh dish to have with a more traditional and heavy meal. Serve this beetroot and orange salad as a beautifully light first course, or make it as a large platter as part of the festive buffet.

Preheat the oven to 220°C. Cover a baking tray with a large piece of foil and top with the raw beetroot wedges. Combine the honey, half the balsamic vinegar and 1 teaspoon of the oil. Drizzle the honey mixture over the uncooked or canned beetroot and season to taste. Enclose the beetroot in the foil and cook for 45 minutes. Open the foil packet and cook for a further 15 minutes.

Meanwhile, combine the remaining oil and balsamic vinegar in a small jug. Arrange the beetroot, orange segments and onion on a plate. Drizzle with dressing and top with mint.

Serves 4

TIP Canned baby beetroot are ideal for this salad if there isn't time to cook and prepare raw beetroot. If you do decide to go with the canned option, rinse and drain the beetroot, and use only half the amount of balsamic vinegar.

8 beetroot, freshly cooked and peeled

1 teaspoon coarse sea salt

1 tablespoon grated fresh horseradish or prepared
   horseradish (not creamed)

1 cup sour cream

1 tablespoon grated orange rind

2 tablespoons snipped dill

Finnish Beetroot Salad

Creamy with a little horseradish bite, this incredibly bright salad is delicious with cold
meats and fish – so is perfect to have with leftovers.

Cut the beetroot into thin strips. Combine the remaining ingredients, except
the dill, and toss with the beetroot. Cover and chill for at least 1–2 hours to
allow the flavours to blend. Just before serving, top with the dill.

Serves 4–6

*TIP To cook beetroot, first cut the tops off, leaving a little stem. Boil in enough
salted water to cover for 30–40 minutes. To bake, wrap in foil and cook in a
180°C oven for 1–1½ hours. Skins will slip off when cooked.*

4 sweet potatoes (about 1.5 kg total), peeled, thinly sliced

1 tablespoon extra-virgin olive oil

salt and freshly ground black pepper, to season

2 teaspoons honey

2 teaspoons cider vinegar

2 tablespoons pine nuts, toasted

1 tablespoon currants

Sweet Potato, Pine Nut and Currant Salad

We look for something a bit different on special occasions and this salad fits that bill – it's a good choice to serve alongside your roast turkey.

Preheat the oven to 220°C. Toss the sweet potato in 1 teaspoon of the oil in a large baking dish and season to taste with salt and pepper. Spread out evenly and cook for 30 minutes, until browned and tender. Remove from the oven and cool slightly.

Meanwhile, combine the remaining oil, honey and vinegar in a small jug.

Arrange the sweet potato on a serving plate. Sprinkle with the pine nuts and currants and drizzle with the dressing. Serve warm or at room temperature.

Serves 6

| 1 kg potatoes, such as kipfler, pink-eye or fir apple, unpeeled |
| salt and freshly ground black pepper, to season |
| 2–3 tablespoons good-quality white wine vinegar |
| 6–7 tablespoons extra-virgin olive oil |
| ⅓ cup chicken or vegetable stock or hot water |
| Continental parsley, chives, chervil and tarragon, chopped |
| 3–4 spring onions, chopped (optional, for a more pungent salad) |
| ¾ cup good-quality mayonnaise (optional) |
| Continental parsley, chopped, to garnish |

Classic Potato Salad

A really good potato salad is one of the best dishes around. Potato salad is a perfect dish for a hot Christmas day.

Boil the potatoes in just enough water to cover, until tender. Drain, peel and cut into thick slices. Spread over a shallow dish. While the potatoes are still hot, season with salt and pepper. Beat the vinegar, stock and oil together with a fork then sprinkle over the potatoes. Add the chopped herbs to taste and spring onions (if using).

Let the salad stand at room temperature until most of the liquid is absorbed. Turn the potato slices carefully to ensure even seasoning. Serve the salad without chilling. For a creamy salad, spoon the mayonnaise over the potatoes. Top with the extra chopped parsley.

Serves 8–10

POTATO AND EGG MAYONNAISE
Make the potato salad as above. Before adding the mayonnaise, top with 6 hard-boiled eggs, halved, then spoon over the mayonnaise. For a festive finish, soak 8 anchovy fillets in milk for 20 minutes, then drain. Slit in two lengthwise and arrange on top in lattice fashion. Set a black olive in each diamond of anchovy and sprinkle with chopped parsley.

For a lighter topping, combine ¾ cup mayonnaise with ¼ cup cream and 1 teaspoon Worcestershire sauce. Spoon the mayonnaise over the egg and sprinkle with paprika.

POTATOES WITH RED CAPSICUM
Make the potato salad as above, without the mayonnaise. Grill 2 red capsicums until the skins blacken and start to flake off, about 10 minutes each side. Remove from the heat. When cool, peel off the skins, remove the seeds and wash the flesh under cold water. Cut into strips and arrange the strips around or in a lattice fashion on top of the potatoes. Sprinkle with chopped parsley.

1 kg baby new potatoes	2 anchovy fillets, finely chopped
1 tablespoon dry white wine	salt and freshly ground black pepper, to season
2 tablespoons lemon juice	⅓ cup semi-dried tomatoes
1 tablespoon extra-virgin olive oil	¼ cup chives snipped into 3 cm lengths
1 clove garlic, crushed	

Baby Potato Salad

With a summery Christmas, light salads are a perfect side dish for your special menu. Quick and easy, they're great for the holiday season. The semi-dried tomato and anchovy dressing drizzled over this potato salad gives it a lively taste.

Cook the potatoes in a saucepan of salted boiling water for 15 minutes, until tender; drain. While still hot, cut in half and add to a serving bowl. Drizzle over the wine and toss to coat.

Combine the lemon juice, oil, garlic and anchovy in a small jug. Season to taste with salt and pepper. Add the tomatoes and chives to the potatoes, drizzle with the dressing and toss to coat.

Serves 6

TIP It's important to pour the wine over hot potatoes – they absorb more when hot than cold.

- -

1 kg potatoes, Tasmanian pink eye or kipfler, unpeeled	2 tablespoons white wine vinegar
½ cup light sour cream	1 tablespoon chopped tarragon or Continental parsley
¼ cup chopped chives	salt and freshly ground black pepper, to season
1 spring onion or eschalot, finely chopped	

Potatoes with Chive Cream

If preparing the potatoes ahead of time, drizzle with an extra tablespoon each of white wine vinegar and olive oil while still warm. Toss to combine and stand at room temperature. When ready, dress with the chive cream just before serving.

Cook the potatoes in a saucepan of salted boiling water for 15 minutes, until tender; drain. When cool enough to handle, peel and slice thickly.

Meanwhile, combine the remaining ingredients in a jug. Season to taste. Pour over the warm potatoes and toss gently to combine.

Serves 8

1 kg new potatoes

⅓ cup dry white wine

½ cup Vinaigrette (page 282)

1 red onion, sliced into rings

1 stalk celery, sliced

2 dill pickles or gherkins, thinly sliced

1 teaspoon capers

4 boiled eggs, peeled and halved

2 tablespoons chopped Continental parsley

salt and freshly ground black pepper, to season

½ cup homemade Mayonnaise (page 274) (optional)

American Potato Salad

Potato salad with all the trimmings. The eggs, capers and pickles are a lovely addition to this American version of one of our favourite salads. Splash the still-hot potatoes with dry white wine to make this special just-warm potato salad.

Scrub and simmer the potatoes gently until tender in salted water. Peel, if liked, and slice while still hot into a bowl. Sprinkle with the white wine, turning the potato slices carefully with a rubber spatula.

Sprinkle over the vinaigrette dressing and gently fold through the remaining ingredients. Season with salt and pepper. For a creamy finish, fold in homemade Mayonnaise.

Serves 6

Green Salad with Chapons

Wash, dry and chill a selection of tender salad greens – lettuce, curly endive, rocket, baby spinach, parsley, watercress. Look also at the bags of mixed greens available, or select your own from the greengrocer. Be selective – look for the freshest, the youngest and the best. Pick over the greens, removing any large, coarse stems or bruised leaves. Wash, spin dry and wrap loosely in a clean tea towel; refrigerate until required.

Take 5–6 handfuls choice salad greens; tear largish leaves into bite-sized pieces.

Crush 2 cloves garlic with salt, put in a small bowl with a few tablespoons of olive oil and a grinding of black pepper; mix well. To make chapons, brush the garlic oil on slices of a small baguette. Add to a large bowl with the salad greens. Just before serving, toss with a little Vinaigrette (page 282).

OTHER INGREDIENTS TO ADD

Olives and grapes make a good addition to salads.

Fresh herbs impart their own distinctive taste to a salad. Chop the herbs into suitable pieces.

Anchovies give a piquant touch to salads, in particular niçoise and caesar. Not too many though – they can easily overpower a salad.

Nuts such as walnuts, pecans, slivered almonds and macadamias give a particular crunch to salads. Dry-roasting the nuts in a small frying pan intensifies the taste and gives extra crunch.

An assortment of **tomatoes** – cherry, teardrop or baby Romas – adds colour and flavour.

Cheese adds richness to salads – cubes of Gruyère or other Swiss-style cheeses, crumbled blue cheese and fresh goat's cheese are all good choices. A Greek salad, of course, can't do without feta.

Avocado pieces are also a welcome addition to a tossed salad.

Adding texture and flavour to a salad, **radish** should be washed and finely sliced, crisped in iced water then drained.

Peel and slice **cucumber**, or cut into batons, crisp in iced water, drain well and toss through salads.

If including **snow peas**, first remove the strings and tops, and blanch in salted boiling water for 2 minutes. Drain and chill in iced water.

NOTES The chapons may be crisped in a hot oven, giving a nice crunch to the salad. Add just before serving.

Before using, wash salad greens in plenty of water. Rinse well to get rid of any sand or grit. Dry the greens in a salad spinner or shake in a large tea towel. Store in plastic bags and chill in the refrigerator until just required.

All salads should have that light, fresh bouffant, just-made look. It is important to remember that crisp salad vegetables droop if mixed too far ahead of serving, so try to do it at the last minute.

1 large iceberg lettuce

5 spring onions, thinly sliced or cut julienne

1 bunch radishes (about 500 g), thinly sliced

¼ cup Continental parsley

DRESSING

1 egg

1 tablespoon white wine vinegar

⅓ cup light olive oil

2 tablespoons chopped cornichons or capers

salt and freshly ground black pepper, to season

Iceberg Lettuce and Radish Salad

When properly chilled, iceberg is the crispest and crunchiest of all lettuce, and makes a refreshing base for a salad. Add a bit more flavour and crunch with bright red radishes.

Remove the dark outside leaves of the lettuce. Wash well, dry thoroughly and chill until crisp and ready to serve.

To make the dressing, process the egg in a food processor with the vinegar. With the motor still running, add the oil in a slow stream until it has thickened. Transfer to a jug and stir in the cornichons or capers. Season to taste with salt and pepper.

Cut the lettuce in halves then cut each half across into 6 wedges, arranging them on a large serving platter. Spoon the dressing over the wedges and scatter with spring onion, sliced radish and parsley leaves.

Serves 8–12

1 tablespoon red wine vinegar

2 teaspoons Dijon mustard

1 tablespoon extra-virgin olive oil

salt and freshly ground black pepper, to season

2 bunches radishes (about 1 kg total), trimmed, thinly sliced

500 g small zucchini, thinly sliced

2 tablespoons chopped dill

crusty bread, to serve

Radish, Zucchini and Dill Salad

Green and red, this salad just seems to say 'Christmas'. This light, crunchy salad goes perfectly with any Christmas meal – whether you've chosen fish, ham or golden roast turkey. If you prefer, Lebanese cucumbers can replace the zucchini, as both are good in this salad.

Combine the vinegar and mustard in a small jug and whisk in the oil. Season to taste.

Put the radish, zucchini and dill in a salad bowl and drizzle with the dressing. Toss to coat and serve with crusty bread, if you like.

Serves 6

TIP Using a mandoline will speed up the chopping time and give you beautiful, thin vegetable slices.

2 mangoes, peeled and cut into strips

1 teaspoon lime juice

6 cups mixed salad greens

125 g snow peas, blanched and refreshed

6 drops Tabasco

2 tablespoons olive oil

salt and freshly ground black pepper, to season

Mango Salad

To me, mangoes are the epitome of Christmas time, so it seems fitting to have them at the table. Serve this deliciously tropical salad with barbecued meats or poultry, roast pork or ham.

Drizzle the mango with the lime juice in a bowl and leave for 30 minutes. Add the chilled salad greens and snow peas to a large salad bowl. Beat the Tabasco and oil together and season with salt and pepper. Just before serving, mix the mango and dressing through the salad and snow peas. Pile on plates and serve with barbecued quail or duck breasts, or leave in the salad bowl for people to serve themselves.

Serves 8

- -

1 teaspoon fish sauce (nam pla)

juice of 1 lime

⅓ cup coconut milk

2 teaspoons caster sugar

½ teaspoon Thai green curry paste

2 cloves garlic, crushed

6 slices ginger, cut julienne

½–1 red chilli, sliced

freshly ground black pepper, to season

1 kg green (raw) prawns, shelled and deveined

8–10 mint leaves

1 punnet snow pea shoots

Minted Prawn Salad

The complex seasonings of Thai cooking intrigue almost everyone who has sampled it – and this dish is no exception. This salad is best served as a first course – a fresh starter, perhaps, before a roast Christmas meal.

Mix the fish sauce, lime juice, coconut milk, sugar, green curry paste, garlic, ginger, chilli and pepper in a bowl. Drop the prawns into a pan of simmering, salted water for 1 minute or until they turn pink. Lift out and toss in the dressing; add the mint leaves and toss.

If serving as a salad, make a mound of snow pea shoots or greens on 8 serving plates and top with the prawns. To serve as a main course, serve with steamed jasmine rice.

Serves 8

JASMINE RICE

Bring 3 cups water to the boil. Add a pinch of salt and 1 cup jasmine rice, and bring back to the boil. Reduce the heat and cook until the water evaporates, about 10–12 minutes. Turn off the heat, cover and leave for a further 5 minutes. Fluff up the rice with a fork and serve.

6 firm, ripe tomatoes

salt and freshly ground black pepper, to season

¼ cup olive oil

1 teaspoon lemon juice or balsamic or wine vinegar

6–8 spring onions

2–3 tablespoons chopped Continental parsley or basil

A Good Tomato Salad

Tomatoes dressed in olive oil and just a touch of lemon juice, topped with blanched spring onions, must be one of the simplest yet most delicious salads.

Cut the tomatoes crosswise into thin slices with a serrated knife and arrange overlapping on a flat dish. Season well with salt and pepper.

Mix the oil and lemon juice or vinegar together and sprinkle over the tomatoes. Chop the spring onions, drop into a saucepan of boiling water for 30 seconds, drain and refresh in cold water. Sprinkle over the tomatoes with the chopped parsley or basil. This salad is improved by covering the flat dish with plastic wrap and refrigerating for 30 minutes.

Serves 6–8

2 bunches English spinach

40 g unsalted butter

2 tablespoons olive oil

1 clove garlic, finely chopped

½ teaspoon salt

¼ cup pine nuts, toasted

⅓ cup sultanas

Spinach with Sultanas and Pine Nuts

Sweet sultanas and toasted pine nuts add interest to spinach in this simple salad.

Remove the stalks from the spinach, wash and shake dry. In a large pan, heat the butter and oil, and add the garlic and salt. Add the spinach and sauté over a moderate heat for 3–5 minutes or until tender, covering with a lid if necessary for the last minute or so. Add the pine nuts and sultanas, and toss to combine. Serve warm.

Serves 6–8

375 g green beans, trimmed

375 g yellow beans, trimmed

250 g cherry tomatoes, quartered

1 spring onion or eschalot, finely chopped

grated rind of 1 lemon (see Tip)

1 tablespoon lemon juice

2 tablespoons baby capers, rinsed, drained

2 tablespoons extra-virgin olive oil

Green and Yellow Bean Salad

This is one of the prettiest and best tasting salads. Look for baby beans and mixed cherry tomatoes – red, yellow, teardrop – as a mix looks lovely. This salad could be served as a first course, or put out on the buffet table during the main course. Green and red, it just belongs on the Christmas table.

Cook the beans in a large saucepan of salted boiling water for 4 minutes, until just tender. Drain and put in a bowl of iced water. Once cool, drain again. Add to a serving dish with the tomatoes and spring onion or eschalot.

Combine the lemon zest and juice, baby capers and oil in a small jug. Season to taste. Drizzle over the beans and tomatoes, and toss to coat.

Serves 6

TIP If you haven't got a zester, peel the lemon and remove the bitter white pith. Slice very thinly and soak in iced water for 10–15 minutes, until curled.

CHAPTER FIVE

Puddings & Other Desserts

Puddings & Other Desserts

Making the special treats of Christmas is mostly a family affair. Take making the Christmas pudding, with the children taking their turns in stirring the pudding, making a secret wish as they do so. This is meant to bring good luck. But, according to old English lore, the pudding should only be stirred clockwise because this is the direction in which the Sun was presumed to move around the Earth. To stir in the opposite direction was supposed to invite disaster.

While some people enjoy a rich, fruity, spicy plum pudding, others know that there are special desserts more suited to hot climates and as a finale to a rich meal. Trifles are perhaps a first choice. Easy to make – and made ahead is the way to go – a trifle can be as lavish and decorative as you wish. I give a recipe for a trifle finished off with Persian fairy floss and silver leaf (page 194) – as exotic as Aladdin and *One Thousand and One Nights*.

Should pavlova be a favourite, make a rolled pavlova into a log – it could be an Australian version of the French yule log made with chocolate. A traditional pavlova also gets a big tick.

Tipsy cake is another favourite; ours is made with an Italian Christmas bread base – panettone.

If you want to celebrate Christmas on winter solstice, keep your rich plum pudding and serve a light dessert knowing that the plum pudding can only improve in time and be even more enjoyable on a cold wintry day.

5 egg yolks

½ cup sifted icing sugar

½ cup rum

1 tablespoon powdered gelatine

¼ cup water

2½ cups cream, whipped

5 egg whites, stiffly beaten

Raspberry Sauce (page 284)

Danish Rum Cream

While the English enjoy a rich spiced fruit pudding brought flaming to the table as the final course of a Christmas meal, the Danes choose a delicate rum cream as white as the driven snow. I have included this lovely pudding for those who would like to finish their Christmas dinner on a Danish theme.

Beat the egg yolks with the icing sugar in a bowl and stir in the rum. Soften the gelatine in the water and dissolve over a gentle heat. Stir into the rum mixture until well combined. Fold in the cream and the beaten egg whites. Pour into a glass bowl and chill for at least 3 hours. Serve with raspberry sauce.

Serves 6–8

250 g raisins	1¼ cups light brown sugar
60 g mixed peel	grated rind of 1 orange
250 g sultanas	4 eggs
250 g currants	1 cup plain flour
125 g chopped blanched almonds	1 teaspoon mixed spice
¼ cup rum or brandy, plus extra, for flaming	1 teaspoon ground ginger
250 g unsalted butter	125 g soft white breadcrumbs

Rich Christmas Pudding

Christmas pudding, stuck with a piece of holly, flaming with brandy or rum, served with a rich custard or rum butter, is one of the highlights of Christmas.

Sprinkle all the fruits and the almonds with the brandy or rum into a large bowl, cover and leave overnight.

Cream the butter until soft, add the sugar and orange rind and beat until light and fluffy. Add the eggs one at a time, beating well after each addition. Sift the flour and spices into a bowl and then fold into the sugar and butter mixture. Stir in the breadcrumbs and the marinated fruit and almonds until well combined.

Place the mixture into a well-greased pudding basin lined with a circle of greased baking paper cut to fit the base. Cover with another circle of greased baking paper to fit the top of the pudding basin. Cover the pudding with a large sheet of baking paper with a pleat in the centre, to allow for any rising. Tie firmly with string, placing a plate on top of the bowl to hold the paper in place while doing so. Make a handle of string from side to side of the bowl, latching it onto the string around the bowl, and use to lower the pudding gently into boiling water. [CONTINUED OVERLEAF]

Rich Christmas Pudding [CONTINUED]

Steam, covered, for 6 hours. The water should come halfway up the side of the pudding bowl. It is a good idea to sit the pudding on a metal ring or an old, upturned saucer. Top up the water with boiling water from time to time. Remove from the water, cover with fresh baking paper and string. Store until needed.

To serve, put the pudding into a saucepan of boiling water to come halfway up the sides of the basin and steam for 2½ hours. Invert the pudding onto a heated plate. To flame, warm a tablespoon or so of rum or brandy, light and pour over the pudding at the table – turn the lights low first to enjoy the flame and be amazed at the spectacle. Serve accompanied by Vanilla Egg Custard (page 285), Brandy Sauce (page 283), Brandied Butter (page 283) or heavy cream.

Serves 8

TIP This pudding will keep for many months. For this quantity you will need a 1.7 litre pudding bowl, or you can make two puddings using two smaller basins.

250 g butter

1¼ cups brown sugar

4 eggs

grated rind of 1 orange

1 tablespoon golden syrup

1 tablespoon treacle

2¾ cups mixed dried fruit

¾ cup mixed peel

½ cup chopped almonds

1 apple, peeled and chopped

1½ cups fresh breadcrumbs

1 cup plain flour, sifted

1 teaspoon ground mixed spice

¼ cup brandy

Microwave Christmas Pudding

Cream the butter and sugar together until light and fluffy. Add the eggs one at a time, beating well after each addition. Beat in the orange rind, golden syrup and treacle.

Stir in the mixed fruit, peel, almonds and apple. Fold in the breadcrumbs, flour and spice alternately with the brandy.

Spoon the pudding mixture into an oven bag and put the bag inside another oven bag. Tie the top loosely with kitchen string. Place in the centre of the microwave turntable and cook for 40 minutes on medium.

Allow to stand for 10 minutes before removing from the oven bag. Serve with Brandy Sauce (page 283) or whipped cream.

To reheat, remove the pudding from the oven bag and place on a microwave-proof plate. Sprinkle 1½ tablespoons water or brandy over the pudding. Cover with plastic wrap and cook on medium for 10 minutes.

Serves 8

TIP Do not tie the top of bag too close to the pudding as it may burst the bag.

2 tablespoons sago

1 cup milk

60 g butter

¾ cup caster sugar

1 teaspoon bicarbonate of soda

pinch of salt

1 cup fine dry breadcrumbs

1 cup mixed dried fruit

2 teaspoons grated lemon rind

1 teaspoon mixed spice

Sago Plum Pudding

If you find rich pudding too much after a hearty main course, you may enjoy a lovely sago plum pudding. It has a light texture, lovely flavour and can be quickly mixed and steamed on Christmas morning. Double the recipe or make two separate puddings to serve eight or more.

Pour the milk over the sago in a bowl and soak overnight.

Cream the butter and sugar in a bowl and stir in the sago, bicarbonate of soda and salt. Add the remaining ingredients and mix well. Spoon into a well-greased 4-cup pudding basin. Cover with a double thickness of greaseproof paper or foil, or a tight-fitting lid, and steam for 2½–3 hours. Serve hot with custard or cream.

Serves 4–6

TIP If making double the quantity, increase the cooking time to 3 hours. This dessert may be made ahead, stored and reheated in the microwave on Christmas Day – see instructions for the Microwave Christmas Pudding, (page 187), but allow 4–5 minutes on medium

2½ cups milk

1 vanilla bean, split lengthwise and seeds scraped,
   or 2 teaspoons vanilla extract

5 egg yolks

¾ cup caster sugar

pinch of salt

1 tablespoon plus 1 teaspoon powdered gelatine,
   softened in ⅓ cup cold water

2 cups cream

fresh raspberries or strawberries, to decorate

RASPBERRY COULIS

2 cups raspberries or hulled strawberries, fresh or frozen

1 tablespoon red currant jelly

½ cup caster sugar

juice of ½ lemon

Vanilla Bavarois with Raspberry Coulis

Bavarois, or Bavarian cream, is a timeless classic and is the perfect choice for a hot climate Christmas dessert. These days, it is moulded individually and accompanied by a little fruit coulis. I like to use a fresh vanilla bean to flavour the milk and scrape out some of the seeds to add a fleck to the bavarois.

Bring the milk, split vanilla bean and scraped seeds (if using) almost to the boil in a saucepan over a moderate heat, then cover and cool. Beat the egg yolks with the sugar and salt until thick and lemon coloured. Pour into a clean heavy-based saucepan with the milk and stir over a low heat until the mixture coats the back of a spoon. Remove the vanilla bean and cool slightly. Add the softened gelatine, stir until dissolved then add the vanilla essence if not using the vanilla bean.

Cool, then chill until the mixture is beginning to set, stirring frequently. Whip the cream until soft peaks form and fold through the custard. Pour into 8 individual dariole moulds which have been lightly oiled and chill for several hours until firm.

Meanwhile, to make the raspberry coulis, gently heat the raspberries or strawberries until just lukewarm. Add the red currant jelly, caster sugar and lemon juice, lightly mashing the fruit. Mash to a pulp, then push through a sieve. Cool and set aside until needed.

Unmould the bavarois carefully onto serving plates and surround each with a little raspberry coulis, decorating with the fresh berries.

Serves 8

½ loaf sliced white bread, crusts removed

750 g mixed fruit, choosing from strawberries, raspberries, blueberries or other berry fruits, red currants, blackcurrants, stoned cherries, fresh or frozen

⅔ cup caster sugar

Summer Pudding

Most good greengrocers have fresh raspberries and blueberries around Christmas time. Look out for red currants too. If you have no luck with fresh berries, try the frozen ones from large supermarkets. Summer Pudding needs to be made at least a day before it is to be served. It makes a great festive dessert and is perfect for a warm Christmas.

Reserve 3 slices of the bread, cut the remaining slices into wedges or oblongs and use to line the base and sides of a 4-cup pudding basin, soufflé dish or charlotte mould. Cook the fruit and sugar in a heavy-based saucepan, covered, over a low heat for 5 minutes, stirring occasionally. This encourages the fruit juices to flow. Allow to cool.

Spoon half the fruit into the pudding basin and lay one of the reserved slices of bread on top. This gives the dessert the body needed to turn out later. Spoon in the remaining fruit, top with the 2 remaining reserved slices of bread, then spoon the remaining fruit juice over, reserving 1–2 tablespoons for coating any patches once the pudding is turned out.

Place a small plate on top of the pudding, making sure it sits inside the basin. Place weights or heavy tins on top (about 500 g is needed) to compress and place the basin on a large plate to catch juices. Refrigerate overnight.

Turn out onto a plate and serve whipped cream separately, if liked.

Serves 8

panettone, or butter cake, sliced and cut into fingers
300 g raspberries, fresh or frozen
2 punnets strawberries, hulled and sliced
pulp of 2 passionfruit
⅓ cup flaked almonds, toasted
½ cup dry sherry or brandy
½ cup orange juice
1 cup thickened cream, whipped
1 quantity Vanilla Egg Custard (page 284)
6–8 strawberries, extra, for decorating

Tipsy Cake

Tipsy cake used to be a whole butter cake soaked with sweet wine or sherry mixed with brandy. This was garnished with almonds and surrounded by custard. An old fashioned trifle was made on somewhat the same lines and covered with fluffy whipped cream. The trifle of today may be a combination of the two. One thing is for certain, whether you call it 'trifle' or 'tipsy cake', it is always a popular and fitting end to a Christmas dinner.

Place half the panettone in a glass serving bowl. Top with raspberries, strawberries and passionfruit. Top with the remaining panettone and half of the almonds. Drizzle with the combined sherry or brandy and juice. Cover and set aside for 30 minutes.

Gently fold the cream into the custard. Spoon over the panettone, allowing excess to drizzle down the sides of the cake. Chill in the fridge for 3 hours or overnight. To serve, sprinkle with the remaining almonds and top with the extra strawberries.

Serves 6–8

TIP This cake is best made the day before. If you have been given a panettone for Christmas, this is a great way to use it.

½ cup Marsala, rum or brandy

½ cup strong black coffee

250 g sponge finger biscuits (savoiardi)

500 g mascarpone cheese

1 quantity Pastry Cream (page 205)

100 g dark chocolate, grated

2 tablespoons cocoa powder

Tiramisu

This is a great Italian dessert, with the added bonus that it is easy to make ahead. This recipe for tiramisu calls for pastry cream, which is a very thick custard professional pastry cooks use to great advantage – it helps to make this recipe a standout. *Tiramisu* translates to 'pick me up' – why not test it out for Christmas Day?

Combine the Marsala and coffee in a jug. Lay half of the sponge fingers in the base of a 28 x 18 x 5 cm dish and pour over half the Marsala mixture.

In another bowl, stir the mascarpone until smooth then fold through the vanilla Pastry Cream. Spoon half over the sponge fingers and sprinkle with half of the grated chocolate. Top with the remaining sponge fingers then pour over the remaining Marsala mixture.

Spoon over the remaining pastry cream mixture, sprinkle with the remaining chocolate and dust with cocoa powder. Cover with plastic wrap and refrigerate for at least 3 hours or up to 24 hours before serving. Serve cut into squares.

Serves 8

250 g sponge finger biscuits (savoiardi)

125 g amaretti biscuits (almond macaroons), coarsely crushed

300 g raspberries, fresh or frozen

3 mangoes, flesh cubed

½ cup dry sherry

½ cup apple juice

1 cup thickened cream, whipped

1 quantity Vanilla Egg Custard (page 284)

Persian fairy floss and silver leaf (optional), to decorate

Christmas Trifle

A summery version of this soft Italian dessert, the fresh raspberries and mangoes are a lovely addition. The ingredients can all be bought from a good supermarket or delicatessen – even the custard, although homemade is better.

Lay half of the sponge fingers in the base of a large glass serving bowl or divide equally between eight individual dishes or glasses. Sprinkle with the crushed amaretti. Scatter with three-quarters of the fruit. Top with the remaining sponge fingers. Drizzle with the combined sherry and juice. Cover and set aside for 30 minutes.

Gently fold the cream into the custard. Spoon over the sponge fingers, allowing excess to drizzle down the sides of the sponge. Top with the remaining fruit, Persian fairy floss and silver leaf, if desired.

Serves 8

TIP Persian fairy floss and silver leaf are available from some supermarkets and delicatessens or fine food stores.

Here are three easy ice cream desserts embodying the true spirit of Christmas with Fruit Mincemeat, nuts, flames and good spirits.

20 g butter	½ cup firmly packed brown sugar
¾ cup coarsely chopped Brazil nuts or hazelnuts, plus extra, to decorate	¾ cup Fruit Mincemeat (page 286)
½ cup cream	2 litres coffee ice cream

Brazil Sundaes

Melt the butter in a small saucepan, add the chopped nuts and stir until lightly toasted. Add the cream and brown sugar, bring to the boil, then simmer until well blended, stirring constantly. Add the Fruit Mincemeat. Spoon the hot sauce over individual servings of ice cream and sprinkle with a few extra chopped nuts.

Serves 8

- -

1 cup Fruit Mincemeat (page 286)	2 litres vanilla ice cream
2 tablespoons brandy or maple syrup	maple syrup, for topping
⅓ cup finely chopped walnuts or toasted almonds	

Christmas Ice Cream

Soften the Fruit Mincemeat with brandy or maple syrup. Add the chopped nuts. Let the ice cream soften slightly and stir in the mincemeat and nuts (don't over mix, a rippled effect is attractive). Return to the freezer until serving time, then serve in individual scoops with a little maple syrup poured over the top.

Serves 8

- -

2 litres vanilla ice cream
2 cups Fruit Mincemeat (page 286)
¼ cup brandy

Ice Cream Balls with Fruit Mince Flambé

Freeze the ice cream balls a day ahead so they're very firm.

Scoop the ice cream into balls with an ice cream scoop. Freeze until ready to serve. At serving time, pile the ice cream balls into a serving bowl, heat the mincemeat in a saucepan and spoon over the frozen ice cream. Warm the brandy in the same pan, ignite, and pour flaming over the mincemeat and ice cream. Serve at once.

Serves 8

½ cup desiccated coconut

4 egg whites, at room temperature

⅔ cup caster sugar

1 teaspoon cornflour

½ teaspoon white vinegar

1 teaspoon vanilla extract

2 tablespoons icing sugar, sifted, plus extra, for dusting

1¼ cups mascarpone cheese

pulp of 3 passionfruit

1 punnet strawberries, hulled and sliced, plus extra to serve

Coconut and Mascarpone Pavlova Log

A new take on a pavlova, this coconut and mascarpone log is easy to slice and serve and caters for those who love pavlovas. It pays homage to the yule log, popular in France.

Preheat the oven to 180°C. Line a 26 x 30 cm Swiss roll pan with baking paper. Sprinkle the base with 2 tablespoons of the coconut.

Beat the egg whites in a clean, dry bowl with an electric beater until soft peaks form. Gradually beat in the caster sugar, 1 tablespoon at a time, until firm, thick and glossy. Beat in the cornflour, vinegar and vanilla. Carefully fold through remaining coconut with a large metal spoon.

Pour the mixture into the prepared pan. Bake for 12–15 minutes, until risen and golden. Turn out onto a clean tea towel that has been dusted with icing sugar. Remove the baking paper. With short side facing you, carefully roll up using the tea towel as a guide. Allow to cool.

Unroll the pavlova, spread with mascarpone almost to the edges and top with the passionfruit pulp and strawberries. Re-roll and refrigerate for several hours. To serve, dust with icing sugar and serve sliced with extra strawberries.

Serves 8

TIP If you wish, replace the mascarpone with the same amount of whipped cream.

6 egg whites, at room temperature

pinch of salt

2 cups caster sugar

1½ teaspoons white vinegar

1½ teaspoons vanilla extract

300 ml cream, whipped

1 punnet strawberries, hulled and sliced

1–2 tablespoons icing sugar

pulp of 3 passionfruit

Pavlova

Pavlova has to be one of the most popular party desserts in Australia and New Zealand. This is my favourite version – it has a crisp meringue outside, delicate marshmallow softness inside, a topping of perfectly whipped cream and the welcome addition of passionfruit. Have the base ready and finish it off with cream and fruit just before it's needed.

Toppings can vary although passionfruit and sliced strawberries are always a good combination. A tablespoon of icing sugar may be added to sweeten them if you like. Sliced strawberries macerated with a tablespoon of kirsch or orange-flavoured liqueur are also a delicious topping. A New Zealand favourite, sliced kiwi fruit, can add a fresh flavour and colour.

Preheat the oven to 200–210°C. Place a piece of baking paper on a baking tray and mark a 23 cm circle (the pavlova will spread a little).

Beat the egg whites and salt with an electric mixer at full speed until they stand in stiff peaks. Sift the sugar and gradually sprinkle in 1 tablespoon at a time, beating at high speed only until all the sugar has been added. Lastly, fold in the vinegar and vanilla. Spoon large dollops inside the circle on the baking sheet and smooth over the top lightly. Reduce the oven to 150°C and cook the pavlova for 1 hour. Turn off the heat and leave in the oven until cold. If using a gas oven, bake at 150°C for 1 hour, reduce the heat to 120°C for a further 30 minutes and then turn off the oven and leave the pavlova in the oven until cooled.

When the pavlova is cooled, slide onto a large cake plate, removing the baking paper. Don't worry if it collapses slightly; also expect cracks on the surface. Whip the cream until stiff but still shiny and spoon over the top of the pavlova. Top with sliced strawberries sweetened with the icing sugar. Spoon the passionfruit pulp over the top and serve.

Serves 8–10

4 egg whites, at room temperature

1 cup caster sugar

1 teaspoon white vinegar

1 teaspoon vanilla extract

300 ml cream, whipped

1 punnet strawberries, hulled and sliced, or 4 kiwi fruit, peeled and sliced, or pulp of 5 passionfruits (or a combination of all of these)

Pavlova Nests

Everyone gets their own little pavlova in this lovely version.

Preheat the oven to 130°C. Line two baking trays with baking paper. Trace 8 circles 11 cm in diameter onto the baking paper.

Beat the egg whites with an electric mixer until soft peaks are formed. Add the sugar, 1 tablespoon at a time, beating constantly, until thick and glossy. Lastly, fold in the vinegar and vanilla. Spoon or pipe the meringue onto the circles on the prepared trays. Using a spoon, make an indent in the top of each meringue. Bake for 30 minutes. Turn the oven off and leave the meringues in the oven until completely cooled. Store in airtight containers until ready to use.

When ready to serve, place a dollop of cream into the centre of each meringue and top with fruit.

Makes 8

90 g unsalted butter, plus 10 g extra

½ cup soft brown sugar

1 teaspoon ground cardamom

¾ cup water

8 ripe pears, peeled, halved and cored (see Notes)

¼ cup dark rum

mascarpone cheese, to serve

Caramelised Cardamom Pears

Pears are perfect poached, baked, grilled or sautéed, or simply wash and eat. Choose firm but ripe pears for this superb dish, perfect for those who want a fruit dessert for Christmas.

Preheat the oven to 220°C. Melt the butter in a saucepan over a moderate heat and stir in the sugar, cardamom and water, until the sugar dissolves. Arrange the pears in a greased shallow ovenproof baking dish. Spoon over the caramel and toss to coat; dot with the extra butter. Bake in the oven, uncovered, for 30–45 minutes, basting the pears several times with the pan juices. Transfer the pears with a slotted spoon onto 8 dessert plates. Stir the rum into the syrup until well combined. Scoop a spoonful of mascarpone onto each plate and spoon the syrup over the pears. Serve warm or cold.

Serves 8

NOTES *Beurre bosc is an elegant pear with greenish-brown skin that warms to a dark cinnamon brown when ripe. It has a delicate texture and flavour and is an ideal dessert pear for this recipe. Bartlett and packham pears are also suitable.*

If oven space is at a premium on Christmas Day, pears can be ready to go into the oven when it's free of a main dish, or prepare and cook well ahead.

PROFITEROLES

125 g unsalted butter, cut into cubes

1 teaspoon caster sugar

½ teaspoon salt

1 cup plain flour, sifted

5 eggs

2 quantities Pastry Cream (opposite)

Croquembouche

Literally 'crunch in the mouth', croquembouche is actually a traditional French wedding cake made of profiteroles filled with cream or pastry cream and stacked into a cone shape. It is often decorated with spun sugar and sometimes with roses, other real flowers. For Christmas, try using holly.

I was reluctant to include a recipe for croquembouche in a book of Christmas food because in Australia, and particularly Sydney, the weather can be so humid at this time of year – and humidity is the enemy of both profiteroles and toffee. But for those who like a challenge, here it is.

To help, you can make and bake all the choux puffs (profiteroles) ahead, cool them thoroughly and keep them in a snap-lock bag in the freezer. The pastry cream can be made the day before and stored in piping bags in the fridge. On the morning, the profiteroles should be refreshed in the oven to crisp them up again. Once cooled again, they can then be filled, dipped in toffee and stacked – but should be served within 4 hours.

When made by pastry cooks, the profiteroles are stacked around a special stainless steel mould and attached to each other with toffee. The finished dessert is then lifted off the mould.

PROFITEROLES

Preheat the oven to 200°C. Lightly grease 2 baking trays. Bring the butter, sugar, salt and 1 cup water to the boil over a moderate heat in a saucepan. Stir in the flour. Cook, stirring constantly, until pastry comes away from the sides of the saucepan.

Transfer to a large bowl and allow to cool slightly. Beat in the eggs, one at a time, with an electric mixer on low speed, until combined, shiny and smooth. The mixture should be thick and glossy and a wooden spoon should stand upright in it.

PASTRY CREAM

2 cups milk

1 vanilla bean, split lengthwise and seeds scraped

4 egg yolks

2 tablespoons cornflour

2 tablespoons plain flour

¼ cup caster sugar

Using a pastry bag and a plain 1.5 cm nozzle, pipe 2.5 cm wide and high mounds onto the prepared trays, leaving space between for spreading. Alternatively, use a spoon to make well-shaped mounds of pastry. Bake in the oven for 20 minutes, then reduce the heat to 190°C and bake for 10 minutes, until golden brown and crisp, and hollow sounding when the base is tapped. Turn off the oven and leave the puffs to dry out completely.

A few hours before you want to serve, pipe the pastry cream into the profiteroles through the base which you have first poked a small hole into, or split and fill with cream.

Makes 45

PASTRY CREAM

Combine the milk, split vanilla bean and scraped seeds in a saucepan over a moderate heat, until simmering. Remove from the heat, cover and set aside for 15 minutes.

Beat the egg yolks and cornflour with an electric mixer. Add the plain flour and sugar, and beat until pale and thick.

Reheat the milk back to simmering point. Pour onto the egg yolks, whisking continuously. Return the mixture to a clean saucepan. Cook over a low heat for 8 minutes, stirring, until the mixture is thick and beginning to bubble. Use a spatula to scrape the pastry cream into a bowl and cover the surface with a piece of baking paper before cooling and using, or storing in the fridge. For a fluffier pastry cream fold in ½ cup whipped cream.

Use a piping bag to fill your profiteroles with this smooth cream.

Makes 2½ cups

[CONTINUED OVERLEAF]

TOFFEE

Heat 2 cups sugar and 1 cup water in a saucepan over a low heat, without boiling, until the sugar dissolves. Bring to the boil and cook until lightly golden. Remove from the heat and plunge the base of the pan in cold water to stop further browning. Once it has stopped, put the pan of toffee into a bowl of hot water to keep it runny. It will need to be just thick enough to run in continuous streams from the ends of the forks.

TO ASSEMBLE

Begin with the large puffs (there usually are some that are bigger than others). Dip the puffs in enough toffee to coat and arrange in a large circle, about 20 cm, with the sides touching. Build up into a cone shape, using smaller puffs nearer the top, and in ever decreasing circles.

Reheat the remaining toffee gently and then dip two forks in it. Rub the backs of the forks together until tacky, and then gently pull them apart. Spin toffee around the croquembouche. Continue re-dipping the forks and making more spun sugar until you are happy with the results. Once you become organised, you can shape the threads around the croquembouche by gently moulding them with your hands.

TIPS Use a heavy-based saucepan which gives an even heat all over the base. Non-stick pans with those dark linings are harder to use as you cannot easily see the colour of the caramel. White or granulated sugar is best as it dissolves easily and is not too refined.

If you boil before the sugar has completely dissolved, it will crystallise. Do not stir the syrup as it boils, or crystals will form on the spoon. Do not allow any crystals to form on the side of the pan from splashes – if they do, dip a clean dry pastry brush in cold water and brush down the side of the pan.

To dip profiteroles in hot toffee, use a small, sharp-pointed knife. Use a similar knife to remove toffee-coated choux puffs to build the pyramid.

CHAPTER SIX

Christmas Treats

Christmas Treats

Christmas time is the one time of the year when baking must be done in advance, not only to clear the way and avoid the Christmas rush, but to allow the flavours of the marvellous Christmas foods – the puddings, fruit minces and cakes – to mature to delicious perfection.

European Christmas food is unique and especially rich in butter, fruits, spices and alcohol (which need time to settle down and mature). Even the hard sauces are all the better for sitting in the cool of the refrigerator for a few weeks.

One month before Christmas Day is a good time to set aside a few days for the making and the baking. There is quite a bit of preparation: the shopping, the cake tins to be lined, the fruits to be cut up, almonds to be blanched and so on, before the actual baking takes place.

Christmas food makes a wonderful gift for friends who don't have time or are unable to make their own. Christmas cake or pudding are some of the nicest gifts and all the more so for being made with love and care.

2¼ cups raisins, roughly chopped

2⅓ cups sultanas

1⅔ cups currants

6 each dried apricots, nectarines and peaches, finely chopped

¾ cup mixed peel

¾ cup blanched almonds, chopped

½ cup glacé cherries, halved

⅓ cup brandy

⅓ cup rum

250 g butter

1 cup brown sugar

5 eggs

finely grated rind of 1 lemon

2 tablespoons marmalade

2½ cups plain flour

1 teaspoon mixed spice

½ teaspoon baking powder

2–3 tablespoons rum or brandy, extra

500 g ready-made fondant

1 egg white, lightly beaten

½ cup icing sugar

Rich Christmas Cake

Christmas cake means a large, rich fruitcake. This rich spicy cake made a few weeks or even a month or two before Christmas will age and mature, ripening to a truly festive cake. Top with a pattern of blanched almonds before baking. Some people prefer to top with almond paste and a sprig of holly, while others like the more elaborate and very beautiful iced version.

Toss the dried fruit, mixed peel, almonds, cherries, brandy and rum together in a large bowl, separating the fruit pieces. Cover and set aside to soak overnight.

Preheat the oven to 150°C. Grease a 24 cm square cake tin. Line the base and sides with 1 layer of brown paper and 2 layers of baking paper.

Cream the butter and sugar together in a bowl until light and fluffy. Add the eggs one at a time, beating well after each addition. Stir in the lemon rind and marmalade.

Sift the flour, mixed spice and baking powder together. Add 2 tablespoons of the sifted mixture to the dried fruits and toss through to prevent the fruit sinking to the bottom of the cake. Mix the remaining flour into the creamed mixture. Fold in the fruit. At this point it is easier to mix using your hands.

Pour the mixture into the prepared pan. Level the top and drop the tin sharply onto the kitchen bench to settle the mixture. If your decoration is to be blanched almonds, arrange in a pattern around the top.

[CONTINUED OVERLEAF]

Rich Christmas Cake [CONTINUED]

Bake for 2¾–3¼ hours, until a skewer inserted into the centre of the cake comes out clean. Remove from the tin. Sprinkle the hot cake with extra rum or brandy. Wrap in a clean tea towel and leave on a cake rack until completely cold. Wrap the cake in baking paper and foil and store in a cool dark place until ready to use.

To cover the cake with fondant, trim the top of the cake to ensure it sits flat. Patch any holes on the cake with small pieces of fondant. Knead the fondant on a surface dusted with icing sugar until smooth. Roll to 7 mm thickness, approximately the size and shape of the top of the cake.

Brush the cake with the egg white. Lift the fondant onto the cake with a rolling pin. Smooth the fondant with hands dusted with icing sugar. Trim the excess from the edge of the cake. Cut stars from scraps of fondant and decorate the cake with ribbon and stars.

Makes 1 x 24 cm square cake

TIPS If desired, you can replace the marmalade with golden syrup instead.

If the cake appears to be browning too much, cover with several thicknesses of paper.

To colour fondant, add a few drops of food colouring to the prepared fondant. Knead to evenly disperse the colour, adding more colouring if necessary so as to reach desired colour.

If you like to put a topping of marzipan on your cake under the fondant, buy a good ready-made marzipan, about 375 g, knead on a board dusted with icing sugar and roll out to fit the top of the cake. Brush the top of the cake with a little warm apricot jam. Gently lift the marzipan onto the cake and press it lightly into place. Roll lightly to make a smooth top. Trim the edge. Allow 1 day to dry out then brush with egg white and top with fondant (as above).

250 g butter

4 cups flour

3 cups brown sugar

large pinch of mixed spice

1 cup raisins

½ cup currants

½ cup sultanas

1 cup glacé cherries, halved

1 cup blanched almonds, chopped

1 cup mixed peel

4 eggs

1¼ cups warm Guinness

1 teaspoon bicarbonate of soda

Guinness Cake

This is today's version of an old Irish recipe for Porter Cake (porter was a weak form of stout). Guinness gives an intriguing flavour and makes the cake moist and rich.

Preheat the oven to 120°C. Line a deep 23 cm round cake tin with baking paper. Rub the butter into the flour with fingertips until resembling breadcrumbs. Add the sugar, spice, dried fruits, nuts and peel, and mix well. In a seperate bowl, beat the eggs, add the Guinness and stir in the bicarbonate of soda. Mix this very well with the flour mixture and turn into the prepared tin. Lay a sheet of baking paper over the top.

Bake in the centre of the oven for 3–3½ hours or until a skewer inserted in the centre comes out clean. Remove the paper for the last 30 minutes. Cool on a wire rack and store in an airtight container for a week before cutting. Guinness cake may be iced or decorated with almonds and used as a Christmas cake.

Makes 1 x 23 cm round cake

750 g mixed dried fruit

185 g butter

¼ cup water

1¾ cups firmly packed brown sugar

¼ cup whisky

3 large eggs

1 cup plain flour

1½ cups self-raising flour

1½ teaspoons mixed spice

¼ teaspoon salt

½ teaspoon bicarbonate of soda

Boiled Whisky Fruit Cake

Whisky does more than buck you up. It does wonders in a fruit cake.
Try it and see – it's easy to make too.

Preheat the oven to 180°C. Grease a deep 20 cm cake tin and line with greased brown paper or two layers of greased baking paper.

Bring the dried fruit, butter, water and brown sugar slowly to the boil in a large saucepan, then simmer for 5 minutes. Remove from the heat and cool until lukewarm. Stir in the whisky and add the eggs one at a time, beating well each time with a wooden spoon. Sift the flours with the spice, salt and bicarbonate of soda and stir into the mixture, combining thoroughly.

Spoon into the prepared tin and bake for 45 minutes. Reduce the heat to 160°C and cook for a further 45 minutes or until a skewer inserted in the centre of the cake comes out clean. Leave the cake for a few minutes in the tin, then turn out onto a wire rack and cool before removing the paper.

Makes 1 x 20 cm round cake

300 g unsalted butter	4 large eggs, lightly beaten
1¾ cups demerara sugar	1⅓ cups plain flour
2 cups raisins	1 cup wholemeal plain flour, plus 1 tablespoon extra
1 cup sultanas	2 teaspoons ground cinnamon
⅔ cups currants	2 teaspoons ground nutmeg
250 g pitted dessert prunes, quartered	¾ cups walnut halves
2 teaspoons bicarbonate of soda	¾ cup blanched almonds
½ cup brandy, plus ¼ cup extra, to sprinkle	

Eleventh Hour Christmas Cake

We all know that rich fruit cakes mature, so taste better when made a few months ahead. This cake, however, has all that rich flavour we expect at Christmas without the time.

Melt the butter in a large saucepan over a moderate heat and stir in the sugar. Add the dried fruit, bicarbonate of soda, brandy and 1½ cups water. Increase heat to high and stir thoroughly until the sugar has melted. Reduce heat to low and cook for another 5 minutes, stirring once or twice. Cover and set aside to soak overnight.

Preheat the oven to 150°C. Grease a 22 cm square cake pan. Line the base and sides first with 1 layer of brown paper then 2 layers of baking paper.

Stir the eggs thoroughly into the fruit mixture. Sift the flours and spices together and fold into the fruit mixture. Turn the mixture into the prepared pan. Level the top and drop the pan sharply onto the kitchen bench to settle the mixture. Decorate the top with nuts.

Bake for 2 hours 40 minutes, until a skewer inserted into the centre of the cake comes out clean. Remove from the pan. Sprinkle the hot cake with extra rum or brandy. Wrap in a clean tea towel and leave on a cake rack until completely cold. Wrap the cake in baking paper and foil and store in a cool dark place until ready to use.

Makes 1 x 22 cm square cake

1 cup dried cranberries

1 cup chopped dried apricots

grated rind and juice of 1 orange

¼ cup brandy

100 g butter, at room temperature

½ cup brown sugar

2 eggs

½ cup gluten-free self-raising flour

¼ cup maize cornflour

⅓ cup white rice flour

1 teaspoon baking powder

1 teaspoon ground ginger

1 teaspoon ground cinnamon

¼ cup chopped pecans

sifted icing sugar, to decorate

Cranberry and Apricot Cake (Gluten-free)

This cake is rich in spice, fruits and nuts, and is perfect for those on a gluten-free regime.

Combine the cranberries, apricots, orange rind and juice with the brandy in a saucepan over a low heat. Simmer for 10 minutes, until the liquid is nearly absorbed. Set aside for about 20 minutes, until completely cooled.

Preheat the oven to 180°C. Grease and line a 20 cm round cake pan. Cream the butter and sugar together in a bowl until light and fluffy. Add the eggs one at a time, beating well after each addition.

Sift the flours, baking powder and spices into a large bowl. Add the creamed mixture, cooled fruits and chopped pecans, folding together until just combined. Spoon into the prepared tin and smooth the top with a spatula.

Bake for 50 minutes, until a skewer inserted in the centre of the cake comes out clean. Cool in the pan before turning out.

To store, wrap the cake in baking paper and foil and store in a cool, dark place until ready to use. To serve, cut a star shape out of cardboard, place it on the centre of the cake, dust with icing sugar and carefully remove the star.

Serves plenty

½ cup plain flour

½ teaspoon baking powder

¼ teaspoon salt

60 g dark chocolate, chopped

4 eggs

¾ cup caster sugar, plus extra, to dust

1 teaspoon vanilla essence

¼ teaspoon bicarbonate of soda

2 tablespoons cold water

CHOCOLATE BUTTER CREAM

2 egg yolks

¼ cup caster sugar

½ cup sugar

½ cup milk

250 g unsalted butter, softened

60 g dark chocolate

Yule Log

The French enjoy their main feast on Christmas Eve, after returning from midnight mass. This feast always ends with a yule log – a tradition stemming from the custom of bringing in a log for the fire on Christmas Eve. Decorate with holly or Christmas decorations.

Preheat the oven to 200°C. Grease a 38 x 25 x 2.5 cm Swiss roll tin and line with baking paper. Sift together the flour, baking powder and salt. Melt the chocolate in a basin over hot water.

Break the eggs into a bowl, add the sugar and beat over hot water, or on the highest speed of the electric mixer, until the mixture is very light and thick and increased in volume. Fold in the sifted mixture and vanilla into the egg mixture.

Stir the bicarbonate of soda and cold water into the melted chocolate and fold quickly and evenly into the cake mixture. Turn into the prepared tin and bake for 15 minutes or until the cake top springs back when the centre is lightly touched. Loosen the edges and turn out onto a tea towel thickly dusted with caster sugar. Peel off the paper and trim the edges of the cake with a sharp knife. Roll immediately in the towel and leave to cool on a wire rack for at least 1 hour.

Meanwhile, to make the chocolate butter cream, cream the egg yolks with the caster sugar. Dissolve the remaining sugar with the milk over a low heat and bring to the boil. Add gradually to the creamed mixture, then return to the saucepan and heat until the mixture coats the back of a spoon. Strain and allow to cool.

Cream the butter until it resembles whipped cream and gradually beat into the cooled custard. Melt the chocolate over hot water, cool, then beat into the butter mixture.

When the cake is cold, carefully unroll and spread with one-third of the chocolate butter cream. Roll the cake once more and cut off one end of the cake at an angle. Place the cake on plate or board, arrange the cut piece of cake to resemble a stump and cover the yule log with the remaining butter cream. Chill until serving time.

Serves 8

2 cups plain flour
¼ teaspoon baking powder
185 g unsalted butter, chopped
¼ cup caster sugar
2 egg yolks
1–2 tablespoons lemon juice or iced water
1 cup Fruit Mincemeat (page 286)
1 egg white, lightly beaten
icing sugar, to dust (optional)

Christmas Mince Pies

Little mince pies are a universal favourite at Christmas time. We make them by the dozen to offer when friends drop in over the festive season. They store and keep well and some say improved by gently heating in the oven before serving.

Preheat the oven to 200°C. Grease 2 x 12-hole small patty pans. Make the pastry by sifting the flour and baking powder into a bowl. Rub in the butter using fingertips until the mixture resembles breadcrumbs. Stir in the sugar. Add the egg yolks and enough lemon juice or water to bring the ingredients together to form a dough.

Knead the dough gently on a lightly floured surface until smooth. Halve, wrap in plastic wrap and chill for at least 30 minutes. Roll out one of the pastry parcels between 2 sheets of baking paper until 3–5 mm thick. Using a 6.5 cm round cutter, cut out 12 rounds. Place the rounds into the prepared pans. Spoon 2 teaspoons fruit mince into each. Re-knead the scraps and chill before rolling out again and using to line pans. Repeat with remaining dough, reserving some pastry for decorating the tops.

Re-roll scraps of pastry and cut into small stars. Top each pie with a star. Brush with egg white. Bake for 20 minutes, until golden. Leave to cool completely in the pans. Serve warm or at room temperature, dusted with a little icing sugar, if you like.

Makes 24

NOTES *The amount of Fruit Mincemeat used and number of pies made will vary. Mince pies can be made ahead, frozen and reheated as required.*

PASTRY

2 cups plain flour

pinch of salt

¼ teaspoon baking powder

185 g unsalted butter, cut into pieces

2 egg yolks

1–2 tablespoons iced water

squeeze of lemon juice

FILLING

2 cups Fruit Mincemeat (page 286)

2 apples, grated

1 egg white

sugar, for sprinkling

Latticed Mincemeat Tart

A traditional Christmas treat with rich fruit mince nestled between a crisp pastry base and lattice top. This beautiful tart, served warm with ice cream and Brandied Butter (page 283), can take the place of a Christmas pudding.

You can make tiny little pies with this quantity of pastry and mincemeat, to have on hand when friends drop in over Christmas. The grated apple is a way of making the mince tart lighter. But, if you prefer, mincemeat only could be used.

Sift the flour, salt and baking powder into a bowl. Rub the butter into the flour until the mixture resembles breadcrumbs. Using a fork, mix the egg yolks with the iced water and lemon juice, then use a knife to stir into the flour mixture and form a dough. Knead lightly, wrap and chill for about 1 hour.

Cut away one-quarter of the dough for the lattice top and roll out the rest to line a 25 cm pie tin or flan ring. Trim the edges.

Mix together the mincemeat and grated apple and fill the pastry shell with it. Spread the fruit filling as evenly as possible. Chill. Roll out the reserved pastry and cut into 1 cm wide strips. Weave these pastry strips into a lattice on a piece of baking paper. Chill. After chilling, shake the lattice top carefully on to the mincemeat filling. Press the edges well together and trim. Beat the egg white until just foamy, brush over the pastry top and sprinkle with sugar. Bake in a preheated 190°C oven for 45 minutes, until the pastry is golden brown.

Serve warm with whipped cream or vanilla ice cream. Alternatively, flavour softened vanilla ice cream with finely sliced preserved ginger and a little rum, return to the freezer to firm and serve with the tart. One of the best options is to top with brandy or rum butter and allow it to melt into the filling.

Serves 8–10

1⅓ cups self-raising flour

⅓ cup demerara sugar

1 egg, lightly beaten

½ cup rice bran oil

⅓ cup milk

1 cup Fruit Mincemeat (page 286)

Christmas Mini Muffins

I love the sight of little Christmas muffins, tied with a ribbon and topped with a tiny sprig of holly to add to the festive spirit. With the mixture made ahead, they could be served as a treat for breakfast – just heat at a low temperature in the microwave.

Preheat the oven to 200°C. Put mini patty cases inside 4 x 12-hole mini muffin pans. Sift the flour into a bowl and mix in the sugar. In a small bowl, combine the egg, oil, milk and Fruit Mincemeat. Fold the mixture through the flour.

Spoon just under a tablespoon of the mixture into the prepared mini muffin cases and bake for 15 minutes, until well risen and golden. Serve warm or at room temperature.

Makes about 42

TIP You can use this mixture to make patty pan-sized muffins. It won't make as many muffins and they will take a little longer to cook, but are a little less fiddly to manage.

125 g butter

¾ cup caster sugar

2 eggs

1 teaspoon vanilla essence

¼ cup dark choc bits

2 cups self-raising flour, sifted

⅔ cup milk

GLACÉ ICING

1½ cups icing sugar

2–3 tablespoons boiling water

20 g butter

Festive Cupcakes

These favourites of children's parties are now appreciated for all occasions. So why not introduce them at Christmas? I like to decorate them with tiny holly sprigs found in cake decorating shops and some supermarkets.

Preheat the oven to 190°C. Line 2 x 12-hole deep patty pans with paper cases. Cream the butter and sugar together in a bowl until light and fluffy. Add the eggs one at a time, beating well after each addition. Beat in the vanilla essence and choc bits.

Lightly fold the flour and milk into the butter mixture, beginning and ending with flour. Spoon into the patty cases to three-quarters full. Bake for 12–15 minutes, until a skewer inserted comes out clean. Cool in the pans for 5 minutes, then transfer to wire racks to cool completely.

To make the glacé icing, sift the icing sugar into a bowl. Make a well in the centre and add the boiling water and butter. Stir until smooth and shiny. Spread the top of each cake with the icing and decorate with tiny holly sprigs moulded from a firm icing, or cut holly with leaves from red and green glacé cherries.

Makes 24

⅔ cup mixed peel	
⅓ cup raisins	
⅓ cup currants	
⅓ cup green glacé cherries, halved	
⅓ cup red glacé cherries, halved	
½ cup slivered almonds	
⅓ cup rum	
1 tablespoon plain flour	

YEAST DOUGH

4 cups plain flour, sifted

large pinch of salt

7 g packet instant dry yeast

125 g butter, melted, plus extra, to brush

¼ cup lukewarm milk

½ cup caster sugar

2 eggs, lightly beaten

TOPPING

¾ cup icing sugar

2 tablespoons warm water

mixed peel and toasted flaked almonds, to decorate

Stollen

This traditional German bread is a specialty of Dresden, from where they are exported around the world. Stollen is not at all difficult to make at home. Being a rich, moist fruit bread, it improves with keeping. Germans often make two loaves of this bread for Christmas – one for keeping and one for giving.

Mix the fruit, almonds and rum together in a bowl. Cover and set aside to soak overnight. Drain and dry the fruit well with paper towel. Sprinkle with the flour and toss to coat.

To make the yeast dough, combine the flour, salt and yeast in a large bowl. Make a well in the centre and pour in the combined butter, milk, sugar and eggs. Bring the ingredients together to form a dough. Knead the dough gently on a lightly floured surface for 10–15 minutes, until smooth and elastic.

Place the dough in a lightly greased bowl. Cover with plastic wrap and a dry cloth. Set aside in a warm place for 1 hour, until the dough has doubled in size. Knock down the dough and turn onto a lightly floured surface. Shape into a square. Spoon the prepared fruit and nut mixture into the centre and knead gently, until

well incorporated. Return to the bowl, cover and leave in a warm place for a further 30 minutes.

Preheat the oven to 190°C. Line an oven tray with baking paper. Halve the dough and roll each half on a lightly floured surface into a 23 x 18 cm oblong. Fold lengthwise into three. Lightly flour hands, taper the ends slightly and pat the sides to mound the stollen in the centre. Place on the prepared tray, seam side down, and brush with extra melted butter. Stand in a warm place for 30 minutes, until doubled in size. Bake for 40–45 minutes, until golden. Transfer to a rack. Mix the icing sugar and warm water together and brush a thin coating over the stollen while still warm. Finish with a sprinkle of mixed peel and toasted flaked almonds.

Makes 2 loaves

3 cups Brazil nuts

½ cup pitted dates

1 cup mixed red and green glacé cherries

¾ cup plain flour

¾ cup caster sugar

½ teaspoon baking powder

½ teaspoon salt

3 eggs

1 teaspoon vanilla essence

Bishop's Cake

This cake gets its name from the stained glass appearance of each slice. 'Bishop's cake' is also known as 'American Christmas cake' – but is really more a fruit and nut slab than a cake.

Preheat the oven to 150°C. Grease and line a 21 x 11 cm loaf tin. Combine the nuts, dates and cherries in a bowl. Sift the flour, sugar, baking powder and salt over the fruit mixture. Mix well.

Whisk the eggs and vanilla until frothy and pour over the fruit. Stir well and spoon into the prepared tin. Bake for 1 hour 45 minutes, until a skewer inserted comes out clean. Remove from the tin and cool on a wire rack. Wrap in foil and store in the refrigerator.

Using a sharp serrated knife, cut the cake into very thin slices or small finger lengths before serving.

Makes one 21 x 11 cm loaf

1¼ cups whole almonds, peeled

125 g pine nuts

4 cups plain flour

4 eggs, beaten

1 tablespoon grated orange rind

1 teaspoon vanilla essence

½ teaspoon baking powder

2 cups caster sugar

pinch of salt

Biscotti di Prato

These biscuits are a Tuscan favourite. Curiously hard, they will keep for months in an airtight container, ready at any time for dunking into a sweet wine or coffee. Great to have on hand for all that chatting to be had with friends over coffee at Christmas time.

Preheat the oven to 190°C. Grease a baking tray and dust with flour. Toast the almonds in the oven for a couple of minutes and chop roughly with the pine nuts. Sift the flour into a large bowl and make a well in the centre. Pour in the eggs, orange rind, vanilla, baking powder, sugar and salt. Work to a smooth consistency with your hands, then mix in the nuts.

Divide the dough into three and roll the pieces of dough into long loaves to fit the length of the baking tray.

Place the loaves on the prepared tray and bake for about 20 minutes. Remove and cut the loaves on the diagonal into about 1 cm thick slices. Bake for a further 20 minutes, until lightly browned. Store in airtight containers.

Makes plenty

| 3 egg whites |
| ½ cup caster sugar |
| 1 cup plain flour, sifted |
| ¾ cup whole almonds |
| ¼ cup shelled pistachios |
| 1 teaspoon vanilla essence |

Almond and Pistachio Bread

This is like the delicious almond bread you find in good delicatessens. Simple to make at home, almond bread is first made then sliced very thinly and baked again to achieve the lovely thin wafers. A perfect Christmas hamper treat for friends.

Preheat the oven to 180°C. Grease a small non-stick loaf tin. Beat the egg whites until stiff without being dry, then gradually beat in the caster sugar. Continue beating until the mixture is thick and glossy. Using a metal spoon, fold in the sifted flour, almonds, pistachios and vanilla essence, mixing well. Turn the mixture into the prepared tin.

Bake for about 30 minutes, until pale golden and firm to the touch. Leave to cool in the tin, then turn out and wrap in foil. Place in the refrigerator and leave overnight – this will help to cut thin, even slices.

Cut into thin slices and place on an ungreased baking tray. Bake in a preheated 180°C oven, until pale golden and crisp. Cool and store in an airtight container. Serve with fruit or creamy desserts or with coffee.

Makes plenty

NOTE You can leave out the pistachios if you prefer, in which case use 1 cup of almonds.

250 g unsalted butter, melted and cooled
3 large eggs, lightly beaten
¼ cup milk
½ teaspoon vanilla essence
grated rind of ½ lemon (see Tips)
3 cups self-raising flour, sifted
1 cup caster sugar
1 cup dried mixed fruit
¼ cup choc bits (see Tips)
icing sugar, to dust

Italian Soft Biscotti

These little biscuits are not unlike the twice-baked thin and crisp almond biscuit bread (page 230), but they are also great to dip into coffee or wine.

Preheat the oven to 180°C. Line 2 baking trays with baking paper. Combine the butter, eggs, milk, vanilla and lemon rind in a jug. Combine the flour, sugar, fruit and choc bits in a bowl. Make a well in the centre and stir in the butter mixture until a soft dough. Rest for 10 minutes covered with a tea towel.

Divide the dough into 4 pieces and shape each piece, twisting slightly, into a 30 cm long log. Place onto the prepared trays. Bake for 25 minutes, until golden. Cool on the tray for 15 minutes. Sprinkle with icing sugar and cut into 2 cm slices while still slightly warm.

Makes about 80

TIPS There is nothing nicer than the distinct flavour of freshly grated lemon rind. It is important to grate only the yellow rind, not the white pith as this tends to be bitter. Use a small, sharp microplane or citrus grater for the best results.

The choc bits can be substituted with pinenuts, pistachios, or chopped almonds if you prefer.

2 cups blanched almonds

¾ cup caster sugar

¾ cup icing sugar, plus extra, for dusting

½ teaspoon vanilla essence

2 egg whites

Ricciarelli

These delectable little almond biscuits from Italy are good to have on hand or make as a gift. This recipe makes so many, there will be plenty to go around.

Grind the almonds as finely as possible, using a food processor, or use 3 cups ground almonds. Process the ground almonds with the caster sugar in a food processor until almost a paste. Remove to a large bowl.

Sift the icing sugar and add to the almond mixture with the vanilla essence. Beat the egg whites until frothy and fold into the almond mixture. Add a little more icing sugar if necessary to make a stiff paste. Pinch off small pieces of paste and form into oval or large almond shapes. Place on wire racks, cover loosely with a cloth and leave in a dry place for about 24 hours, to dry out a little.

Preheat the oven to 140°C. Arrange the ricciarelli on baking trays and bake for 30–40 minutes, until dry but still very pale. Remove to wire racks to cool and dust with sifted icing sugar before storing in airtight containers.

Makes about 50

1 sheet ready-rolled puff pastry, thawed

1 egg, beaten

2 tablespoons sugar

FILLING

90 g unsalted butter

¼ cup caster sugar

1 egg yolk

100 g ground almonds

1 tablespoon rum

Pithiviers

This is the traditional cake served on Twelfth Night, the 5th of January, in France, usually made in a round. It is so easy to make long strips now that frozen puff pastry sheets are available. You can, of course, make your own puff pastry.

For the filling, cream the butter and sugar together in a large bowl, then beat in the egg yolk, ground almonds and rum.

Cut the pastry in half. Place one strip on a greased baking sheet and fill the centre with the almond filling, flattening it out but leaving the edges clear. Top with the remaining pastry and press the edges together. With a sharp knife, cut the top of the pastry (but not through) in a decorative pattern, swirls or herringbone. Chill until ready to bake as this is delicious served warm. Brush with the beaten egg.

Bake in a preheated 200°C oven for 15 minutes, then reduce the heat to 180°C and bake for a further 10 minutes. Sprinkle with the sugar and return to the oven for 5–10 minutes to give the pastry a crisp, caramelised glaze. Serve warm with coffee or with whipped cream as a dessert.

Serves 6–8

3 cups plain flour, plus extra, for kneading

1 tablespoon baking powder

1 tablespoon ground cinnamon

1 teaspoon ground cloves

1 teaspoon ground nutmeg

½ teaspoon ground aniseed

½ teaspoon salt

½ teaspoon ground ginger or ground white pepper

250 g butter

1½ cups firmly packed brown sugar

3 tablespoons rum or brandy

1 egg white, beaten

125 g slivered blanched almonds, for decoration

Speculaas

These are special crisp biscuits, rich in butter and flavoured with brown sugar, spices and rum, made especially for Saint Nicholas' Eve in Holland. The biscuits are sometimes in the shape of small rectangles sprinkled with almonds, or the biscuit mixture is pressed into elaborate moulds in the shape of men and women or Saint Nicholas himself.

Preheat the oven to 190°C. Sift the flour, baking powder, cinnamon, cloves, nutmeg, aniseed, salt and ginger or pepper together in a bowl. Beat the butter until creamy in a large bowl, then add the brown sugar gradually, beating until the mixture is light and fluffy. Stir in the rum or brandy.

Gradually add the flour and spices to the creamed mixture, stirring until well combined, then form the dough into a ball. Knead the dough on a board sprinkled with about ¼ cup sifted flour. Roll the dough out into a rectangle about 5 mm thick. With a sharp knife or cutter, cut the dough into 6 x 3 cm rectangles. Lay on a greased baking tray, brush with the egg white and decorate with slivered almonds. Bake for 12 minutes or until they are browned and firm. Cool and store in an airtight container.

Makes about 40

From top: Vanilla Kippels, Ginger Daisies and Speculaas

½ cup brown sugar		2 eggs, lightly beaten	
½ cup golden syrup		cachous and chocolate buttons or drops, to decorate	
90 g butter			
2 teaspoons bicarbonate of soda		**ICING**	
3⅓ cups plain flour		1 cup icing sugar	
1 tablespoon ground ginger		2–4 tablespoons boiling water	
pinch of salt		20 g butter	

Ginger Daisies

Pretty little biscuits, such as these, are good to have on hand and also make a lovely gift.

Heat the sugar, syrup and butter in a small saucepan over a low heat, stirring, until the sugar has melted. Remove from the heat, cool for 2 minutes then stir in the bicarbonate of soda.

Sift the flour, ginger and salt into a large bowl. Make a well in the centre and stir in the butter mixture and eggs to form a soft dough. Wrap the dough in plastic wrap and chill for 1 hour.

Preheat the oven to 200°C. Line baking trays with baking paper. Divide the dough into four and roll each out to a 3 mm thickness. Cut flower shapes from the dough, using a 5 cm cutter. Arrange on the prepared trays and

continue with the remaining dough. Bake for 6 minutes. Leave on the trays until cool enough to handle. Transfer to wire racks to cool completely.

To make the icing, sift the icing sugar into a bowl, make a well in the centre and stir in the combined boiling water and butter until smooth. Spread lightly on each biscuit and decorate with cachous and chocolate buttons or drops.

Makes about 90

TIP These biscuits can be made ahead of time and stored in an airtight container un-iced. Simply ice and decorate as required.

- -

1¼ cups plain flour		½ cup very finely chopped hazelnuts	
2 tablespoons caster sugar, plus extra, for dusting		1 egg yolk	
125 g butter			

Hazelnut Crescents

These are one of the most delicious biscuits – especially when the hazelnuts are good and fresh.

Sift the flour into a bowl, stir in the sugar and rub in the butter until the mixture resembles coarse breadcrumbs. Mix in the nuts and stir in the egg yolk to make a dough. Cover and chill for 30 minutes.

Preheat the oven to 180°C. Grease 2 baking trays. Take about 2 teaspoons of dough at a time,

roll into 6 cm lengths and shape into crescents. Arrange on the trays and bake for 12 minutes or until lightly coloured. Remove the crescents and roll in extra caster sugar while still warm. Cool on a wire rack and store in an airtight container.

Makes about 35

2⅔ cups self-raising flour	½ cup caster sugar
pinch of salt	½ cup brown sugar
1½ teaspoons ground cinnamon	250 g butter, cut into small cubes
1½ teaspoons ground cloves	⅓ cup milk
1½ teaspoons ground nutmeg	¼ teaspoon bicarbonate of soda
1 teaspoon ground white pepper	sifted icing sugar, for dusting

Christmas Spice Biscuits

If you want to hang these biscuits on the Christmas tree, make a hole at a top point of each biscuit and thread a fine ribbon through the hole to tie it to a branch. The baked biscuit may also be decorated with icing to serve. Or, if you prefer, these biscuits can be slipped into small cellophane bags and sealed, to make pretty little gifts for visitors.

Preheat the oven to 180°C. Line 2 large baking trays with baking paper. Sift the flour, salt, spices and sugars into a large bowl. Add the butter and rub into the flour mixture until it looks like breadcrumbs.

Combine the milk and bicarbonate of soda in a bowl and stir into the flour mixture. Knead lightly to form a firm but elastic dough. Halve the dough and wrap each piece in plastic wrap. Chill for 30 minutes.

Roll out one half of the dough (leaving the other half in the fridge) to 4 mm thickness and cut out biscuits with fancy biscuit cutters, such as hearts, angels, reindeer, stars and trees. Arrange on the trays, allowing room for spreading. Re-knead the dough scraps and chill before rolling out again. Repeat with the remaining dough. Bake for 15–20 minutes, until golden. Cool on wire racks and store in airtight containers. Dust with icing sugar if you like before serving.

Makes about 80–100 depending on size of cutters used

TIPS Baking trays should always be cold before arranging uncooked biscuits on top, othewise the biscuits will lose their shape.

These biscuits can be decorated with a soft icing (see Ginger Crisp Biscuits, page 241). This is a job children enjoy doing, as they get to use their own imagination.

250 g golden syrup

250 g unsalted butter, at room temperature

¾ cup caster sugar

3 cups plain flour

3 teaspoons ground ginger

2 teaspoons baking powder

2 teaspoons bicarbonate of soda

1 egg, lightly beaten

silver cachous (optional), to decorate

ICING

½ cup icing sugar

2 tablespoons hot water

Ginger Crisp Biscuits

Triangles of spicy and crisp biscuits are decorated in the shape of a Christmas tree – all very festive for the holiday season.

Heat the golden syrup, butter and sugar in a small saucepan over a low heat for 3-4 minutes, stirring, until the sugar has dissolved.

Sift the flour with the remaining dry ingredients in a large bowl. Add the butter mixture alternately with the beaten egg and mix until well combined. Divide the dough into a few batches, cover in plastic wrap and chill for 1 hour, until firm.

Preheat the oven to 190°C. Line 2 baking trays with baking paper. Roll out the dough thinly on a lightly floured board. Cut into triangles and place on the prepared baking trays. Re-knead the scraps and chill before rolling out again. Repeat with the remaining dough.

Bake in batches for 8–10 minutes or until very lightly golden. Cool on a wire rack. Repeat with the remaining dough. Store in an airtight container.

To make the icing, beat the icing sugar and hot water together in a bowl until smooth. Using an icing pipe with a fine point (or make baking paper triangles into cones for piping), ice the biscuits and decorate with the cachous to resemble Christmas trees.

Makes about 25

TIP To be sure these biscuits are fully cooked, check underneath – the base should also be pale golden.

¼ cup golden syrup

¼ cup brown sugar

1 tablespoon ground ginger

1 teaspoon ground cinnamon

½ teaspoon ground cloves

1 teaspoon bicarbonate of soda

125 g unsalted butter, chopped

1 large egg, lightly beaten

2¼ cups plain flour, sifted

currants and glacé cherries, to decorate

Icing (page 241) (optional), to decorate

Gingerbread Men (and Boys and Girls)

Gingerbread men bring out the cannibal in everyone – nibbling away at feet, legs, hands and finally the head. Use your skills with the icing to pipe buttons, eyes, mouths, bikinis, skirts or whatever you like, giving each biscuit its own personality. Kids love to decorate gingerbread people, so let them do their own thing.

Preheat the oven to 180°C. Grease and line 2 baking trays. Combine the golden syrup, sugar and spices in a heatproof bowl over a saucepan of simmering water. When the sugar has dissolved, stir in the bicarbonate of soda. Remove from the heat as soon as the mixture bubbles.

Mix the butter and the warm golden syrup mixture together in a large bowl. Stir until the butter has melted and the mixture is smooth. Set aside to cool.

Add the egg and 1 cup of the flour to the bowl and mix well. Add the remaining flour and bring the dough together using hands. Knead gently on a lightly floured board, until the dough is soft and smooth. Halve the dough and wrap each portion in plastic wrap. Chill for 30 minutes.

Roll a portion of dough between 2 sheets of baking paper to 5 mm thick. Using gingerbread cutters, cut out 14 people shapes. Arrange on the baking trays. Re-knead the dough scraps and chill before rolling out again. Repeat with the remaining dough.

To decorate the biscuits, press in currants for eyes and buttons, and a sliver of glacé cherry for a mouth. Bake for 10–15 minutes, until starting to colour and firm to the touch. Cool on racks before decorating further.

Makes 14, depending on size of cutters

TIPS If the dough is very soft and difficult to handle, place on a baking tray in the refrigerator until firm.

Kids may not want to make the dough, or roll it out, but they have a lot of fun cutting out the men and making eyes, mouths and buttons for their new creations. Look for boy and girl shaped cutters for fun.

1 cup plain flour, sifted

1 teaspoon ground cinnamon, sifted

¼ teaspoon ground ginger, sifted

¼ teaspoon mixed spice, sifted

75 g unsalted butter, diced

¼ cup honey

Honey Spice Cookies

Spice features in many festive treats, as does honey – the early monasteries always kept beehives for collecting honey. Cut the cookies into various shapes such as hearts, gingerbread men or stars to dunk into a sweet wine or coffee.

Preheat the oven to 180°C. Line 2 baking trays with baking paper. Combine flour and spices in a bowl. Using fingertips, rub in the butter until the mixture resembles breadcrumbs. Add the honey and mix gently to form a soft dough. Cover with plastic wrap and chill for 30 minutes.

Roll out the dough between 2 sheets of baking paper until 4–6 mm thick. Cut out shapes using various cutters of choice. Arrange the biscuits, slightly apart, on the prepared trays. Chill for 10 minutes. Bake for 10 minutes, until golden. Stand for 5 minutes before transferring to a wire rack to cool completely.

Makes 30

125 g unsalted butter, softened

¾ cup caster sugar

3 eggs

¼ cup Grand Marnier or other orange liqueur

grated rind of 1 orange

1½ cups plain flour, sifted

¾ cup self-raising flour, sifted

1 cup pine nuts, toasted

Orange Biscotti with Pine Nuts

Like Biscotti di Prato (page 231), these biscuits are another Tuscan favourite. There is something that says Christmas about these orangey biscotti. Deliciously hard, they are perfect for dunking into a sweet wine or coffee over the holiday season.

Preheat the oven to 180°C. Line a baking tray with baking paper. Beat the butter and sugar with an electric mixer until pale and creamy. Add the eggs one at a time, beating well between each addition. Stir in the Grand Marnier and orange rind. Fold in the remaining ingredients until the mixture forms a soft dough.

Divide the dough in half and shape each piece into a 30 x 7 cm log. Place on the prepared tray and bake for 25 minutes, until risen and golden all over. Cool completely.

Cut into 1 cm slices and lay in a single layer on baking trays. Reduce the oven to 160°C. Bake for a further 20 minutes, until crisp and crunchy. Remove and cool on wire racks. Store in an airtight container.

Makes about 50

| 4 large egg whites |
| 500 g ground almonds |
| 1¾ cups caster sugar |
| 2 teaspoons baking powder |
| ¼ teaspoon almond essence (optional) |
| 1 cup icing sugar mixture |
| 200 g red or green glacé cherries (or both) |

Mandorlas (Amaretti)

An Italian specialty, known also as amaretti, Mandorlas are perfect to have on hand over the festive season. Serve with coffee after dinner, or package in a glass jar or nice box for a great gift.

Preheat the oven to 170°C. Line 2 baking trays with baking paper. Beat the egg whites in a bowl with a whisk or fork until foamy.

Combine the ground almonds, caster sugar and baking powder in a bowl. Make a well in the centre and add the almond essence, if using. Add the egg whites gradually, mixing all the time. To mix, use a wooden spoon and begin at the centre of the bowl mixing with a circular motion that gets larger as the ingredients become blended. This method will help to prevent over mixing, which may toughen the dough.

Mix together thoroughly with your hand to form a sticky dough. The dough should be firm enough to hold together but not dry. When mixing dough, use the tips of your fingers as much as you can to keep the dough light.

Roll 1 tablespoon of the dough into a ball. Repeat with the remaining mixture. Roll in icing sugar mixture to coat and arrange on the prepared trays. Press a glacé cherry into the centre of each biscuit. Bake for 15 minutes, until risen, cracked and very lightly coloured. Cool for 5 minutes on the tray before transferring to wire racks to cool completely.

Makes about 80

2 eggs
¾ cup caster sugar
½ teaspoon finely grated lemon rind
1 cup plain flour, sifted
185 g unsalted butter, clarified (see Tip)
1 tablespoon rum (optional)

Madeleines

These plump little cakes are immortalised in Marcel Proust's *In Search of Lost Time*. They are baked in special embossed moulds that, according to Proust, resemble the 'fluted scallop of a pilgrim's shell'. Serve with Christmas drinks.

Preheat the oven to 200°C. Grease madeleine tins and dust them with flour. Mix the eggs and sugar together with an electric mixer, or with a hand-whisk in a bowl set over a saucepan of simmering water, until thick and mousse-like. Remove from the heat and continue to beat until cooled. Add the lemon rind and fold in the flour. Mix in the cooled butter only when everything is blended. Take care not to over-work the mixture at this point and don't allow the butter to sink to the bottom of the bowl – a metal spoon or spatula is the best tool for this job. Lastly, fold in the rum, if using.

Spoon the mixture into the moulds. Bake for about 8 minutes until pale golden. Stand for 1–2 minutes before removing from the pans. Repeat until all the mixture is used.

Makes 32 large or 50 small Madeleines

VARIATIONS

Chocolate Madeleines: Sift the flour with 3 tablespoons cocoa powder.

Orange Madeleines: Add the grated rind of 1 orange in place of the lemon.

TIP To clarify butter, slowly melt the butter in a saucepan. When the butter is clear, remove from the heat, stand for a few minutes and pour the clear butter into a cup, leaving the sediments in the pan. Cool. This can also be done in the microwave.

| 1¼ cups plain flour |
| pinch of salt |
| 155 g butter |
| ¼ cup icing sugar |
| 2 egg yolks |
| ½ teaspoon vanilla essence |
| 1¼ cups ground almonds or hazelnuts |

VANILLA SUGAR

| 2 vanilla beans |
| 1 cup caster sugar |

Vanilla Kippels

These very European shortbread crescents make a lovely gift at Christmas. You can choose different nuts to use, although in Bavaria they are nearly always made with hazelnuts. The vanilla taste is important, so either make your own or buy vanilla sugar.

Sift the flour with the salt on a pastry board. Make a well in the centre and add the butter, sugar, yolks and vanilla. Sprinkle over the ground nuts. Work the ingredients in the centre with your fingertips until thoroughly blended. Using a metal spatula, quickly draw in the flour and ground almonds. Knead the dough lightly until smooth then form into a ball. Cover in plastic wrap and chill for 1 hour.

Preheat the oven to 180°C. Grease 2 baking trays. Divide the dough into small pieces and roll into walnut-sized balls. Roll each ball in the palm of your hand to form a small tube, then curve into a crescent. Arrange on the prepared baking trays. Bake for 10–12 minutes, until lightly coloured.

Meanwhile, to make the vanilla sugar, cut the vanilla beans into pieces and process in a food processor with the sugar, until the beans have processed through the sugar, giving it an ashy look.

Once cooked, remove the biscuits to a wire rack and position a sheet of baking paper under the rack. Dredge the kippels with sifted vanilla sugar or icing sugar while still warm. Cool and store in an airtight container. Store excess vanilla sugar in a small glass jar with a lid.

Makes about 40

TIPS Care should be taken if grinding nuts in a food processor. Use a pulse or on–off action; don't over-process or the nuts will become a paste. They should be finely ground, even with little bits of nuts through the ground mix.

If using walnuts, it is best to buy canned walnuts unless the walnuts are very fresh, just off the trees.

1 cup plain flour

pinch of salt

¼ cup caster sugar

½ cup ground almonds

finely grated peel of 1 lemon

90 g butter

2 egg yolks

sifted icing sugar, for dusting

Sables

An English favourite, these biscuits can be cut into festive shapes, such as stars or angels, to fit the Christmas season. The biscuit's name is derived from the French word for 'sand', which relates to the light, crisp and grainy texture of these lovely shortbreads.

Preheat the oven to 180°C. Grease 2 baking trays. Sift the flour, salt and sugar into a bowl, then mix in the almonds and lemon peel. Rub in the butter with fingertips until the mixture resembles fine breadcrumbs, then mix in the egg yolks to form a soft dough.

Roll out the dough thinly on a floured surface. Using a biscuit cutter, cut 4 cm rounds from the dough. Alternatively, cut the biscuits by hand into long strips 7.5 cm wide, then cut across the strips at 4.5 cm intervals to form oblongs. Arrange, slightly apart, on the prepared baking trays. Refrigerate for 30 minutes.

Bake for 15–20 minutes, until very lightly browned. Using a palette knife, move the biscuits from the baking sheets to wire racks to cool. When cold, dust very lightly with sifted icing sugar.

Makes about 32

250 g butter, at room temperature

1 cup caster sugar

1 large egg

1 teaspoon vanilla essence

2½ cups plain flour, sifted

½ teaspoon salt

2 cups walnuts, very finely chopped

½ cup raspberry conserve, warmed

Jelly Dots

This jolly-looking biscuit with its bright red dot is an American version of the Australian and New Zealand jam thumbprint biscuit. Fig jam also works very well for this recipe.

Preheat the oven to 190°C. Line 2 baking trays with baking paper. Cream the butter and sugar in a bowl with an electric mixer until light and fluffy. Add the egg and vanilla and beat until well combined.

With the mixer on low speed, add the flour and salt, mixing just until the dough comes together to form a ball. Divide the dough in half, pat each into a thick round and cover in plastic wrap. Chill for 1 hour.

Pinch off 1 level tablespoon pieces of dough and roll into balls. As you work, roll balls of dough into the chopped walnuts and arrange on the prepared trays about 5 cm apart. Use a thumb or the end of a wooden spoon handle to make an indentation in the centre of each ball and chill for 20 minutes.

Bake in batches for 15–20 minutes or until very lightly golden. Remove from the oven and use the end of a wooden spoon to redefine the indent. Fill each centre with the warm raspberry jam and leave to cool on a wire rack. Cool completely before storing in airtight containers.

Makes about 40

| ¼ cup ground almonds |
| ¼ cup ground hazelnuts |
| ¾ cup icing sugar, plus extra, for dusting |
| 1 egg white |

Snowballs (Boules de Neige)

Little balls of almond and hazelnut meringue are rolled in snowy white sugar and baked into the most delectable crispy sweet treat. Offer these special treats as a petits four, after Christmas dinner, or package in a pretty box or cellophane bag as a gift.

Preheat the oven to 160°C. Line a baking tray with baking paper. Combine the ground nuts, sugar and egg white together in a large bowl to make a firm paste, which can be rolled in the hand.

Divide the mixture into pieces the size of large hazelnuts. Roll each ball in sifted icing sugar to coat thickly. Arrange on the baking tray and bake for about 10 minutes, until well puffed. Dust with icing sugar if liked. Cool and transfer to paper cases to serve. Store in an airtight container.

Makes about 18

185 g butter

1½ cups finely grated Cheddar cheese

¼ cup grated Parmesan cheese

1½ cups plain flour, sifted

1 teaspoon paprika

1 teaspoon salt

2 tablespoons finely chopped walnuts

Cheese and Walnut Shortbreads

Little savoury shortbreads make a welcome nibble with pre-dinner drinks, and are handy to have on hand when friends drop in over during the festive season. These would also make a welcome gift, sealed in a cellophane bag tied with a festive ribbon.

Preheat the oven to 180°C. Line 2–3 baking trays with baking paper. Cream the butter and grated cheeses in a bowl using an electric mixer. Add the flour, paprika, salt and walnuts. Mix well until the dough comes together to form a ball. Divide the dough in half, pat each into a thick round and cover in plastic wrap. Chill for 1 hour.

Roll the dough out thinly and cut into stars using a 5 cm star-shape or a simple fluted biscuit cutter. Re-roll the trimmings to make more stars. Arrange on the prepared trays. Bake in batches for 12–15 minutes, until golden. Cool completely before storing in airtight containers.

Makes about 60

TIP You can also make these shortbreads in the food processor. To do so, first have the butter well chilled and cut into small pieces. Fit the processor with a metal double-bladed knife. Sift the flour, paprika and salt into the bowl. Add the butter to the flour mixture with the cheeses. Process for about 20 seconds or until the pastry clings together and forms a ball. Lightly knead the mixture together to form a smooth dough. Chill until ready to use.

250 g butter

½ cup caster sugar, plus extra, for dusting

3 cups plain flour

Shortbread

Everyone knows how delicious shortbread is with tea or coffee, but it's also great with a dry sherry or Madeira for visitors. Shortbread is traditionally broken into pieces to serve. We've shaped our shortbread into 'petticoat tails', a traditional Scottish way. The name derives from the English pronounciation of the French *petits gateaux tailles* (little cakes, cut off), the popular style reportedly brought from France by Mary, Queen of Scots.

Preheat the oven to 160°C. Cream the butter in a bowl with an electric beater until it resembles whipped cream, then add the sugar gradually, beating it until light and fluffy. Work in the flour gradually, then knead the dough for about 5 minutes, until the mixture is very smooth.

Halve the dough and press each piece into a 24 cm circle on baking trays, flan rings or sandwich pans. You can make them into smaller, thicker circles if you prefer. Using the palm of a hand, push the dough out until the mixture is very smooth, then smooth over the surface with a rolling pin, or the palm of a hand over plastic wrap.

Crimp the edges by pressing the edge of the pastry with a finger, then pinching the edge together. If using a flan ring or sandwich pan, use a fork to decorate the edges or pinch a frill.

Using a 7 cm round biscuit cutter, cut a circle into the middle. Keeping the smaller circle whole and intact, cut the remaining round into 12 segments. Using a fork, prick the shortbread in a decorative pattern. Dust lightly with extra caster sugar. Bake for 40 minutes, until very lightly coloured and crisp. Cool and store in an airtight container.

Makes 2 rounds

TIPS If you like melt-in-the-mouth shortbread, try 1 cup icing sugar instead of caster sugar and replace 1 cup plain flour with cornflour. Like a grainy finish? Replace ¾ cup plain flour with coarse grained rice flour (not the Chinese variety).

Shortbread is pricked to release the moisture as it cooks, making the shortbread crisp. Shortbread may soften a little when stored. This can be remedied by placing it in a 170°C oven for 15 minutes.

540 g dark chocolate, chopped

250 g white marshmallows

1 cup pistachios or hazelnuts, toasted and chopped

½ cup shredded coconut, toasted

400 g confectionery spearmint leaves

Mint Rocky Road

This is such an easy sweet treat to make. Children love it – and parents love to sample it too! Make it for Christmas holiday visitors or wrap in a pretty box as a gift.

Line the base and sides of a 20 cm square cake pan with baking paper.

Melt the chocolate in a large heatproof bowl over a saucepan of simmering water. Working quickly, stir in the remaining ingredients to coat thoroughly in the chocolate. Turn into the prepared pan and refrigerate for 2 hours, until set. Cut into squares.

Makes about 36 squares

- -

2¾ cups light brown sugar

¾ cup evaporated milk

20 g butter

pinch of salt

2 cups pecan halves

Pecan Pralines

On a visit to Louisiana, Suzanne and I became hooked on these southern confections. You can buy smallish cellophane bags from most newsagents or larger supermarkets. Pop some pralines in, tie with a ribbon and give to guests as a Christmas treat.

Line 2 baking trays with baking paper. Combine the sugar, evaporated milk, butter and salt in a large heavy-based saucepan over a low heat. Stir until the sugar has dissolved. Continue to stir over a moderate heat until the mixture reaches 116°C on a sugar thermometer (see Tips).

Remove from the heat and cool for 5 minutes. Add the pecans and stir rapidly until the mixture thickens and coats the nuts. Drop teaspoons of the mixture onto the prepared trays. Cool until set.

Makes about 28

TIPS If the mixture hardens, stir in a few drops of hot water.

If you don't have a sugar thermometer, drop a teaspoon of mixture into ice cold water. It should form a soft ball and flatten out when pressed between the fingers.

2½ cups plain flour

250 g butter

1 tablespoon white vinegar

⅓ cup water

⅓–½ cup caster sugar

Flaky French Fingers

Simple, light, flaky biscuits, perfect to serve with a Christmas dessert. Or, enjoy them with a cup of tea when you finally get time to relax over this busy time of year.

Sift the flour into a bowl and rub in the butter with fingertips until the mixture resembles breadcrumbs. Add the vinegar to the water and sprinkle over the dry mixture, 1 tablespoon at a time, while tossing with a fork. Continue to add the water mixture until the dough is just moist enough to hold together. Divide the dough into 2 balls, cover in plastic wrap and chill for 20 minutes.

Preheat the oven to 230°C. Roll out the dough on a lightly floured surface to 6 mm thickness. Cut into oblong shapes 7.5 x 2.5 cm. Pour the sugar onto baking paper and press the top of each biscuit shape on, so the sugar clings to it. Transfer, sugar side up, to baking trays and bake for 8–10 minutes, or until the top begins to caramelise. Roll and cook the remaining dough in the same way. Cool completely on wire racks and store in an airtight container.

Makes 48

VARIATION

When sandwiched together with buttercream, these crisp biscuits can stand on their own on the tea or coffee tray. To make a buttercream filling, beat 185 g butter until light and creamy, then beat in ½ cup icing sugar, 1 egg yolk and vanilla essence to taste. Beat until light, smooth and creamy. Before serving, sandwich pairs of biscuits with the filling.

2 cups Rice Bubbles

1 cup desiccated coconut

1 cup milk powder

1 cup icing sugar mixture

½ cup raisins

½ cup currants

½ cup red and green glacé cherries, halved

250 g Copha

White Christmas

A favourite with children – get them involved in the kitchen by helping them make this colourful sweetmeat. If you like, wrap these treats in squares of cellophane, twisted at the ends, and pile into a pretty bowl, mug, jar or box to make an elegant gift. These should be stored in an airtight container in the fridge.

Line the base and sides of a 19 x 29 cm large slice pan with baking paper. Mix the Rice Bubbles, coconut, milk powder and icing sugar mixture in a bowl. Add the raisins, currants and cherries and mix through.

Melt the Copha in a saucepan over a low heat and pour into the Rice Bubble mixture. Stir to mix well. Turn the mixture into the prepared pan and press down well with the back of a large spoon. Refrigerate for 2 hours, until set and chilled. Serve sliced into squares.

Makes about 20 pieces

| 1 sheet (20 x 30 cm) rice paper |
| 2 cups caster sugar |
| 1 cup glucose |
| ½ cup honey |
| 2 egg whites |
| 1 cup almonds, toasted |
| 1 cup shelled unsalted pistachios |
| ½ cup dried cranberries |
| ½ teaspoon vanilla essence |
| 60 g butter, at room temperature |

Pistachio and Cranberry Nougat

This superb sweet is perfect for Christmas celebrations – offer to guests, or box up as a gift.

You might find the nougat will be different each time you make it – sometimes softer, other times firmer, but always delicious. It all depends on how much you beat the mixture and how accurately you gauge the sugar thermometer. A good electric mixer is essential; one with a strong motor that can stand the weight of the mixture. Rice paper is another essential – you'll find it at good health stores.

Line the base and sides of a 20 x 30 cm lamington pan with baking paper. Cover the base with rice paper.

Heat the sugar, glucose, honey and ¼ cup water in a heavy-based saucepan over a low heat until the glucose has melted and the sugar dissolved. Increase the heat to moderate and boil until the syrup reaches 130°C on a sugar thermometer.

Meanwhile, beat the egg whites in a bowl with an electric mixer until stiff. With the mixer running, add half of the syrup in a slow steady stream. Return the remaining syrup to the heat while continuing to beat the egg white and syrup mixture.

Boil the remaining syrup until it reaches 'crack' temperature (154°C). Slowly pour into the egg white mixture with the motor running. Continue beating until the mixture is very thick. Check that the mixer's motor is not overheating. Add the nuts, cranberries, vanilla and butter, mixing thoroughly.

Pour into the prepared pan and top with rice paper to cover, using the palm of your hand to smooth the surface. Leave to cool completely and set. Turn onto a board and cut into 3 cm strips. Wrap each strip in a piece of baking paper and store in an airtight container for up to 2 weeks.

Makes about 60 pieces

1 tablespoon instant coffee
¼ cup boiling water
250 g dark chocolate, broken into pieces
125 g unsalted butter
2–3 tablespoons brandy or rum
cocoa powder, for dusting

Rich Chocolate Truffles

Very rich, very moreish and very French – and shaped into small balls or nuggets to resemble the 'black diamonds' French chefs prize so highly. Once made, they can be finished in a variety of ways and kept in the refrigerator.

In a bowl over a saucepan of gently simmering water add the instant coffee powder, boiling water and chocolate. Melt, stirring a little, until the mixture is smooth.

Cut the butter into small pieces and beat into the chocolate mixture gradually, a little at a time, until all the butter is thoroughly incorporated. Stir in the brandy or rum, adding enough to suit taste and chill for at least 3 hours or until firm enough to handle.

Break off pieces of the chilled mixture and roll into small balls. Place in a dish containing a generous amount of sifted cocoa powder and shake until the truffles are thoroughly coated. To store, place truffles in paper or tiny foil cups, arrange in an airtight container and keep refrigerated.

Makes 18 pieces

VARIATIONS FOR FINISHING THE TRUFFLES:
- Roll in coarsely shredded dark or white chocolate
- Roll gently in toasted desiccated or shredded coconut
- Roll in praline powder (crushed almond toffee)
- Roll in finely chopped toasted hazelnuts or almonds
- Stud with a piece of macadamia nut
- Stud with a piece of glacé ginger

500 g sugar
¾ cup water
375 g ground almonds
2 egg whites
1 teaspoon sherry
⅓ cup icing sugar, sifted

Marzipan

A European Christmas wouldn't be the same without marzipan sweets, often moulded into little fruits and vegetables, pink pigs and other animals to ornament the Christmas tree.

Simple sweets can also be made by moulding delicately coloured marzipan between walnut halves or pressing it into a plump prune or date and coating it in fine sugar. Placed in tiny paper cups and arranged in neat rows in a small box, these little treats make a special gift.

If you don't want to make your own marzipan, a good alternative is the excellent Danish brand, Odense, which is available in rolls.

Dissolve the sugar in the water in a large saucepan over a gentle heat and boil steadily, without stirring, for 10 minutes, until the mixture forms a 'soft ball' when a little is dropped into cold water. Remove from the heat and beat with a wooden spoon until the mixture looks slightly cloudy. Stir in the ground almonds.

Whisk the egg whites in a bowl until just frothy, add to the pan and cook the mixture over a very gentle heat for 1–2 minutes. Add the sherry, then turn the mixture on to a board dusted with a little of the icing sugar.

Once the mixture has cooled a little, knead until quite smooth, working in the remaining icing sugar as you go. While still warm, divide into 2 portions, colour and flavour as desired.

TO COLOUR:

Colour one portion of marzipan with pale green. To the second portion, add rum or brandy and pink colouring. Knead the flavouring and colouring into the marzipan until perfectly distributed, adding the colour a few drops at a time – a little more can always be added. The marzipan may be wrapped in waxed paper or foil and stored in the fridge.

MARZIPAN WALNUTS OR PECANS

Roll small pieces of marzipan, natural coloured or tinted, into balls about the size of a small walnut. Press a perfect walnut or pecan half into each side and roll in caster sugar. Place in paper cups and store in a container in the refrigerator if the weather is warm. Chocolate boxes are ideal for presenting these treats, just cover with a fresh wrapping paper secured with tape or glue.

MARZIPAN PRUNES OR DATES

Remove the stones from prunes or fresh dates by making a slit along one side, not right through, and lifting out the stone with the point of a knife. Roll some marzipan into a coil about 1 cm thick and cut off into even-sized pieces. Shape into oval pieces, press a blanched almond or a piece of glacé ginger in the middle and then insert into each prune or date. Roll in caster sugar. Place in small paper cups and store.

Alternatively, the prunes can be filled with a quince or apricot paste which has been rolled into nuggets and slipped into the prunes. Make two or three light indentations across the filling at a slant for decoration.

MARZIPAN FRUITS AND VEGETABLES

Marzipan may be shaped into tiny fruits and vegetables, which are useful to have on hand for offering with a sweet drink or coffee. They make a charming gift when boxed or presented in a pretty dish. As a cake decoration, they can add a touch of whimsey.

Marzipan shapes may be coloured by painting the shape with diluted vegetable colouring using a small paint brush. Another method is to work the desired colour into pieces of marzipan before moulding.

Following are a few shape ideas. Once you make them, I'm sure you'll feel more confident in creating your own fruits and vegetables.

Strawberries: Break off small pieces of marzipan, roll into balls then into strawberry shapes. Colour a pretty pink. Roll each shape gently on a fine wire sieve, then roll in caster sugar. Make a small coin-sized hull with marzipan, cutting the edges; use a little egg white to secure on the strawberry and colour green. If liked, the marzipan may be tinted bright pink and green before moulding. Set in small confectionary paper cups.

Bananas: Break off small pieces of marzipana and roll into small, long shapes, tapering one end. Paint yellow with small brown splashes. Set in small paper cups.

Peaches: Break off small pieces of marzipan, roll into balls, then, using a toothpick, press an indentation down one side of each ball. Paint a peachy yellow with a brush and roll in icing sugar to give the peach a 'bloom'. Set in small paper cups.

Carrots: Break off small pieces of marzipan, roll into carrot shapes. Using a toothpick, press small creases in the carrot shape. Make a few green stalks and poke them into an indentation on the thick top end of the carrot. Tint orange and green, or tint the marzipan before shaping.

Potatoes: Break off small pieces of marzipan, shape into potato shapes, make a few eyes with the end of a toothpick, roll in cocoa and dust off the excess.

250 g blanched almonds

250 g blanched hazelnuts

310 g caster sugar

310 g honey

2 cups plain flour

1 tablespoon ground cinnamon

1 teaspoon mixed spice

750 g dried mixed fruits, using a mixture of currants,
    raisins and mixed peel

icing sugar, to dust

Panforte

Devotees of panforte, the traditional nut and fruit cake of Siena, Italy, say this recipe is the real thing – it is rich and spicy, as it should be. Small individual ones make wonderful gifts.

Preheat the oven to 180°C. Lay the almonds and hazelnuts on a baking tray and toast in the oven until golden. Melt the sugar and honey together in a heavy-based saucepan over a gentle heat, then allow to boil until it reaches a temperature of 115°C on a sugar thermometer. Alternatively, test a little mixture in cold water; it should not disintegrate but flatten of its own accord when picked up with the fingers.

Meanwhile, sift the flour and spices into a large bowl and add the toasted nuts and dried fruit.

When the syrup has reached temperature, pour into the bowl and mix quickly and thoroughly together. Tip into 2 x 25 cm cake tins or a tin 28 x 38 cm and 2.5 cm deep (or a little larger than this) which have been lined with baking paper. Pat the mixture into the tins using hands which have been dipped in water.

Bake in a 160°C oven for 45 minutes. Dust liberally with icing sugar and store in airtight containers. Cut into wedges or rectangles to serve. The flavours develop and improve with age.

Makes 2 x 25 cm round cakes

| 1 cup sugar |
| ¼ cup water |
| 1 teaspoon salt |
| 1 cup walnuts (see Tip) |
| freshly ground black pepper, to season |

Chinese Toffee Walnuts

Our friend Rebecca Hsu Hui Min introduced us to this Chinese delicacy. A little salt and lots of freshly ground black pepper seems a quirky addition to nut brittle, but gives it a spicy, rather than peppery, taste. It leaves one's mouth feeling fresh and clear. A welcome Christmas gift, put in a glass jar with a lid.

Heat the sugar and water in a heavy-based saucepan over a gentle heat until the sugar is dissolved, then increase the heat until it reaches the 'soft ball' stage, about 121°C on a sugar thermometer.

Add the salt and walnuts. Bring the mixture to the crack stage (154°C), turning the pepper mill about 20 times over the pan between stirs. The nuts will take up the sugar until they are lightly coated and sticking together in a cluster.

Pour out onto a greased baking tray. As the mixture quickly cools, pull it apart into pieces with a couple of forks. These are best eaten the same day.

Makes about 1 cup

TIP The quality of the walnuts is important. Buy canned walnuts, which are always fresh. In Chinatown look for shelled and peeled walnuts – these are an even better choice for this recipe.

| any choice of fresh fruits (see Note) |
| 1–2 egg whites, depending on size of centrepiece |
| caster sugar, to dust |

Frosted Fruits

This makes a festive edible centrepiece for the Christmas table. Use your best piece of silver, china or glass. I use a special family heirloom – a silver fruit stand. Children love to be involved in creating this centrepiece of fruit.

Wash and thoroughly dry the fruit. Beat the egg white until just frothy. Have the sugar ready in a wide, shallow bowl. Brush a piece of fruit with the egg white, draining away any excess, then dip the fruit in the caster sugar. There should be a fairly thin, even layer of caster sugar. Lightly shake off any excess sugar then place the fruit on a wire rack to dry. Continue with the remaining fruit, egg white and sugar.

Arrange the fruits into the centrepiece of your choice.

Makes 1 centrepiece

NOTE *Fruits that work well as a centrepiece include whole unblemished peaches, plums, apricots, cherries, small clusters of grapes, strawberries, dates and tiny red apples. Muscatels or other dried fruits can also work well.*

20 cumquats

500 g caster sugar

1 stick cinnamon

750 ml brandy

Brandied Cumquats

Eat these delights as a dessert with ice cream, or slice and add to Christmas fruitcakes and compotes. The liquid can be sipped as a liqueur with coffee, or used as a syrup over ice cream and custard. For those who love cumquats, this makes a lovely gift in a pretty jar.

Lightly prick the cumquats in several places with a needle or thin skewer. Arrange in layers in a sealable, wide-mouthed glass or earthenware jar, sprinkling the sugar between each layer. Allow to stand overnight.

Add the cinnamon and brandy to the jar. Close tightly with a lid or cork and place the jar on its side, shaking gently every few days to distribute the sugar evenly. When the sugar has completely dissolved, leave the jar undisturbed for at least 2 months before serving in your favourite way.

Makes 20

---

1 cup caster sugar

⅔ cup water

1 kg dessert prunes, pitted

2.5 cm stick of cinnamon

3 tablespoons overproof rum

Rum-laced Prunes

Plump, shiny prunes in a clear glass jar make a good Christmas present for people who have everything and for those who like the good things in life.

Bring the sugar and water to the boil in a heavy-based saucepan. When the sugar has dissolved, simmer the syrup for 5 minutes. Add the prunes and cinnamon. Cook very gently for 5 minutes or until soft. Remove from the heat and stir in the rum. Cover the pan and allow to cool. Seal in a jar.

Makes about 4½ cups

NOTE These are delicious with vanilla ice cream or as a filling for pancakes with whipped cream.

500 g dessert prunes	2 cups white vinegar
1½ cups cold black tea	4 cloves
1 cup caster sugar	1 stick cinnamon

Spiced Prunes

Serve these prunes with roasted pork or cold meats, rillettes and terrines. They also make a handy Christmas gift for those who love prunes.

Cover the prunes with the cold tea in a bowl and soak overnight. Combine the sugar, vinegar and a muslin bag containing the spices, in a heavy-based saucepan. Bring to the boil and boil steadily for 15 minutes. Remove from the heat and discard the spice bag. Pour the prunes and tea into another saucepan and simmer for about 15 minutes or until soft. Drain, reserving 1 cup of the liquid, and pack the prunes into sterilised jars. Add the reserved liquid to the spiced vinegar and pour over the prunes. Seal the jars and store in a cool, dark place. Leave for 24 hours before using. Label the jars and include suggestions for use if giving as a gift.

Makes about 3 cups

- -

2 kg cherries	1 stick cinnamon
3 cloves	1½ cups caster sugar
2.5 cm piece of ginger, bruised	1¾ cups vinegar

Sweet and Sour Cherries

These go wonderfully with cold pork, ham and delicatessen meats. Leave the stalks on the cherries, as they look much more attractive.

Wash the cherries and prick once or twice with a needle or thin skewer. Secure the spices in a muslin bag. Heat the sugar, vinegar and spice bag in a saucepan until the sugar dissolves. Simmer for 20 minutes, then pour the syrup over the cherries in a bowl. Leave to stand for 24 hours.

Drain off the soaking liquid and add to a saucepan, reheat and again pour over the cherries. Leave to stand for another 24 hours.

Now, reheat the liquid with the cherries, bringing it slowly to the boil. Bottle the cherries with the syrup, cover and seal. Label the jars and include suggestions for use if giving as a gift.

Makes about 10 cups

CHAPTER SEVEN

Sauces, Dressings & Accompaniments

Sauces, Dressings & Accompaniments

Roast pork without apple sauce, roast chicken without bread sauce, Christmas pudding without brandy sauce and custard and brandy butter – no thank you, it just wouldn't be right.

We all feel the same about those lovely sauces and accompaniments that make many foods justly famous for what they are and have the right finishing touch of flavour.

Here are recipes for the things that matter – the sauces, dressings and accompaniments that add distinction to everyday and festive meals.

| 2 egg yolks |
| ½ teaspoon salt |
| pinch of freshly ground black pepper |
| 1 teaspoon Dijon mustard or ½ teaspoon dry mustard |
| 2 teaspoons white wine vinegar or lemon juice |
| ¾ cup light-flavoured olive oil or rice bran oil |
| ¼ cup extra-virgin olive oil |

Mayonnaise

Homemade mayonnaise, with its sumptuous texture and fresh, subtle flavour, is one of the great sauces. It's delicious with poached fish or chicken salad, drizzled over sliced tomatoes or eaten with hard-boiled eggs, asparagus, warm baby steamed potatoes, shelled prawns or other seafood. It takes only about 10 minutes to make by hand once you've mastered the technique and is faster still with a food processor.

You will notice two oils are used. First pressing greenish extra-virgin olive oil is too strong on its own for most mayonnaise uses, so a lighter olive oil or rice bran oil is used in larger amounts and a little of the stronger oil added for flavour.

Have the ingredients at room temperature. Warm the egg and oil in hot water if they are cold. Rinse out a mixing bowl with hot water and wrap a damp cloth around the base to keep it steady.

Put the egg, salt, pepper, mustard and 1 teaspoon of the vinegar or lemon juice in the bowl and beat with a wire whisk or hand-held blender to combine. When the mixture becomes thicker, begin to add the oil, drop by drop, whisking constantly and incorporating each addition thoroughly before adding the next. As the mixture thickens, the oil flow can be increased to a steady thin stream, but you must keep beating constantly. When all the oil is incorporated, beat in the remaining vinegar or lemon juice. Store in a cool place, covered.

Makes about 1 cup

MAYONNAISE IN A FOOD PROCESSOR
Process a whole egg, seasonings and 1 teaspoon of the vinegar or lemon juice in a food processor or blender for a few seconds. With the motor running, add 1 cup oil gradually, ensuring that each addition has been absorbed before adding more. When all the oil has been incorporated, add the remaining vinegar or lemon juice.

Lime Mayonnaise: Add the juice of a lime and a little of the grated rind in place of the vinegar or lemon juice. Try adding chopped coriander to serve with seafood.

Sesame Mayonnaise: Instead of extra-virgin olive oil use rice bran oil or a light olive oil, adding a few drops of sesame oil and a tablespoon of lightly ground toasted sesame seeds. Try with chicken or seafood salads.

Garlic Mayonnaise or Aïoli: This is one of the best loved sauces of France. Crush 3 or 4 cloves garlic to a paste with a little salt (this can be done with the flat of a knife blade on a chopping board). Transfer to a bowl. Add the egg yolks and seasonings as for the basic recipe. If making in a food processor add garlic paste with egg and proceed with the recipe. Serve with poached chicken, fish dishes or raw vegetables.

TIP If either handmade or machine-made mayonnaise refuses to thicken or if it curdles, take a clean, warmed bowl and beat an egg yolk with ½ teaspoon each salt and vinegar, then gradually beat in the curdled mayonnaise very slowly at first and then more quickly.

pinch of saffron	1 star anise
¼ cup white wine	1 stick cinnamon
2 tablespoons caster sugar	3 Fuji or other crisp apples, peeled, cored and diced
2 tablespoons white wine vinegar	¼ cup raisins
1 tablespoon Chinese plum sauce	2 tablespoons toasted pine nuts
1 red bird's eye chilli	

Apple and Saffron Chutney

A fresh-tasting chutney adds interest to grilled and barbecued meats. It is equally good with cold meats, Christmas ham or roast duck.

Mix the saffron, wine, sugar, vinegar, plum sauce, red chilli, star anise and cinnamon in a bowl until well combined. Put the saffron mixture in a heavy-based saucepan and bring slowly to the boil. Cook until the liquid has reduced a little. Add the apple, raisins and pine nuts, and cook gently, stirring occasionally. The chutney is ready when the apples are soft. Remove the star anise, cinnamon stick and chilli before serving.

Makes 2½ cups

PEACH AND SAFFRON CHUTNEY

Make as above, but substitute the apple for 3 firm, peeled yellow peaches cut into dice and proceed with the recipe. Mango chutney may be made the same way using the flesh of 3 firm mangoes.

- -

3 cooking apples, such as granny smith
1–2 tablespoons water
2 tablespoons caster sugar
strip of lemon rind
strip of orange rind

Apple Sauce

A must-have for roast pork. Popular in the United States, England and certainly Australia – this sauce is lovely with pork leftovers as well.

Peel, core and slice the apples thinly. Cook the apples gently in a saucepan with the water, sugar and rinds until the mixture turns to a pulp, adding more water if needed. Remove the rinds and serve warm with roast pork.

Makes 2 cups

¼ cup white wine vinegar or dry vermouth	3 egg yolks
¼ cup tarragon vinegar	250 g butter, at room temperature, cubed
1 eschalot or spring onion, finely chopped	salt and ground white pepper
4 peppercorns	1 teaspoon finely chopped tarragon or Continental parsley (optional)
½ teaspoon dried tarragon	

Bearnaise Sauce

This sauce is absolutely wonderful with pan-fried fillet mignon or roasted fillet of beef. Slices of rare cold fillet of beef on buttered small baguette slices and a smear of bearnaise make a delicious cocktail party savoury. Cold roast beef with bearnaise sandwiches are simply divine.

This rich and luscious sauce is thickened by the emulsifying action of egg yolk on butter and vinegar with aromatics. Note that this is a warm, not hot, sauce. If it has to be held for a time before serving, stand the container in a pan of warm water and cover with a piece of plastic wrap placed directly over the surface of the sauce. It may be refrigerated and very gently reheated over some warm water, very gently whipping it back to life.

Boil the wine vinegar or vermouth, tarragon vinegar, eschalot or spring onion, peppercorns and dried tarragon in a saucepan until reduced to 2 tablespoons of liquid. Strain and cool slightly.

Place the reduced liquid and egg yolks in a mixing bowl set over a saucepan of simmering water. Whisk until the mixture thickens a little, then beat in the butter, piece by piece, slipping it through your fingers to soften it slightly and whisking constantly. When all the butter has been added, remove the sauce from the heat and season to taste with salt and white pepper. Add tarragon or parsley if desired.

Makes approximately 1 cup

- -

1½ cups milk	freshly ground black pepper, to season
½ onion	1 cup dry homemade breadcrumbs
1 bay leaf	10 g butter
4 cloves	

Bread Sauce

Some wouldn't consider turkey or roast chicken without this sauce. It seems thin when you start adding the breadcrumbs but it will soon thicken.

Combine the milk, onion, bay leaf and cloves in a saucepan over a moderate heat. Season with pepper and bring to the boil. Remove from the heat and stand for 1 hour. Remove the onion, bay leaf and cloves from the milk and return the pan to a moderate heat. Stir through the breadcrumbs until simmering. Simmer for 2 minutes, stir in the butter and check the seasoning.

Makes 2 cups

5 tablespoons red currant jelly	2 teaspoons arrowroot
¼ cup marmalade	rind and juice of 1 orange
2 teaspoons dry mustard	rind and juice of 1 lemon
⅔ cup good-quality port or red wine	1–2 tablespoons Grand Marnier (optional)

Cumberland Sauce

This is the classic sauce to be served with ham or turkey. It improves if made a day or two before it is to be used. Here is my version.

Heat the jelly and marmalade in a saucepan over a moderate heat. Mix the mustard with a little of the wine then add to the pan with the remaining wine. Bring to the boil and simmer for about 5 minutes. Mix the arrowroot with a little water and stir into the simmering sauce, drawing the pan away from the heat immediately. Add the rind and juice of the orange and lemon.

For a very special lift to this already good sauce, add a tablespoon or two of Grand Marnier at the end.

Makes approximately 1 cup

- -

2 mangoes or 1½ cups drained canned mango slices
⅓ cup olive oil
2 tablespoons balsamic or wine vinegar
8 mint leaves, shredded

Mango and Mint Sauce

Tropical fruits go so well with choice seafood. This beautiful sauce is excellent with Atlantic salmon or trout, or any choice of fish and even prawns and lobster salad.

Cut the cheeks off the mango, scrape off all the flesh from the skin and around the stone and purée the mango flesh in a blender or food processor. While the motor is still running, add the oil gradually, then add the vinegar and mint leaves – the mixture should thicken, like mayonnaise. Transfer to a bowl and keep at room temperature until ready to serve.

Makes 1 cup

⅔ cup currants	¾ cup brown sugar
½ cup port	½ cup red wine
50 g unsalted butter	¼ cup red wine vinegar
2 kg red, white or brown onions, thinly sliced	1 tablespoon balsamic vinegar

Onion and Currant Marmalade

This marmalade makes a delicious topping for bruschetta and goes well on grilled meats, with pâtés, in sandwiches and with fresh goat's cheese. It is perfect for snacks over the Christmas holiday, or give little jars as gifts – but don't forget to label the marmalade and include suggestions for using.

In a bowl, soak the currants in the port. Meanwhile, melt the butter in a large heavy-based saucepan over a moderate heat and cook the onions, stirring frequently, for 30 minutes, until very soft and lightly coloured.

Stir in the sugar and cook for a further 15 minutes. Add the wine, vinegars, soaked currants and port. Increase the heat to high and cook, uncovered and stirring frequently, for 30 minutes, until the onion mixture is a thick jam consistency. Season to taste. Cool slightly, then ladle into jars, cover and refrigerate for up to 3 weeks.

Makes about 5 cups

- -

300 g frozen cranberries
1 cup caster sugar
½ cup orange juice
⅓ cup water
grated rind of 1 orange

Cranberry and Orange Relish

A sauce favoured by Americans for their Thanksgiving turkey, we Australians also enjoy it with Christmas turkey and ham.

Simmer all the ingredients in a large heavy-based saucepan over a moderate heat for 10 minutes, until the mixture is thick. Cool before serving.

Makes 2 cups

TIP This relish can be prepared several days ahead and kept in the refrigerator until ready to use.

3 kg red onions

¼ cup light olive oil

2 cups caster sugar

½ cup balsamic vinegar or sherry vinegar

2 cups red wine

Red Onion Marmalade

Onion marmalade has a rich, robust flavour. Try it to dress up simple grilled meats, sandwiches and cold ham. It also makes a welcome Christmas gift.

First halve the onions then pull away the peel. Leaving the root end attached, start from the top of each onion half and cut across into fairly thin slices down to the root end.

Heat the oil in a large heavy-based saucepan and cook the onion over a gentle heat for 15 minutes or until soft but not coloured, stirring occasionally. Stir in the sugar and simmer over a gentle heat for 30 minutes. Add the vinegar and red wine and cook uncovered for 45–60 minutes or until the liquid has reduced and the onion mixture is of a jam consistency. Pour into prepared jars and seal with lids while still hot. This marmalade can also be made with brown onions with great success.

Makes about 4 cups

TIP To bottle the onion marmalade, allow to stand for 15 minutes before bottling. Make sure the jars are dry, warm and clean. The easiest way to fill the jars is to pour the marmalade from a jug. Fill jars to within 5 mm of the top. Cover with a lid and wipe the filled jars carefully with a cloth wrung out with hot water before storing, while the marmalade is warm. Label carefully and store in a cool, dry place.

- -

2 tablespoons Dijon mustard

2 tablespoons caster sugar

pinch of salt

1 teaspoon white wine vinegar

⅓ cup light olive oil

2 tablespoons chopped dill

1 teaspoon lemon juice

Dill Sauce

This is a perfect sauce to go with a special salmon dish for Christmas lunch, be it smoked salmon, gravlax or poached salmon. It also makes a lovely dipping sauce for prawns.

Combine the mustard, sugar and salt in a small bowl. Add the vinegar and slowly whisk in the oil until slightly thickened. Add the chopped dill and lemon juice.

Makes about ½ cup

30 g butter

2 tablespoons plain flour

3 cups chicken stock

1–2 tablespoons dry sherry or port

Gravy

Pour off excess turkey drippings, leaving about ¼ cup. Add butter and melt
on medium heat. Stir in flour and cook for 3 minutes, until browned lightly.
Stir in stock, scraping up crusty pan residue. Bring to boil. Simmer for
3 minutes, until thickened. Stir in sherry or port and strain.

Adjust seasonings if necessary and skim excess fat from the top.
Serve piping hot in a gravy boat or jug.

Makes 3 cups

2 tablespoons good-quality vinegar (if using balsamic use 2 teaspoons)
1 teaspoon Dijon mustard or ½ teaspoon dry mustard
¼ teaspoon salt
freshly ground black pepper, to season
½ cup oil

Vinaigrette

Vinaigrette, or French dressing as it is often called, is essential for a classic green salad and is used with other vegetables and salads.

Salad greens must be washed and dried well – in a salad spinner or wrapped loosely in a dry tea towel – so that the dressing will cling to the leaves.

When dressing rice, potato or cooked vegetable salads, pour the dressing over and toss gently while still warm so that the flavour is absorbed more readily.

The usual proportion of oil to vinegar or lemon juice is three parts oil to one part vinegar. I prefer less vinegar. Look for good-quality vinegars and interesting oils for your vinaigrette. Cider vinegar, red or white wine vinegar, and flavoured vinegars such as tarragon or other herbs are excellent. Olive oil is traditional and superb, but walnut, rice bran, mustard or macadamia oils give a subtle variation.

Mix the vinegar in a small bowl with the mustard, salt and pepper. Slowly add the oil, beating well with a fork or small whisk. Taste as you go to get the flavour you like.

Makes about ⅔ cup

GARLIC DRESSING
For a delicate garlic flavour, peel 1 or 2 cloves garlic, bruise and steep in the vinegar for an hour. For a pungent flavour, crush 1 or 2 cloves garlic to a paste with the salt, add the vinegar and other seasonings, then the oil.

250 g unsalted butter	¼ whole nutmeg, grated
2	
¾ cup icing sugar	1 teaspoon Grand Marnier
1 teaspoon grated orange rind	3 tablespoons brandy

Brandied Butter

Christmas pudding or warm mincemeat tart wouldn't be quite the same without this gorgeous hard sauce – brandy butter melting into the spicy, fruity, delectable pudding. If rum is your fancy use a strong rum instead of brandy.

Cream the butter until soft and white, then beat in the icing sugar. When creamy, beat in the orange rind, nutmeg and Grand Marnier. Lastly, add the brandy, drop by drop, beating all the time so the mixture doesn't curdle (a liqueur brandy is the best if you have it).

This may be made on the same day as the pudding. Pack it into a bowl with a lid, first covering it with foil, and store in the fridge. Remove it from the fridge well beforehand on Christmas Day, spoon it into a bowl and fluff up with a fork. If it is preferred hard, leave it in the fridge until ready to serve.

Makes 1½ cups

- -

45 g unsalted butter	½ cup cream
2 tablespoons plain flour	½ cup milk
¼ cup caster sugar	¼ cup brandy
1 tablespoon golden syrup	

Brandy Sauce

Some prefer brandied butter, some brandy sauce. Why not have both? After all, it's Christmas.

Melt the butter in a small saucepan and stir in the flour. Cook for a minute without colouring then add the sugar, golden syrup, cream and milk. Stir to combine and continue cooking over a gentle heat until thick and creamy. Stir in brandy and serve hot with Christmas pudding.

Makes 1½ cups

MICROWAVE ALTERNATIVE
Put the butter in a heatproof jug and melt for 30 seconds on high. Blend in the flour and cook a further 1 minute on high. Combine the sugar, golden syrup, cream and milk and heat on high for 2 minutes. Gradually add the cream mixture to the butter and flour. Heat for 5–7 minutes on medium, stirring every minute.

60 g butter

½ cup firmly packed brown sugar

2 tablespoons cold water

1 egg yolk, beaten

¼ cup cream, whipped

½ teaspoon vanilla essence

Easy Butterscotch Sauce

Wicked, yes, but so delicious. This easy-to-make sauce is perfect with ice cream for those who choose to go without Christmas pudding.

Melt the butter in a saucepan over a low heat, add the brown sugar and cook for 2 minutes, stirring. Add the water and egg yolk and continue stirring until the mixture thickens. Do not allow it to boil. Remove from the heat and cool, then chill. Fold in the whipped cream and vanilla just before serving.

Serves 4

- -

2 cups fresh or frozen raspberries

juice of ½ lemon

¼ cup caster sugar

2 tablespoons framboise liqueur or Grand Marnier

Raspberry Sauce

Bright red and festive, this sauce livens up ice cream, creamy set desserts like panna cotta, crème caramel, steamed puddings, meringues and Danish rum cream.

Process the raspberries, lemon juice and sugar in a food processor until well combined. Just before serving mix through the framboise or Grand Marnier.

Makes about 1½ cups

2 cups milk

1 vanilla bean, split lengthwise, seeds scraped

4 egg yolks

1 tablespoon cornflour

¼ cup caster sugar

Vanilla Egg Custard

This is a rich vanilla custard, used to serve with many sweets. It's a great favourite with plum pudding and is also good with stewed fruit, light steamed pudding, apple pie and trifle. Pastry cream is a thicker custard used as a filling for fruit tarts, éclairs, profiteroles and pastries such as cream horns, neapolitans or as an alternative to cream in sponge cakes.

Combine the milk, vanilla bean and seeds in a saucepan over a moderate heat, until simmering. Remove from the heat, cover and set aside for 15 minutes. Remove the vanilla bean.

Beat the egg yolks and cornflour in a bowl with an electric mixer. Add the sugar and beat until pale and thick.

Reheat the milk back to simmering point. Pour onto the egg yolks, whisking continuously. Return to a clean saucepan. Cook over a low heat for 8 minutes, stirring, until the mixture thickens and coats the back of a spoon. Cool.

Makes 2½ cups

PASTRY CREAM VARIATION

Make as for vanilla custard, adding 2 tablespoons each plain flour and cornflour to the egg yolks and sugar. Cook over a low heat until thick and beginning to bubble. Use a spatula to scrape the pastry cream into a bowl and cover the surface with a piece of baking paper before cooling and using or storing in the fridge. For a fluffier pastry cream, fold in ½ cup whipped cream.

TIPS If you have a sweet tooth, the custard can easily be made with double the amount of sugar. For a richer vanilla custard, substitute 1 cup of the milk with 1 cup cream.

3 cups raisins

3 cups currants

3 cups sultanas

¾ cup blanched almonds, chopped

2 large cooking apples, grated

1½ cups brown sugar

150 g butter, melted

¾ cup brandy or rum

½ teaspoon grated nutmeg

½ teaspoon ground cloves

1 teaspoon ground cinnamon

grated rind and juice of 2 oranges

Fruit Mincemeat

The heart of the delicious mince pie, this fruit mince stores for months, covered, in the fridge. Make it well ahead of time – at least a few days before needed and up to several months.

Process batches of dried fruit and almonds in a food processor. Pulse to coarsely chop. Spoon into a bowl and combine with the grated apple, sugar, butter, brandy or rum, spices and orange rind and juice. Cover and chill, stirring daily, for at least 2 days before use.

Makes about 9 cups

| 2¾ cups sugar |
| 2 cups water |
| 4 cups red wine |
| 4 sticks cinnamon |
| 10 cloves |

Red Wine Caramel Sauce

A good sauce is important to have on hand over the festive season for casual visits from friends and family. For a perfectly sweet treat, serve this delicious sauce with ice cream or meringues.

Combine the sugar and water in a large saucepan over a low heat, until the sugar is dissolved. Bring to the boil and cook, without stirring, for about 10 minutes, until the sugar starts to caramelise to a darkish golden colour.

Meanwhile, combine the remaining ingredients in a separate saucepan over a moderate heat until warm.

Remove the caramel from the heat and, standing back to prevent steam scorching, add the warm red wine mixture. Return to the heat and stir until smooth. Simmer for 30 minutes, until reduced to 3 cups and a syrupy consistency. Cool and bottle before storing in the refrigerator.

Makes 3 cups

TIP Drop prunes or cherries in and poach until just cooked. Cool and serve over ice cream with some of the syrup.

CHAPTER EIGHT
Drinks

Drinks

What will we have to drink for Christmas? It's a common question. Top of the list for many is chilled Champagne – one bottle serving eight is modest enough to start. Make sure the Champagne is well chilled – have an ice bucket half-filled with ice to keep it cool. Get out tall glass flutes and ask the most likely person to pop the cork – it should be a gentle whisper not a vulgar pop. It's all part of the fun.

Cold beer seems to be the choice of many and there is a wide range to choose from; each drinker seems to be emphatic about the best.

To fit into the festive spirit and give it a special zing, a bit of a change is welcome. I have included some alcoholic and non-alcoholic punch drinks and coolers. These are good to have on a table where guests can help themselves. Just one punch with alcohol should do it – we all have to be responsible for our guests (and ourselves). A large glass jug of simple lemonade or elderflower syrup with ice cubes and plain or sparkling water, lemon slices and mint is refreshing.

What wines to serve with Christmas dinner? You don't have to be a connoisseur of fine wine to know what types of wine go with certain foods. If you are uncertain, rely on a good wine merchant, as almost anyone who sells wine has a good idea of which wines best go with certain dishes.

Champagne can be served at the beginning and throughout the meal, but don't serve a dry Champagne with desserts, as it makes them taste sour. However, dry Champagne does go well with cheese and fruit.

Pep Drinks

There are people who just can't get started in the morning. Get them going on Christmas morning with one of the following pep drinks, which are recommended for health and vitality. Some are pick-me-ups after a late or heavy night, others will keep you going through a full and busy day and keep you in good humour for Christmas.

GRAPE AND HONEY DRINK

Blend 1 cup unsweetened grape juice with 1–2 teaspoons mild honey until smooth. Especially good for slimmers, this drink curbs the desire for rich, fattening foods and contains goodness and minerals.

QUICK PEP JUICE

Beat 1 fresh egg yolk into 1 cup of unsweetened orange or any other fruit juice. This makes an ideal protein breakfast. Fresh egg yolk is considered to be one of the richest sources of lecithin, which is good for the nerves.

FRUIT AND NUT DRINK

Blend ¼ cup nuts (almonds, pecans or walnuts are a good choice) until finely ground. Add 1 cup fruit juice and 1 teaspoon honey, and blend together for about 30 seconds until smooth.

½ cup sugar

1 cup water

8 mint sprigs

2 sticks cinnamon

2 litres apple juice

1 cup strained lemon juice

2 litres sparkling mineral water or lemonade

ice cubes

flowers and mint sprigs, to garnish

Apple Blossom Cooler

This drink is so pretty and inviting, especially on a hot Christmas Day. Put out a large glass jug of this cooler with tumbler glasses on a handy table, allowing all the family and guests to help themselves throughout the day.

Dissolve the sugar in the water with the mint and cinnamon in a saucepan over a gentle heat and bring to the boil. Simmer for about 10 minutes, then cool and strain. Combine half the sugar mixture in a jug with half the apple and lemon juice and half the mineral water or lemonade, and fill with ice cubes. Garnish with small flowers from the garden and mint sprigs. Repeat with remaining syrup, juices and mineral water or lemonade as the cooler runs out.

Serves 12

¼ cup pearl barley

4 cups water

thinly peeled rind and juice of 2 lemons

2 lemons, juiced

caster sugar, to taste

Lemon Barley Water

This refreshing drink, which was very popular during Victorian times, is enjoying a revival today – and is especially welcome over the festive season. It keeps well in the refrigerator, so you can always have it on hand.

Put the barley, water and lemon rind in a saucepan and bring to the boil. Lower the heat and simmer as gently as possible, with the lid on, for 2 hours. Strain into a container and add lemon juice and sugar to taste. Cool, then chill.

Serves 4–6

1 bunch of mint	ice cubes
¾ cup caster sugar	3 x 1.25 litre bottles dry ginger ale, well chilled
1 cup strained lemon juice	1 lemon, thinly sliced, for garnish

Ginger Julep

The idea of combining tender mint sprigs chopped with sugar and lemon in a drink – the refreshing flavour infusing the sugar – comes from Kentucky in the United States, where they also used to add bourbon. Making the drink in three stages keeps it tasting fresh and bubbly. The spicy ginger also seems to go well with Christmas.

Remove the leaves from the mint stalks and chop finely in a blender or food processor with the sugar and lemon juice. Scoop the mixture into a jug or bowl, cover and leave to stand for 2 hours, stirring occasionally.

When ready to serve, half-fill a tall jug with ice cubes and strain (or pour unstrained) a third of the mint mixture over the top of the ice. Fill up the jug with one of the bottles of dry ginger ale, stir and garnish with the lemon slices and a sprig of mint.

Repeat with the remaining ingredients once the jug has emptied.

Makes 10–15 drinks

- -

10–12 young mint leaves	crushed ice (see Tip), to serve
1 tablespoon sugar	½ cup whisky or bourbon
2 tablespoons hot water	

Mint Julep

Cool, summery, but potent if you have more than one! In New Orleans, Juleps are served on tiered stands, with perhaps 20 glasses, under shady trees – it's southern hospitality at its best. A lovely shade of green, they're perfect for a hot Christmas Day.

Crush half the mint with the sugar using a spoon. Add the hot water and mix until all the mint flavour is extracted and the sugar has dissolved. Take 2 tumblers or large balloon wine glasses, fill almost full with crushed ice and push the remaining mint leaves downwards. Strain the crushed mint mixture into the glasses and pour in the whisky or bourbon. Put in two drinking straws and serve.

Makes 2 drinks

TIP To crush the ice, put ice cubes in a blender or food processor, pulse at first to break up the cubes, then let the motor run a little longer, pushing the ice down with a spatula every now and then until you have finely crushed ice.

1 cup fresh pineapple cubes	2 tablespoons honey
1 cup strained orange juice	2 tablespoons freshly squeezed lime or lemon juice
3 cups sparkling ginger beer	ice, to serve
⅔ cup rum	pomegranate seeds, to garnish (optional)

Pineapple and Orange Cooler

Rum leads us to thoughts of Jamaica or Queensland sugar plantations, pineapples and other tropical delights. Try this cooler with a few friends on a warm Christmas Day and dream you're in the Havana Club.

Blend all the ingredients (except the ice and pomegranate seeds) together in a blender or food processor and pour into 4 tall glasses filled with ice cubes. Scoop in some pomegranate seeds to garnish.

Serves 4

---

500 g raspberries
2 cups white or red wine vinegar
2 cups sugar

Raspberry Vinegar

An antidote for sore throats in Victorian times, raspberry vinegar features in a variety of salads and sauces. It also makes a great cordial – just a spoonful topped up with chilled mineral or soda water makes a refreshing drink.

Crush the raspberries and tip into a non-metallic bowl. Pour the vinegar over and leave to marinate overnight.

Strain the marinated raspberries into a heatproof jar and add the sugar. Stand the jar in a saucepan and add water to come halfway up the sides. Simmer for an hour, then strain the raspberry mixture into sterilised jars or bottles. This vinegar is ready to use immediately, or can be stored for several months, where it becomes more mellow as it ages.

Makes about 4 cups

¼ cup black tea leaves

5 cups boiling water

5 cups sweet white wine, such as Sauternes or Barsac

½ cup lemon juice

ice cubes

fresh fruit, such as orange and lemon slices, strawberries, cherries, sliced peaches or pineapple chunks, to garnish

Iced Tea Punch

Here's a light alcoholic punch for the older family members on a hot day. A pretty punchbowl or large glass jug of this waiting to welcome friends to a Christmas lunch will help them cool off.

Steep the tea leaves in the boiling water for 5 minutes. Strain into a bowl and allow to cool. Add the wine and lemon juice and pour the mixture over ice in a punch bowl. Float fresh fruit on top and stand for 10 minutes before serving.

Serves 10

---

3 litres dry apple cider

2 tablespoons cloves

8 sticks cinnamon

ice cubes

mint sprigs, to garnish

Iced Spiced Cider

This cider is so easy – select a large glass jug for the cider, with a small bowl of mint leaves for people to garnish their own drinks, and punch glasses or wine glasses, ready to welcome guests. For an alcoholic punch add half a cup of brandy and half a cup of Cointreau or Grand Marnier, but do warn guests – with alcohol it's not for children.

Put the cider, cloves and cinnamon in a large non-corrosive saucepan and bring to the boil, then remove from the heat. Cover and leave to cool and infuse for at least 1 hour. Strain into a glass jug half filled with ice and leave to chill. Add a sprig of mint to each glass.

Makes 12–18 drinks

Spider Drinks

Sparkling Champagne, red wines and moreish fruit punch – so much about drinking on Christmas Day is adult-only. But there are lots of options to keep the kids happy.

All kids love spiders, otherwise known as ice cream sodas, and over the Christmas celebrations and holidays, it's okay to give them a treat. Let them prepare their own – they'll have fun scooping ice cream into glasses and adding their favourite flavours so they can top them up with bubbles. Each recipe makes one drink

1–2 scoops of vanilla ice cream
sparkling apple cider
4–5 unpeeled apple slices, to garnish

APPLE SPIDER

Scoop the ice cream into a glass. Pour in the apple cider to three-quarters fill. When it begins to foam, top up the glass with more cider.

Top with apple slices, pop in a straw and drink.

1–2 scoops of vanilla ice cream
1 tablespoon lime cordial
chilled soda water

COOL LIME SPIDER

Scoop the ice cream into a glass. Add the lime cordial and pour in the soda water to three-quarters fill. When it begins to foam, top up the glass with more soda water.

1–2 scoops of vanilla ice cream

orange Fanta

1 orange slice

ORANGE SPIDER

Scoop the ice cream into a glass. Pour in the orange Fanta to three-quarters fill. When it begins to foam, top up the glass with more Fanta.

Make a cut from the edge to the centre of the orange slice and slide it onto the glass to decorate.

1–2 scoops of vanilla ice cream

1 tablespoon blackcurrant cordial

chilled soda water

BLACK SPIDER

Scoop the ice cream into a glass. Add the blackcurrant cordial and pour in the soda water to three-quarters fill. When it begins to foam, top up the glass with more soda water.

- -

1–2 scoops of passionfruit ice cream or gelato

1 tablespoon passionfruit pulp

chilled lemonade or soda water

SPOTTED SPIDER

Scoop the ice cream into a glass. Add the passionfruit pulp and pour in the lemonade or soda water to three-quarters full. When it begins to foam, top up the glass with more lemonade or soda water.

1–2 scoops of vanilla, chocolate or chocolate ripple ice cream

1 tablespoon chocolate topping or syrup

chilled soda water

SPIDER RIPPLE

Scoop the ice cream into a glass. Add the chocolate topping or syrup and pour in the soda water to three-quarters fill. When it begins to foam, top up the glass with more soda water.

TIP Use low-kilojoule cordial and fizzy fruit drinks to lower the sugar content of these drinks, if you prefer.

2 roughly chopped mangoes

½ cup white rum

1 tablespoon sugar

2 tablespoons freshly squeezed lime or lemon juice

4 cups crushed ice

thin slices of lime and mint sprigs (optional), to garnish

Mango Daiquiri

A tropical cocktail is a great summer drink. Daiquiris were created in Havana, Cuba – where there is an abundance of tropical fruit and rum. Here in Australia, there is nothing like the smell of mango to remind us that Christmas is on its way. Sip the rummy mango through the finely crushed ice, using a straw or not, and know the festive season is definitely here. But be warned – it packs a punch.

Put everything apart from the garnish in a blender or food processor and process, scraping down the sides a few times, until the mixture is very smooth but still frozen.

Pour the mixture into stemmed glasses and garnish each with a slices of lime and mint if desired.

Makes 6 drinks

1½ tablespoons Cointreau, or other orange-based liqueur

⅓ cup white rum

1 tablespoon caster sugar

1 tablespoon freshly squeezed lime or lemon juice

2 cups fresh pineapple, cut into small cubes

4 cups crushed ice

Pineapple Daiquiri

Like most rum-based cocktails, this drink sure packs a punch

Process everything together in a blender or food processor, scraping down the sides a few times until the mixture is very smooth but still frozen.

Pour the mixture into two stemmed glasses and finish each off with a sprig of mint or a pineapple leaf if you like.

Makes 2 drinks

- -

6 eggs, separated

½ cup caster sugar

2 cups brandy, rum or whisky

4 cups cream

pinch of salt

freshly grated nutmeg, to sprinkle

Egg Nog

Whether the celebrations are over or just beginning, this is a popular drink – almost a dish in itself. It gets a party off to a good start or bucks us up if we're winding down or feeling tired.

Beat the egg yolks with the sugar in a bowl until thick. Beat in the brandy, rum or whisky, and the cream. In a separate bowl, beat the egg whites with the salt until they form soft peaks, then fold into the cream mixture. Serve in small punch cups or coffee cups, sprinkled with grated nutmeg.

Serves 10–12

1 orange

½ small lemon

750 ml dry red wine

½ cup sugar

5 black peppercorns

6 cloves

3 star anise

¼ teaspoon freshly grated nutmeg

Mulled Wine

Wrap your hands around this fragrant warm mulled wine and drink to your health – this wine holds undisputed tonic properties for the heart and breathing. Add a cinnamon quill as well if you like and enjoy on a cooler Christmas evening.

Peel the rind from the orange and lemon without taking any of the white pith (which makes it bitter). Squeeze the juice from the fruit and set aside.

Put the wine in a saucepan with the orange and lemon rinds, sugar, peppercorns, cloves, star anise and nutmeg, and bring slowly to a simmer, stirring occasionally, until the sugar is dissolved. Add the reserved fruit juice and simmer a further 5 minutes. Pour into heatproof glasses or mugs and serve hot.

Serves 6–8

1 cup water
½ cup sugar
1 stick cinnamon
1 orange
1 lemon
ice cubes
750 ml dry red wine (Spanish, if available)
1 x 1.25 litre bottle soda water

Sangria

Outdoor summer parties in Spain always include big jugs of this fruity, spiced wine punch. You can add seasonal fruit to give an extra burst of variety and colour – it seems so festive and is the perfect drink for a summer Christmas.

Combine the water, sugar and cinnamon stick in a saucepan and boil for 5 minutes. Remove from the heat and allow the syrup to cool.

Slice the orange and lemon, place them in a bowl and pour the syrup over the fruit slices. Marinate for at least 4 hours.

Fill a large glass pitcher one-quarter full of ice. Add the marinated fruit, 1 cup of the syrup and the red wine. Stir well with a sangria stick or a wooden spoon and add soda water to taste. Serve in chilled wine glasses.

Serves 8–10

TIP Peach slices, strawberries or other fruit in season may replace the orange and lemon.

½ cup crème de cassis

750 ml Champagne or chablis, well chilled

Kir and Kir Royal

The blackcurrant liqueur crème de cassis is rather expensive, but for very special friends or a festive occasion, why not splash out and buy a bottle? It goes a long way mixed with Champagne (no need to use a costly one) for Kir Royal, or a crisp white wine such as chablis for Kir – both are great drinks to whet the appetite.

Have champagne glasses well chilled and the Champagne or wine still on ice. Pour a little crème de cassis into each glass and top with the wine. Stir and serve.

Makes 6–8 drinks

¼ cup Grand Marnier

sparkling wine or Champagne

⅔ cup fresh orange juice

Mimosa

A classy, welcoming first drink of the day – a fitting start to Christmas.

Divide the Grand Marnier between 4 champagne flutes. Fill almost to the top with sparkling wine or Champagne and top each glass with about 2 tablespoons orange juice. Serve immediately.

Makes 4 drinks

2 tablespoons puréed fresh peach

1 teaspoon peach schnapps

½ teaspoon lemon juice

chilled Champagne or Prosecco

Peach Bellini

You would think little could improve on Champagne, but sometimes we just fancy a twist on this classic. The legendary bellini from Harry's Bar in Venice was given its name in 1948 to honour the fifteenth century artist Giovanni Bellini, whose work was in exposition in Venice at the time. The authentic mixture is made with a white peach purée, sometimes with a little sugar syrup added, mixed with Prosecco, an Italian version of Champagne.

Pour the peach purée, schnapps and lemon juice into a champagne flute.
Fill almost to the top with the chilled Champagne or Prosecco and stir.

Makes 1 drink

CHAPTER NINE
Leftovers

Leftovers

It is one consolation when Christmas is over that we still have all those leftovers to enjoy. Whether you choose turkey or ham, there is likely still a lot of food to get through. Something about the Christmas season just makes our eyes so much bigger than our stomachs. You can almost repeat the Christmas meal a few times over after the day – and often it tastes even better.

My granddaughters love a simple turkey and gravy sandwich, and who doesn't want another slice of that Christmas pudding with custard? But if you're still in the mood for cooking, there are some great ways to use up all those leftovers by creating something new.

1 tablespoon oil	DRESSING
4 small peaches, stoned and halved	2 tablespoons olive oil
4 thickly sliced ham steaks or slices	1 tablespoon white balsamic vinegar
2 baby cos lettuces, leaves separated	2 teaspoons honey
¼ cup toasted pistachios, roughly chopped	1 teaspoon wholegrain mustard
	salt and freshly ground black pepper, to season

Grilled Ham and Peach Salad

Brush a chargrill pan or grilling racks with oil and heat on high. Cook the peaches, cut side down, for 1–2 minutes. Remove and set aside. Cook the ham in batches for 2–3 minutes each side, until charred nicely. Tear into bite-sized pieces.

Arrange the cos leaves, peach halves and ham on serving plates. Sprinkle with pistachios. Whisk together the dressing ingredients in a jug, season to taste and drizzle over the salad.

Serves 4

- -

2 large pears, cored, quartered (see Tips)	VINAIGRETTE DRESSING
juice of 1 lemon	2 tablespoons white wine vinegar
150 g mesclun or baby mixed salad leaves (see Tips)	1 tablespoon walnut or olive oil
400 g cooked lean pork or turkey, fat removed, thinly sliced, cut into strips	1–2 teaspoons honey
30 g toasted macadamias, chopped	1 teaspoon Dijon mustard

Pork and Pear Salad with Macadamias

Cut each pear quarter into thin slices and pour the lemon juice over. Divide the mesclun or salad greens between four serving bowls. Top with the pear, pork or turkey and macadamias.

To make the vinaigrette dressing, whisk all the ingredients together in a small bowl. To serve, drizzle a little dressing over each salad and toss very gently to coat.

Serves 4

TIPS Choose ripe but firm pears, and salad greens should be very fresh and not show signs of browning or wilting. Buy only enough for a day or two, and wash in cold water to remove any sand or grit.

60 g unsalted butter	¾ cup chicken stock
3 bundles of asparagus, tough ends removed	1 cup fresh breadcrumbs
185 g sliced leg ham, cut into julienne	½ cup grated Gruyère cheese
½ teaspoon salt	2 tablespoons chopped continental parsley
freshly ground black pepper, to season	1 lemon, cut into wedges
¼ cup double cream	

Asparagus and Ham Gratin

This classic French dish is suitable for a Boxing Day brunch, lunch or a light supper. And, if you have a lot of people around, you can easily expand it for a crowd.

Preheat the oven to 190°C. Butter a gratin dish with 20 g of the butter. Wash the asparagus and arrange them in the gratin dish. Position the ham in the crevices between the asparagus. Sprinkle with the salt and freshly ground black pepper.

Mix together the cream and stock in a small bowl and pour over the asparagus. Melt the remaining butter and mix together with the breadcrumbs, cheese and parsley. Spread this mixture over the gratin. Bake for 50–60 minutes, until most of the liquid is absorbed and the crust is golden. Serve hot, garnished with lemon wedges.

Serves 4–6

- -

1 teaspoon oil	2½ cups boiling chicken stock
1 onion, chopped	100 g rocket leaves
100 g ham, chopped	2 tablespoons grated parmesan cheese
2 cups arborio rice	salt and freshly ground black pepper, to season

Ham and Rocket Risotto

This no-stir risotto makes a wonderful alternative to the traditional method.

Heat the oil in a large heavy-based saucepan over a moderate heat. Cook the onion and ham for 5 minutes, until the onion is tender. Add the rice and stir for 2 minutes, until the rice is translucent and lightly toasted. Stir through the hot stock and reduce the heat to very low. Cover with a tight-fitting lid and simmer gently for 12–14 minutes, until all the liquid has been absorbed.

Remove from the heat, add the rocket and cheese and mix very well with a wooden spoon, until creamy. Season to taste and serve.

Serves 4

6 desiree, pontiac or Dutch cream potatoes, peeled

2 tablespoons plain flour

salt and freshly ground black pepper, to season

¼ teaspoon baking powder

2 eggs, well beaten

1 teaspoon grated onion

1–1½ cups chopped ham or pork

60 g butter

Apple Sauce (page 276), warmed, to serve

Potato Ham Pancakes

Something for a late breakfast or light lunch? This is a great way of using leftover ham or pork.

Grate the potatoes on the coarse side of a grater into a colander. Combine the flour, salt, pepper, baking powder, egg and onion. Squeeze the potato as dry as possible, and mix thoroughly with the egg mixture. Lightly mix in the ham or pork.

Heat a heavy-based frying pan with half of the butter. When the foaming subsides, ladle the egg mixture, about 2 tablespoons at a time, into the pan, leaving about 2.5 cm between the pancakes. Cook the pancakes over a moderate heat until golden-brown and crisp on the underside, turn, and brown the other side. Repeat this with the remaining mixture, adding more butter as needed. Drain the pancakes on crumpled paper towel and serve piping hot with warmed Apple Sauce.

Serves 4–6

8 slices rye or sourdough bread

butter, margarine or mayonnaise, to spread

mixed salad greens, such as oak leaves, watercress and curly endive

200 g thinly sliced turkey

MANGO SALSA

1 ripe mango, diced

2 spring onions, sliced

½ small red chilli, seeded and finely sliced

¼ cup lemon or lime juice

1 tablespoon olive oil

freshly ground black pepper, to season

Turkey Sandwich with Mango Salsa

To make the mango salsa, mix together the chopped mango, spring onion and chilli in a bowl. Whisk the lemon or lime juice and oil together until amalgamated. Pour over the mango mixture and lightly toss to coat. Season, cover and store in the refrigerator until ready to serve.

To serve, spread the bread slices with the butter, margarine or mayonnaise. Pile the salad greens on half the bread slices and top with slices of turkey. Place a good spoonful of the mango salsa on top of each then finish with the remaining bread.

Serves 4

- -

1 teaspoon oil

4 salad onions, peeled, halved

2 tablespoons plain flour

2 cups chicken stock

1 bunch baby carrots, quartered, blanched

1 cup frozen peas

2 cups roughly chopped cooked turkey

1 tablespoon sour cream

1 tablespoon chopped tarragon

salt and freshly ground black pepper, to season

6 sheets filo pastry

spray oil

Turkey and Vegetable Pot Pie

Preheat the oven to 200°C. Heat the oil in a saucepan over a moderate heat. Cook the onion for 5 minutes, until beginning to soften. Increase the heat to high, add the flour and cook, stirring, for 2 minutes. Add the stock, stirring constantly, and simmer for 5 minutes, until the sauce has thickened slightly. Add the carrots, peas, turkey, sour cream and tarragon and season well. Simmer for 3 minutes. Spoon into a 6-cup ovenproof dish.

Spray each sheet of filo with oil and stack on top of each other. With the short end facing you, roll tightly to form a log. With a sharp knife cut 1 cm slices from the roll. Scatter the slices over the turkey mixture and spray with oil. Bake for 15–20 minutes, until the pastry is golden.

Serves 4

1 cup leftover chopped potato

1 cup leftover chopped mixed vegetables, such as pumpkin, sweet potato and peas

1 cup finely chopped cooked pork or turkey

3 spring onions, finely chopped

flour, for dusting

1 tablespoon oil

lemon wedges, to serve

Bubble and Squeak Patties

Mash the potato and mixed vegetables together in a bowl. Add the pork or turkey and spring onion and combine with the mashed vegetables. Using a ⅓-cup measure, form the mixture into patties. Chill for 30 minutes.

Heat the oil in a non-stick frying pan over a moderate heat. Cook the bubble and squeak patties for 3–4 minutes each side, until golden. Serve with lemon wedges, or a tomato chutney and a freshly tossed mixed salad.

Serves 4

- -

½ cup self-raising flour

40 g unsalted butter, melted

3 eggs, lightly beaten

1 cup finely diced ham

2 cups fresh corn kernels, cut from the cob

1 tablespoon mixed chopped herbs, such as continental parsley and chives

salt and freshly ground black pepper, to season

¼–½ cup milk

olive oil, for frying

2 tomatoes, diced and snipped basil to garnish

Corn and Ham Fritters

Sift the flour into a bowl. Pour in the melted butter and eggs, blend well, then add the diced ham, corn kernels and herbs. Season with salt and plenty of freshly ground black pepper. Add enough milk to make a batter which should be smooth, not runny, and you should only just be able to shake the batter from the spoon. Keep adding the milk and mixing until you reach this consistency.

Heat a 1 mm layer of olive oil in a large frying pan until hot but not smoking. Drop tablespoons of the batter and cook until golden, turning gently once to cook the other side. Test one fritter first to ensure you are cooking it the right length of time.

Drain the fritters on crumpled paper towel, then place in a warm oven until all are cooked. Serve warm or at room temperature with the tomato and basil garnish or a tomato chutney.

Serves 4

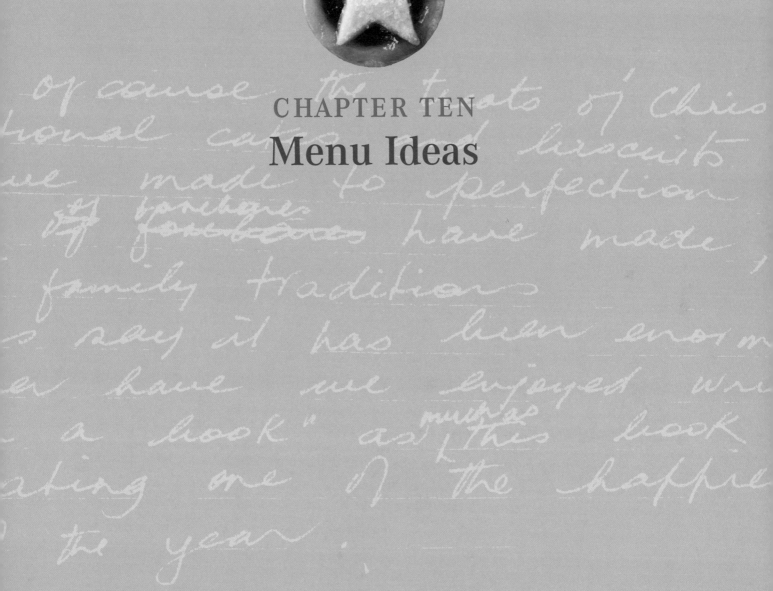

CHAPTER TEN

Menu Ideas

Planning the menu

Plan a traditional Christmas dinner – turkey and all the trimmings or perhaps a European Christmas dinner – that's with goose and ending with Stollen. Christmas buffet for 20, a cold do-ahead lunch, a small dinner for 4 with a great duckling dish, two ideas for a cold seafood lunch, a Christmas picnic and a barbecue and by popular demand, how to do a glistening glazed ham and not forgetting roast pork with crispy crackling. It's all here.

Enjoy planning the menu for your Christmas festivities. We have planned some menus to give you ideas, for there are lots of choices. Dinner like your mother used to make or you may prefer a contemporary celebration. We have included nibbles to welcome guests, drinks, starters for a first course, mains with all the trimmings and accompaniments plus the puddings, the rich Christmas puddings and some lighter ones. We've also included the special treats of Christmas, the cakes, biscuits, sweetmeats, some just right for Christmas giving. So, it's over to you. Mix and match as you bring out your planning skills and create the perfect festive meal for your family and friends.

A Cold Do-Ahead Lunch

For 6-8

Champagne, Beer

Ginger Julep

Tapenade

Black or rye bread

Nuts and Olives

Salmon Gravlax with Dill Sauce and Horseradish Mousse

Poached Turkey Breast with Lime Mayonnaise

Crunchy Cranberry & Rice Salad

Beetroot & Orange Salad

Tomato Salad

Green Salad with Chapons

Baked Ham on the sideboard

with 3 mustards

Danish Rum Cream

With Madeleines or Pistachio Bread

Coffee or Tea

Christmas Mince Pies

Wines – your personal choice

Christmas Buffet

For 20
Champagne, Beer
Ginger Julep
Blinis with Smoked Salmon or Gravlax
Crudités
Nuts and Olives
Baked Salmon with Herb Mayonnaise

∽∾

Baked Guinness Ham with choice of mustards
Cumberland Sauce
Cranberry & Orange Relish

∽∾

Roasted Turkey Buffe
served warm or cold

∽∾

Potato Salad
Green Salad with Chapons
Crunchy Cranberry & Rice Salad
Tomato Salad
Broad Beans with Pancetta
Sour Cream Coleslaw

∽∾

Tipsy Cake
Large Platter Christmas Mince Pies
Festive Cupcakes

∽∾

Wines – your personal choice

Note: Double quantities of vegetables, salads, Tipsy Cake and Mince Pies
and any foods you think will be in demand.

For fewer guests say 10–12 drop the salmon or ham.

Christmas Picnic

For 6-8
Champagne, Beer
Drinks for children
Smoked Salmon Pancake Rolls
Watermelon with Gin
Nuts and Olives

⁓⊙⁓

Crudités
Summer Beetroot Soup

⁓⊙⁓

Seafood and Pasta Salad
Green Salad with Chapons

⁓⊙⁓

Pithiviers
Christmas Mince Pies
Christmas Mini Muffins

⁓⊙⁓

Wine – your personal choice

Cold Seafood Christmas Lunch

For 8
Champagne, Beer
Ice Tea Punch
Gougères / Nuts and Olives
Horseradish Mousse with Gravlax

Seafood Platter

OR

Baked Salmon with Herb Mayonnaise
Asparagus with Lemon Butter
Baby Potato Salad
Finnish Beetroot Salad
Green Salad with Chapons

Vanilla Bavarois
with Fresh Raspberry Coulis

Coffee
Christmas Mince Pies

Wines – your personal choice

Duckling Dinner

For 4
Champagne, Beer
Gougères
Hot Olive & Cheese Puffs

Blinis with Smoked Salmon or Gravlax

Roast Duck with Cherries
Scalloped Potatoes
Asparagus
Green Salad with Chapons

Coconut & Mascarpone Log
with strawberries

Coffee
Christmas Mince Pies
Wines – your personal choice

European Goose Christmas Dinner

For 6-8

Champagne, Beer
Elderflower Cooler
Iced Tea Punch
Gougères
Oysters Coriander

Tropical Seafood Cocktails

Red Currant Glazed Roast Goose with Apples & Prunes
Gravy
Braised Red Cabbage with Apples
Mousseline Potatoes
Green Peas with Mushrooms

Tipsy Cake
Madeleines

Coffee
Stollen
Wines – your personal choice

Garden Barbecue at Home

For 8-10
Champagne, Beer
Drinks for children
Ginger Julep
Nuts and Olives
Watermelon with Gin
Salmon on Rye with Dill Sauce

Barbecued Vegetables with Sage & Garlic Mayonnaise
Barbecued Tiger Prawns
Crusty Bread Mayonnaise
Turkey in the Barbecue
Cranberry & Orange Relish
Baby Potato Salad
Crunchy Cranberry & Rice Salad
Sour Cream Coleslaw
Green Salad with Chapons

Christmas Trifle
Madeleines

Coffee
Christmas Mince Pies
Wines – your personal choice

Roast Pork Christmas Dinner

For 6-8
Champagne, Beer
Sangria
Nuts and Olives
Anchovy Turnovers
Caviar Bowl

⁓

Tropical Seafood Cocktails

⁓

Roast Pork with rhubarb & orange
Apple Sauce
Roast Potatoes
Sugar-fried Sweet Potatoes
Parsnip Purée with Peas
Green Beans with Almonds
Braised Cabbage with Apples

⁓

Christmas Mince Pies with
Brandied Butter

OR

Summer Pudding

⁓

Coffee or Tea
Orange Biscotti with Pinenuts
Hazelnut Crescents
Wine – your personal choice

Grand Traditional Christmas Dinner

For 6-8
10-12 if Baked Guinness Ham is on sideboard
Champagne
Iced Tea Punch
Tomato and Bocconcini Spears
Blinis with Gravlax
Crudités

Summer Beetroot Soup

Roast Turkey with Two Stuffings
Pork, Sage and Apple
Lemon and Parsley
Chipolata Sausages
Gravy
Cranberry & Orange Relish

Baked Guinness Ham
(on side table)
with 3 assorted mustards

Best Ever Roasted Potatoes
Brussel Sprouts with Hazelnuts
French Peas
Sugar-Fried Sweet Potatoes

Rich Christmas Pudding
Vanilla Egg Custard
Brandied Butter

Coffee
Christmas Mince Pies
Wines – your personal choice

Turkey Breast Dinner

For 6-8
Champagne, Beer
Apple Blossom Cooler
Hot Olive and Cheese Puffs
Mixed Nuts and Olives
Pineapple Japonaise

Roasted Stuffed Turkey Breast
Apple, Prune & Pistachio Stuffing
Gravy
Cumberland Sauce
Scalloped Potatoes
Green Beans with Almonds
Glazed Carrots
Truss Tomatoes

Latticed Mincemeat Tart
Brandied Butter

Coffee or Tea
Vanilla Kippels
Wines – your personal choice

Acknowledgements

It is delightful to have this new book of my favourite festive recipes, a book made possible with the help of many talented people. Suzanne and I would like to thank the Hardie Grant Books team for their hard work in bringing this sumptuous book to fruition, especially Mary Small and Ellie Smith, and editor Paul McNally.

To all our fabulous foodie helpers, thank you: Michele Curtis and Mara Szoeke, for their cooking prowess; Deborah Kaloper, for her mouth-watering styling of each dish; Leesa O'Reilly, for sourcing the interesting and unusual props used in the photography; and Mark Roper and assistant John Laurie, for their delicious photographs that bring the dishes to life.

We also extend our thanks to Trisha Garner for her beautiful design, bringing a fresh, Australian approach to these Christmas classics, and Michelle Macintosh for her arresting cover.

A final special thanks to our dear friend Jannie Brown, who allowed us access to her lovely home for the photoshoot – the perfect setting for a fun-filled, festive celebration.

Recipe Index